The Bell Tolls

Tomorrow's Truncated India

"....never send to know for whom the
bell tolls; it tolls for thee".

John Donne

Attention Authors

Manas Publications is fighting a war to tell the world that India can win the battle not only by bullet but also by pen. We are converting fighters into writers since our country is full of intellectuals but their knowledge is only confined to them. No sincere effort has been made by any publisher to give the right direction to their knowledge and the talent of intellectual is still hidden. An author always gives the raw material in the shape of manuscript and it is the sense of publisher to make it a finished product. We are motivating the intellectuals' mind and publishing their manuscripts for more than two decades and would like to publish your manuscript too. If you or your colleagues have any manuscript or are working on, please don't hesitate to contact us with detailed synopsis and contents for its publication. We take utmost care in production and give a wide publicity to the book and its author. We can also suggest you the title for writing related to your subject since we are the publishers who believe more in quality than in quantity.

The Bell Tolls

Tomorrow's Truncated India

R.K. Ohri, IPS (Retd.)

Manas Publications
New Delhi-110002 (INDIA)

Manas Publications
(Publishers, Distributors, Importers & Exporters)
4858, Prahlad Street,
24, Ansari Road, Darya Ganj,
New Delhi - 110 002 (INDIA)
Ph.: 23260783, 23265523:, 23842660 (R)
Fax: 011-23272766
E-mail: manaspublications@vsnl.com

2006

ISBN 81-7049-294-7
Rs. 495/-

Typeset at
Manas Publications

Printed in India at
Nice Printing Press, Delhi
and Published by Mrs. Suman Lata for
Manas Publications,
4858, Prahlad Street,
24, Ansari Road, Darya Ganj,
New Delhi - 110 002 (INDIA).

Dedicated

To eternal glory of Mother India

Contents

Appendices

Foreword

Democracy based on the rule of law and social justice has given voice, identity, dignity and opportunity to millions of men and women belonging to traditionally deprived and disadvantaged sections of Indian society. The remarkable resilience of Indian democracy has manifested itself time and again. Yet that very model reminds us that India's national security, as well as its external standing, depend on its internal cohesiveness.

India is one of the oldest civilizations that has successfully assimilated people of all ethnicities, including those who came from outside. It is proud of its pluralistic and secular ethos. Its secular ethos actually dates back to ancient times. It has a heritage of a benign and humane civilization, with its wealth of philosophy and a generally spiritualised worldview. That is a unique attribute. In contemporary times, however, the markedly changing demographic patterns are beginning to have an important bearing on internal security.

Internal security, historically, has been India's Achilles' heel, leading to extended periods of subjugation and exploitation of its people by invaders from outside. Despite the central importance of internal cohesion and consolidation, the Indian state has since Independence not paid adequate attention to that need. As a consequence, the Indian Army has been saddled with significant internal-security responsibilities. It is critical to the country's long-term interests that its policy-makers focus on domestic cohesion and consolidation.

Broadly, India's principal strategic interests are to safeguard its territorial integrity, aim to be the dominant influence in the Indian Ocean region, and craft an international role commensurate with its size and capabilities. But one of India's vital interests is to ensure stability in terms of patterns of demographic growth. That objective is centrally connected with internal security, including the goal of ensuring national unity and territorial integrity. This book brings out that linkage.

Any country's internal security would be seriously undermined if there are wild fluctuations or rapid changes in demographic patterns in terms of ethnicity, religion, race or culture. Maintaining demographic stability in terms of racial, ethnic or religious patterns is an important component of national security in Western nations. In fact, even immigration policy in the United States or Australia, for instance, is openly pivoted on keeping the country as a White-majority state.

Rapid changes in India's demographic patterns will inevitably spur national and provincial problems, and embolden states hostile to Indian interests to consciously seek to exploit those changes in order to prejudice and weaken Indian security. Let us not forget that at the root of the various insurgencies prevailing in the North-East, other than the Naga guerrilla movement, is ethnic discontent and antagonism over rapid changes in demographic patterns due to the influx of immigrants from Bangladesh and other Indian states. The All-Assam Students' Union movement in the 1980s, for example, began in response to such influx.

The author of the book has done a commendable job in analyzing the fundamentals of India's changing demographic situation and underlining the importance of a national strategy and policy to contain potentially destabilising shifts in population patterns. For example, the unchecked influx of millions of illegal migrants from Bangladesh has changed the demographic composition of 21 districts in eastern and north-eastern India, as per official admission.

The Bangladeshi influx has been allowed to strain the already fragile ethnic balance in several parts of the diverse North-East and exacerbate internal security challenges there. Such has been the level of influx that some of the eastern and north-eastern areas of India geographically contiguous to Bangladesh have, ethnically and socially, become an extension of Bangladesh, with all the attendant Bangladeshi problems, including the spreading virus of Islamic fundamentalism.

Given the exceptionally narrow neck that connects the North-East with the rest of India, the changing ethnic picture there has implications starker than the spectre of native populations becoming minorities in their own homelands, as has already happened in Tripura, Sikkim and parts of Lower Assam. The ethnic expansion of Bangladesh beyond its political borders sets up enduring trans-border links, undermining India's task of border management. In the long run, it threatens to make India's hold over the North-East more taxing and tenuous, as this book concludes. The uneasy ethnic mix in the North-East, made more tense by the continuing refugee influx and the rise of sub-ethnic identities, has made this region a fertile ground for external trouble-makers.

Nationally, the most disturbing aspect is that the demographic patterns are changing most rapidly in the areas along India's borders with neighbouring states. For a country that has land borders with six countries stretching more than 15,200 kilometres, this poses a direct security challenge. Indeed, it makes India's already complex task of border management more onerous.

Effective border management is an important issue tied to national security and well-being. This is underscored by Pakistan's continuing dispatch of armed terrorist and saboteurs into India and the use by foreign interests of Nepal's long open border with India to undermine Indian security. The porous border with Bangladesh traverses five Indian states, each with different demographic features.

What the book highlights is that India has to be deeply conscious of the significance of the changing demographic patterns and their impact on its national security. India was once partitioned on the basis of religious demography and now has to counter the threat of another partition on the same basis in Kashmir. There can be no effective border management if the frontier areas are transformed demographically and become a hub for political or religious militants.

Building internal cohesion is an essential political task that has to draw on India's societal strengths. India epitomizes the celebration of many diversities that fashion its rich social fabric. It is a land that supports and encourages varied social identities to flower and flourish within a framework of nationhood built on the strength of multiple characteristics. The continued political fusion of those diverse identities in one nation-state demands greater national priority to meeting the challenges of internal security.

Brahma Chellaney

Acknowledgments

I owe a debt of gratitude to my Chennai-based friend, Ashok Joshi, for his hard work and invaluable contribution to the writing of this book. Like me, Ashok has been a keen observer of the tectonic demographic changes sweeping across the Indian subcontinent which have the potential to tear asunder the socio-political fabric of our country and trigger an era of instability in not-too-distant future. During last century almost copycat demographic changes in which Christians were outnumbered by Muslims had led to civil strife and armed conflicts in Lebanon and the Balkans. Some political analysts have attributed the recent violence in France in October-November 2005 to the fast-paced demographic changes. Mathew Campbell, a well known columnist, highlighted in an article published in *The Sunday Times,* London, in early November 2005, the strong demographic under-pinnings of the widespread violence which rocked 300 cities of France, a demographically challenged civilization.

I must thank the Centre for Policy Studies, Chennai, for their kindness in allowing me to make use of their database.

My special thanks are due to late Shri A.K. Dave, I.P. (Retd), a former doyen of India's intelligence fraternity, for drawing attention to the possibility of balkanization of India, highlighted by Selig S. Harrison in his tome, *India: The Most Dangerous Decades,* though in an altogether different context. That threat seems more relevant today than it was forty-six years ago. But for Shri Dave's timely alert and my intense interaction with him in two long sessions I might have altogether missed Harrison's four decades old treatise which has suddenly become highly relevant to the currrent politics of India.

I make a bow to the well known strategic analyst, Prof. Brahma Chellaney, for finding time from his busy schedule to go through the manuscript of my book and write its Foreword.

In the end I should like to place on record my gratitude to Shri N.N. Sharma for editing the manuscript and making some very useful suggestions. His vast knowledge of the subject and unflinching commitment to the glory of Mother India have been a source of enormous encouragement.

R.K. Ohri

Introduction

During last 50 years, among all Asian countries India alone has undergone the most far reaching and dramatic demographic changes which threaten to erase its secular and democratic identity. The tragedy, however, is that neither any frontline political party nor mainstream media analysts have shown full awareness of these tectonic demographic changes taking place across the country which have the potential of changing the course of India's history, nay even the history of South Asia. India has witnessed a relentless fast-paced growth in percentage terms of one single community, i.e., the Muslims, to the exclusion of every other community. In percentage terms all other religious groups, i.e., the Hindus, Sikhs, Jains, Buddhists and Christians have been in a declining mode, while the growth rate of Muslims has been perpetually in a fast forward mode. Though this fact has been known to the successive central governments as well as Chief Ministers of the affected states for several years, the long term consequences of adverse demography have been kept under wraps. Whenever any concerned citizen or wide-awake group tried to bring up the matter for an objective analysis of the problem, it was deliberately sidetracked and the persons or groups seeking a rational and objective discourse were peremptorily dubbed as anti-secular right wing Hindu fundamentalists. Even after conclusive re-confirmation of the problem by the Census 2001, clumsy attempts were made to camouflage the truth in a bid to keep the vexatious topic beyond legitimate public discourse. For reasons not altogether inscrutable, the mainstream political leadership has found the fig-leaf of self-styled secularism as a convenient tool to maintain and strengthen their stranglehold on the state apparatus. Unfortunately the national media too continues to ignore the problem in the holy name of secularism. Nowhere in the world the term secularism is used so extensively and in a such a devious manner as it is in India by the casteist and leftist groups to feather their nests and grab political power. An example of the anguish felt by genuine secular Hindus was reflected in a column titled "I am a Hindu, but........." written by Gurcharan Das, a versatile writer and former Chief Executive of the well known multinational Proctor and Gamble, in *The Times of India*, New Delhi, on October 9, 2005. He cited two typical instances of denial of Hindu identity by spineless Hindus themselves out of which I am citing only one. The Principal of one of Delhi's best schools asked Gurcharan Das to speak to its students. But when he conveyed that he will speak about *"dharma"* and the moral dilemmas in *Mahabharata,* an ancient literary epic, the Principal's "horrified reaction" was "oh don't please!" "There are important secularists on our governing body and I don't want a controversy about teaching religion". Nothing more could unveil the ugly face of India's sham secularism than this episode. In today's secular India there will be no takers for the lament of Gurcharan Das that if "Italians are proud of *Divine Comedy*, the Spanish of *Don Quixote*, and the Greeks of *Iliad*, why should 'secularist' Indians be ambivalent about *Mahabharata*? Why should it become untouchable for a sensitive, modern, school Principal?" An intellectual of the stature of Gurcharan Das ought to have known better. India is passing through a peculiar phase where a Hindu is considered secular only if he is rabidly anti-Hindu. It is expected of him that he will support the patently communal demands of fundamentalist outfits and acquiesce in casteist shenanigans of the self-styled secular groups. If he does not fit into that regressive political format he will stand condemned as a right wing Hindu communalist, howsoever progressive and rational he might be. Frankly, in India secularism has assumed the hideous form of a regressive and obscurantist religious dogma, sort of a terminal disease which could be appropriately called 'secularitis'. It may be recalled that in quite a few countries, e.g., Lebanon, Bosnia,

Kosovo and Serbia, the comparable political infection caused by secularitis has already taken heavy toll of life, property and multicultural ethos during the last century. Nearer home it is threatening to destroy the cultural identity of the fast thinning majority Hindu community in Assam and West Bengal and might impact even the Christian identity of Nagaland, though perhaps a little later. In due course of time it could further undermine the tottering law and order machinery of Bihar, a state overawed till recently by the cult figure of a Bin Laden look-alike and the unending political refrain seeking a Muslim Chief Minister. The inglorious decline and decimation of similarly secularitis-seized nations of the Balkans reveals that Islamist fundamentalism thrives more vigorously in communist and leftist countries than under any other political dispensation.

In India, the frightening dimensions of the fast-paced adverse demographic changes have been deliberately concealed not only from the opinion-makers and middle class, but the whole lot of gullible Indian masses, spread out in rural areas. Worse still, though the menacing contours of the problem were effectively highlighted in the Census 2001 (Religion Data) Report in September 2004 by the former Registrar General of Census, neither the central government nor the country's opinion-makers tried to comprehend the geopolitical consequences of the sharp population changes writ large across the country. On the contrary, a clumsy attempt was made to harass and humiliate the then Registrar, J.K. Banthia, and finally, the vote-bank besotted leftist politicians hounded him out.

It is distressing to find that most of our political leaders and bureaucrats appear (or pretend) to be blissfully unaware of the latest demographic developments across the globe, as is evident from their obsessive occupation with promotion of family planning, a hackneyed concept already junked even by the U.N.D.P.(United Nations Development Programme). Today the problem facing the world is too few babies and not their growing numbers, excepting Islamic countries where relentless population growth continues apace. In the circumstances, it has become necessary to speak frankly to dispel the abysmal ignorance of Indian middle class and opinion-makers about the latest population changes across the globe so that the bureaucracy stops transmitting incorrect and outmoded information to millions of ignorant and illiterate rural masses.

The latest census data also confirmed two worst fears of the miniscule fraternity of the nation's concerned population watchers. First, the percentage growth of Muslims has been galloping ahead ever since independence and their growth rate is now higher by almost forty-five per cent than that of Hindus. And second, this trend of increasing growth rate of Muslims is likely to pick up more speed and culminate in a dramatically higher growth decade after decade which trend is likely to continue at least for the next 40 to 50 years, may be even 100 years! Sounds incredible? Perhaps it does. But that is a statistically established truth, which our 'secularitis-seized' politicians will never like to admit lest they lose minority votes and their high-backed political chairs, too.

In an in-depth demographic study published in the January 29, 2005, issue of *Economic and Political Weekly*, Mumbai, it was reiterated by Mari Bhat and A. J. Francis Zavier, two professional demographers, that "the fertility of Muslims which was about 10 per cent higher than that of Hindus before independence, is now 25 to 30 per cent higher than the Hindu rate". In other words, the growth rate of Muslims is now almost 45 to 50 per cent higher than that of the Hindus. The difference in T.F.R. (Total Fertility Rate) between the Hindus and Muslims is higher even than the fertility difference between the forward castes and depressed scheduled castes and tribes of Hindu community. The problem of growing demographic asymmetry has been compounded further by the sharply growing influx of Bangladeshis and their progeny whose total number in our country could now be anywhere between 3 crores and 5 crores, as estimated by knowledgeable analysts. Like proverbial late-risers, the Marxist Chief Minister of West Bengal, sounded a red alert on June 23, 2005, at a B.S.F. seminar, about threat of Islamic fundamentalism posed by Bangladeshi infiltrators. In doing so he displayed a singularly better vision and wisdom than his self-deluding leftist peers. Apparently Buddhadev Bhattacharjee remembers the treatment meted out to the communist fraternity of Afghanistan when the Taliban overran that country and the tragic fate of the communist-ruled Serbian identity, ravaged by the civil war of 1980s and 1990s. He knows that once the Islamists take over West Bengal, or a part of that state, Marxism and communists will disappear quite fast — as indeed they have in the next-door Bangladesh. It may be recalled that earlier Jyoti Basu and other Marxist leaders had persistently supported the hyperactive pro-infiltration lobby in West Bengal and elsewhere.

It is clear from Statement 1-a (page xxviii) of Census 2001 Religion Data Report (Appendix A) that the Muslims recorded an abnormally high decadal growth of 36 per cent, or at least 29.3 per cent if one were to accept the fudged census data (arrived at by the government by omitting 3.6 crore Indians residing in Assam and Jammu & Kashmir).

This alarmingly high growth rate, however, tells only one part of the story. The real clue to the future demographic changes destined to burst upon the Indian scene lies in the religion-wise percentages of young cohorts in the 0-6 years age group the data of which is available in Statement 7 (page xlii) of the Census 2001 Religion Data Report (Appendix 1) where at all India level the Muslims have a headstart of 21 per cent more cohorts than the Hindus and allied faiths. That one single page of Census 2001 Report spells out the huge demographic change waiting to overwhelm India. As analysed in chapter 2, the 0-6 years age cohorts hold the key to the future population changes during the next 50 years because these youngsters will enter the reproductive age between 2010 and 2016 A.D. and thereafter continue to be reproductively active for the next forty to fifty years. A mere glance at the religion-wise distribution of 0-6 age group shows that in percentage terms the ratio of Muslim cohorts is higher by a whopping 21 points vis a vis the cohorts of Hindus and allied faiths which term includes, Hindus, Sikhs, Jains and Buddhists, all counted together. Excepting Madhya Pradesh and Sikkim and two Union Territories of Andaman and Nicobar Islands and Diu and Daman, in the remaining 31 states the percentage of Muslim cohorts is higher than Hindu cohorts. And to fully grasp the future profile of India's population one has just to take into account the fact that the acceptance of family planning among Muslims is at least 25 per cent lower than that among members of the Hindu and allied faiths.

The biggest demographic change during the next 4 to 5 decades will be noticed in Haryana where the percentage of Muslim cohorts in 0-6 years age group is 24.5, as against 15.4 of Hindus. The difference in the ratio of two communities comes to a huge high of nearly 60 per cent more Muslim cohorts the impact of which will cause political tremors from 2011 A.D. onwards. Next in the descending order are Assam (Muslims cohorts 21.8, Hindus 14.5 per cent), West Bengal (Muslims 18.7, Hindus 12.7 per cent), Delhi (Muslims 18.5, Hindus 14.3), Uttaranchal (Muslims 21.2, Hindus 16.0 per cent), Jharkhand (Muslims 21.2, Hindus 17.9) and Bihar (Muslims 22.0, Hindus 19.9 per cent), and so on. Interestingly, in the so-called highly educated state of Kerala where the literacy percentages of Hindus and Muslims are almost equal and the latter enjoy a higher level of economic prosperity (perhaps due to remittances from Gulf countries) there is a big difference in the percentages of 0-6 age cohorts, with Muslim percentage at 15.0 as against 10.8 of Hindus which effectively translates into more than 40 per cent more Muslim cohorts. Next 20 to 40 years will thus witness earth-shaking demographic changes in Kerala as well. The challenge of adverse demography now threatens to envelope the Christian-dominated state of Nagaland too, where the percentage of Muslim cohorts (0-6 age group) is now 19.2 as against 14.6 of Christians which means that the Muslim cohorts in 0-6 years group are higher by nearly thirtythree per cent over their Christian counterparts. And according to well informed sources the proportion of Muslims has already grown to 20 per cent in Nagaland largely due to illegal immigration from Bangladesh. These cold statistics are pointers to the shape of things to come, say during the next four to five decades.

It requires no great arithmetical skill to assess the overall impact on the country's future population profile caused by 21 per cent more reproductively active Muslims among whom the acceptance of small family norm will be lower by at least 25 per cent, if not more. The fast-paced growth in Muslim population will impact on the unity and integrity of India, apart from posing a threat to our peace-loving citizens. Its long term consequences have to be assessed against the backdrop of the rising crescendo of Jihadi ideology fuelling multiple faultline conflicts across the globe and the ongoing relentless silent invasion of our country by illegal Bangaldeshi immigrants.

It looks as though India's political class and mainstream media has no knowledge, nor the slightest understanding, about the havoc played in several countries by adverse demographic changes during the twentieth century. The death knell of secularism, plural ethos and democratic institutions of the once-upon-a-time Christian-dominated Lebanon, Kosovo and Bosnia was sounded only by the sharp demographic changes in which Muslims outpaced the Christians. Similarly the fate of Macedonia, the famed land of Alexander the Great, is likely to be sealed within the next few decades because of the rapidly growing Muslim numbers, now estimated to constitute one-third of that country's population.

Few Indians and fewer political analysts and column writers of our country, seem to be aware that in the beginning of the twentieth century Muslims constituted only 12 per cent of the world population which proportion rose to 18 per cent in 1990s. In tandem with that dramatic increase erupted a rash of multiple jihads and secessionist movements in more than one dozen countries from Bosnia and Kosovo in the Balkans to the Philippines in southeast Asia. And now, hold your breath, the percentage of Muslims worldwide is likely to be 30 per cent or more by 2025, barely two decades away from now. Meanwhile, as warned by Niall Ferguson, who teaches contemporary history at Harvard University, in another 50 years time, Europe could become a Muslim-majority continent.

India has a plethora of experts, economists and geopolitical analysts. Many of them have been trying to figure out causes of the growing ungovernability of India's north-eastern region. Those who have been familiar with the region, or had the privilege of serving there in any capacity, know that no amount of mere pumping of money or rushing of security forces will solve the problem of deep-seated distrust among lakhs of frustrated indigenous people angered by the savage trampling of their hearths and homes and civilizational values by millions of infiltrators. They suspect the intentions of the union government and its ability to stem the rot. If the problem of silent Bangladeshi infiltration had been tackled firmly and in good time, there might not have been any separatist ULFA (United Liberation Front of Assam), nor any NDFB (National Democratic Front of Bodoland), nor TIWA tribals' movement.

Way back in 1980s, people in the north-east used to say: "Dilli ooncha sunti hai" meaning that the government in Delhi is hard of hearing. The new refrain is "Dilli ki sarkar andhi hai" which conveys that the government in Delhi is blind. That succinctly sums up the tragedy of India's north-east.

The high-decibel campaign launched sometime ago by a political party to opt for a Muslim Chief Minister in Bihar, too, has a loud and clear message flowing from the ongoing demographic transformation of the state. During an informal interactive discourse, held in Delhi, on population changes taking place in eastern India, one of the participants narrated the contours of the problem of identity being faced by the miniscule minority group of Hindus living in a remote village of Kishanganj district of Bihar. The village in question has an overwhelming Muslim majority and the situation has come to such a pass that the left-over remnants of the small Hindu community have to seek permission of the village Imam for taking out a marriage procession with band in attendance. If this incident narrated at random during an interactive session on India's demography is true, it should serve as an eye-opener for the somnolent Hindu society and perhaps more for the central government about growing non-governance in remote areas of Bihar where Islamic fundamentalism seems to have struck deep roots. The fact of rampant non-governance in the two heartland states of Bihar and Uttar Pradesh was candidly voiced by Rahul Gandhi, the young Member of Parliament from Amethi, in an interview to a Delhi weekly, *Tehelka*, in the second week of September 2005. In a scathing, but truthful, observation he asserted that there is "no functioning government in U. P. and Bihar and so there is no governance. There is a total collapse of the administrative system in these states. Nothing happens there". According to Census 2001, the proportion of

Muslims in Kishanganj district has now grown to 67 per cent and it is growing rapidly. Kishanganj district happens to be the pocket borrough of Taslimuddin, a Minister in the central government. There is a strong undercurrent of belief, nay conviction, among enlightened citizens that the vast land mass from Assam to Bihar and Uttar Pradesh, West Bengal included, is likely to witness further sharpening of communal divide and likely outbreak of religion-based faultline conflicts in the coming decades, unless effective remedial measures are initiated immediately. As revealed by Prafful Goradia, a well known author and political analyst, in an article published in *The Pioneer*, New Delhi, on June 2, 2005, some NRIs wanting to buy houses in the prestigious Salt Lake area of Kolkata are being advised by their well-wishers not to invest in property in Kolkata because the city is likely to be overwhelmed and over-run soon by fundamentalist Bangladeshis thereby making life difficult for Hindus. This is not surprising because according to census 2001, the decadal growth-rate of Hindus was 0.7 per cent in Kolkata district while that of Muslims was a whopping 18.9 per cent which translates into 27 times higher than Hindus.

In a perceptive analysis about the likely future turns and twists in India's polity, Selig S. Harrison, a U.S. based strategic analyst, now working for the Center for International Policy, had prophesied as early as 1960 in his book, *India: The Most Dangerous Decades*, that due to growth of centrifugal forces India was likely to break up into a number of fascist states in the coming decades. He felt that Indian communists will manipulate the divisive casteist and ethnic political outfits in a manner which will destroy democracy and lead to the emergence of a number of fascist states across the country. Though Harrison's forecast about the communists trying to fish in the troubled waters by supporting casteist political groups has come true almost remarkably, the real threat of vivisection of India has emanated from a different source, namely the demographic crisis caused by the galloping increase in the percentage of Muslims coupled with massive silent invasion of Bangladeshis through our porous eastern border. Today both these developments have come to constitute a grave threat to Indian identity and our ancient civilizational values.

It is my considered opinion (but I am always willing to stand corrected through a public discourse) that the problem of growing demographic asymmetry, has the potential to create massive societal upheavals and even change the course of India's history. The problem is far more serious than the Kashmir issue on which we have remained unifocussed now for almost six decades. It looks certain that during the next three to five decades the law and order problems created in the eastern region by the dynamics of adverse demography will become far more intractable than the Kashmir issue. While most countries of Europe and even the far away Australia, sensing threat from jihadi warriors of neighbouring Indonesia, have demonstrated their resolve to meet the demographic threat facing them, in India there is little awareness about the fast approaching civilizational disaster. It is not for nothing that the British Prime Minister, Tony Blair, has started advising British couples to opt for a 5 children norm.

These are some of the important reasons for undertaking the writing of this somewhat controversial, but truthful, tract about the far-reaching consequences of climactic demographic changes taking place in the country which must be understood in the context of political developments in our jihadist neighbourhood. No one dare deny that India will remain a secular and multicultural country only so long as it retains its Hindu majority character. Unfortunately the very Hindu identity has come under pressure in many areas, more specifically in the north-eastern region, West Bengal and some districts of Bihar and even Uttar Pradesh. It is not an existential crisis only for Hindus and allied faiths; it is a challenge to all those who genuinely believe in keeping intact long term secular and democratic identity of India.

If past experience is any guide the central government is not likely to react positively to the growing demographic threat. Hopefully the problem will receive attention of the concerned citizens and opinion-makers rooting for the continuation of our plural societal ethos and preservation of India's civilizational heritage.

R. K. Ohri

1

Demography as Destiny

"The wisest mind has something to learn".

George Santayana

Demography has always played an important role in the history of mankind. Most people, including those who claim to be educated elite, consider census operations as a kind of routine statistical exercise. Yet it is much more than mere headcount. Throughout mankind's history the growth and decline of population has played a singularly important role in shaping the destinies of countries and civilizations. This eternal truth was epitomised by Augustus Comte, the famous French philosopher of nineteenth century, in his well known dictum *"demography is destiny"*. In every age and all over the world, demographic changes have been the source of progress as well as destabilization and decimation of many a country and civilizations.

Demography is the science of population changes and deals with its growth, distribution, density and related social statistics and subterranean shifts resulting therefrom. It has two very important functions. First and foremost, no country can progress without adequate human resource which is just another name for population. Manpower, or human resource, is the most critical component of every human activity and every process of economic development, especially research and scientific progress. Without adequate and skilled human resource no country can make effective and proper utilization of its natural resources. All farms, factories and transport systems need robust and adequate manpower. In every age and every country knowledgeable, trained and technology oriented human resource has been the fountainhead of all scientific research. It has been the most important source of economic development and social progress. The second aspect of demography is equally crucial. No civilization or nation state can defend itself from predators and hostile groups without an adequate reservoir of youthful manpower required for manning its defence forces. That is both an elementary and eternal truth. It applies more rigorously to countries like India, the United States of America, Russia and Australia which have extensive borders and large coastlines. During the last eight decades a great deal of disinformation has been spread across the world, especially in developing countries, that increase in population *per se* is an impediment to the process of economic development. The truth, however, is altogether contrary to what has been propagated by the votaries of Malthusian theory all these years, perhaps now for more than a century. Manpower or human resource, as it is called, is a great asset for economic development and prosperity. The real roadblocks to progress are illiteracy and lack of skill. Youthful population, if it is educated and skilled, is the harbinger of enhanced productivity and a higher Gross Domestic Product (i.e., GDP).

It will surprise most Indians, especially the Indian middle class, that the new threat to the humankind does not come from too many babies, but from too few new arrivals. That is the latest news on the population front. Fertility levels have declined by more than half since 1972—from 6 child births per woman to a mere 2.9 worldwide in 1990s and are still falling rapidly. By 2050 the world population will be around 9 billion, up by a mere 2.6 billion, and after that it may go into a steep downswing.[1] The threat now facing the mankind is depopulation, or too few babies. The continent of Europe, and countries like Russia and Japan are badly trapped in a serious depopulation crisis. According to the United Nations Population Report 2002, Europe's fertility rates are now far short of the replacement level of 2.1 children per woman. France and Ireland with fertility rate of 1.8 top the child-birth chart, while Italy and Spain are at bottom with 1.2. The population of Germany could go down by one-fifth of its 82.5 million people over the next 40 years, while Bulgaria will shrink by 38 per cent, Romania by 27 per cent and Estonia by 25 per cent. Well known demographer, Reiner Klingholz, Director of the Berlin Institute for Population and Development, fears that parts of Eastern Europe, already sparsely populated, "will just empty out."[2] With an annual decrease of 750,000 people, Russia has already landed in a disastrous phase of depopulation, with President Vladimir Putin calling it a "national crisis". In Asia the situation is equally dismal. For instance, Japan with a new low fertility of 1.3 children per woman could lose 25 per cent of its 127 million numbers over the next four decades. And the latest Chinese census data, too, puts the fertility at 1.3. The population of China will peak out at 1.5 billion around 2019. By mid-century it could start losing 20 to 30 per cent of its population in every generation. Ben Watenberg, a well known sociologist, has pointed out that since the Black Plague, never during the last 650 years the fertility rates have fallen so fast, so low and in so many places.[3] The scenario is so grim that recently there were strikes and demonstrations in Germany, Italy, France and Austria by elderly groups due to threatened cuts in social security and pensionary benefits, spilling into confrontationist postures between the older and younger generations. But the worst fate awaits China where the operation of one-child policy has created a 1: 2+4 problem in which each child will be potentially responsible for caring for 2 parents and 4 grandparents in the decades ahead because of increased longevity.[4] Similarly over a long period, India's 2 child norm (e.g., in Kerala the TFR of Hindus is already 1.64 which is far below the replacement level) will prove only a shade less harmful than the myopic Chinese campaign for one child norm primarily because of increased longevity. Statistically, it will mean a high dependency burden of 1:3 on shrinking younger generations by making 2 children responsible for looking after 2 parents and 4 grandparents, i.e., a dependency ratio of 2: 6 (2+4 retired persons). A high dependency ratio of 1: 3 will entail making one youngster look after 3 elderly non-earning persons, in addition to looking after his/her own family. Such high dependency ratio can be quite burdensome and difficult to shoulder. The Chinese are already in the process of abandoning the one-child norm, after realising the damaging long-term consequences of their foolish quick-fix solution for poverty alleviation. To ensure a high percentage of youth in the population and maintain a reasonable dependency ratio, the British Prime Minister, Tony Blair's prescription of adopting a 5 children norm seems to be a more pragmatic option, provided every child could be assured of good education plus technical or occupational skills either by parents or by the state.

There are, however, striking exceptions to the global trend of rapidly declining population. In Europe, Albania and Kosovo are reproducing energetically, and so are Mongolia, Pakistan and the Philippines in Asia. Many Islamic countries continue to grow fast in numbers, with Saudi Arabia at a high fertility rate of 5.7, Palestinian territories at 5.6 and Yemen at 7.2 per woman. According to the projections made by the United Nations the population of Middle East will nearly double from 326 million to 649 million by 2050.[5]

We can assess the wide sweep of the serious mismatch between the youthful component and the ageing population by comparing the fertility and age distribution of two rather extreme cases in each group, namely Saudi Arabia and the Russian Federation, as depicted below.

Table 1.1: Total Population (in million) and Age Distribution

	Saudi Arabia	Russia
Total population (1980)	9.6	138.7
Total population (2025)	39.8	124.4
TFR (1980)	7.2	2.03
TFR (2025)	2.46	1.49
Age distribution (1980)		
Per cent < 0-14	44.3	21.6
Per cent 15-24	18.5	17.7
Per cent > 60	4.4	13.5
Median Age	18.0	31.3
Age distribution (2025)		
Per cent < 0-14	29.4	13.3
Per cent 15-24	18.6	9.8
Per cent > 60	7.9	26.9
Median Age	26.1	43.8

Source: UN 2002 Population data

Chart 1.1: Comparative Age Distribution in1980 and 2025

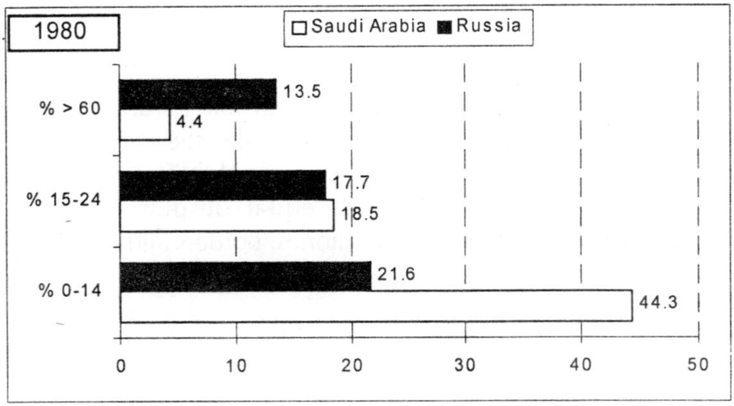

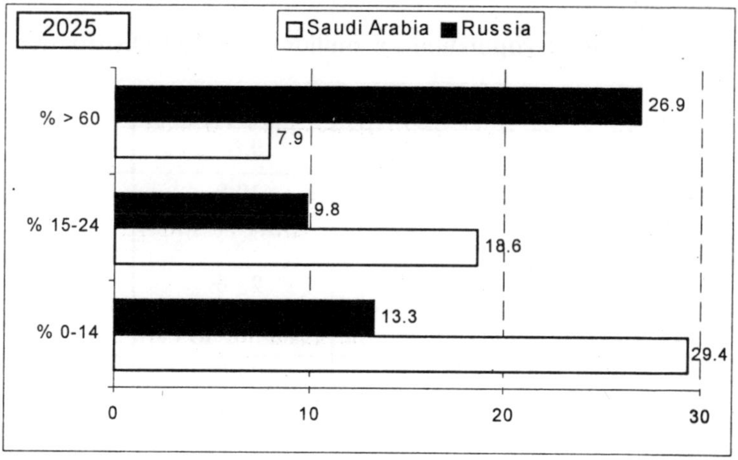

During a time frame of 45 years (1980 to 2025) the population of Saudi Arabia would have *increased* by over four times whereas that of Russia would have *decreased* by 10 per cent. Also the ratio of children and youth in Saudi Arabia will be more than twice that of Russia leading to a much lower median or average age of the population. Therefore although in 2025 the population of Saudi Arabia will be only one-third of Russia, the strength of youth will not be in that proportion. Saudi Arabia will have nearly 7.4 million youth in 15-24 age group, while Russia will have 12.2 million youth in that age group. In effect Russia will have a huge disadvantage vis a vis Saudi Arabia in terms of youth power while burdened with security concerns of a massive territory, huge borders and long coastline. Thus strategically a relative advantage will accrue to Saudi Arabia in terms of the core youthful component available for armed forces of Saudi Arabia in 2025. After a few decades the core youthful component of the two countries, having vastly different security problems, could become almost equal despite enormous differences in their populations, territories, borders and coastlines. That illustrates the importance of youthful component in a country's population.

Historically, the European nations dominated the world in the nineteenth and twentieth centuries because their share in the world population rapidly increased from about 14 per cent in 1500 A.D. to about 40 per cent in 1920 which was further powered by a high youthful component. It facilitated the subjugation of numerous regions by the growing armed forces of European countries, albeit aided by conversion of new technologies into innovative armaments and weapons of war. The might of European stock further led to rapid spread of Christianity because of multiple conquests by the Christian nations which were followed by dedicated efforts of their missionaries. The Table 1.2 below shows the share of different regions in world population from 1650 A.D. onward.

Table 1.2 Share of Different Regions in World Population between 1650-1990 (As percentage of total world population)

Name of Continent/ Country	1650 AD	1850 AD	1933 AD	1990 AD
Europe	18.3	22.7	25.2	13.67
North America	0.2	2.3	6.7	5.34
Latin America	2.2	2.8	6.1	8.29
Oceania	0.4	0.2	0.5	0.50
European Stock	21.1	28.0	38.5	27.79
Africa	18.3	8.1	7.0	11.91
Asia	60.6	63.9	54.5	60.28
India (subcontinent)	Not known	19.04	16.42	20.45
Indian Union (Bharat)	-do-	16.14	13.54	16.02
World Total	**100.0**	**100.0**	**100.0**	**100.0**

[Source: *Religious Demography of India,* Summary Version 2003, Table 1]

From the middle of the twentieth century onwards, there has been a steady decline in the fertility rates of all industrial and modern societies. After the invention and propagation of contraceptives, the process of fertility reduction has gathered pace. According to the United Nations Population Division's *World Fertility Report,* between 1970 and 2000, the world experienced an unprecedented reduction of fertility levels, driven mostly by a declining trend in developing countries. Improved use of contraceptives is behind this fall. The average number of births fell from 5.9 children in the 1970s to 2.9 in 1990s.[6] The use of contraceptives, however, has substantially slowed down the population growth almost all over the globe, except in Islamic societies where its impact has been minimal. During the last three decades throughout Europe, North America, Russia, Japan and China birth rates have fallen so low that many countries have now become acutely apprehensive about the grave consequences of shrinking population on their economic development and defence preparedness.

It is sunset time for a civilization, or country, when its fertility level starts falling below the replacement level of 2.1 children per woman. Such a scenario entails that the future generations of the affected country's workforce will be numerically smaller than the generations to which their parents and grandparents belonged. Furthermore, it will *ipso facto* mean that the proportion of young people in future years will continue to decline in every successive generation, while that of old people, who are economically inactive, will continue to grow. Consequently the GDP (Gross Domestic Product) will shrink because national wealth will be produced by a smaller workforce which will be less than the economically active component in the past. But the smaller GDP will be shared by a disproportionately large number of pensioners and economically inactive population. At the same time, the state and the society will have to make bigger allocations of funds for providing medical and social services to a relatively much larger proportion of retired and elderly people. That critical scenario is already threatening many European nations, Russia and Japan today. This simple but vitally important reason along with the threat of inadequate youthful manpower in the coming decades has forced China to do a rethink on its population policy. A declining population invariably means that over the years the concerned country will have a higher proportion of old people and therefore would find it difficult to meet its requirements of young men and women for its defence forces, as will be seen from the graph below which gives an idea of the likely proportion of youth in the age group 15-24 years in the total population of some important communities from 1965 to 2025:

Chart 1.2: Percentage of 15-24 Age Group

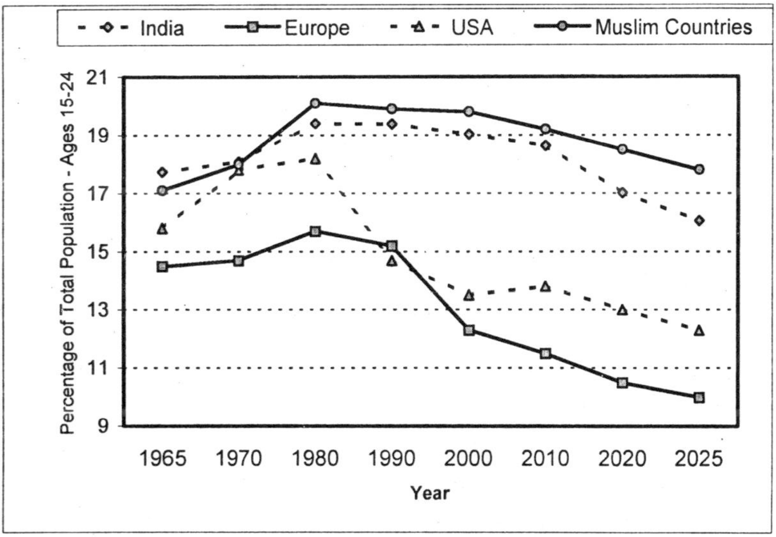

This graph is based on the data given in Samuel Huntington's famous tome, *The Clash of Civilizations and The Remaking of World Order* and indicates the percentage of 15-24 age group in the population of Islamic countries, Europe and the U.S.A. We have also plotted alongside the values for the Indian population based on the United Nations population data published in 1996. It will be seen that the European population is aging so rapidly that by 2025, the proportion of this core youthful group will be less than 10 per cent as compared to about

16 per cent in 1980 (refer to Chart 1.1 and Table 1.1 above). America is somewhat better placed. On the other hand, the proportion of youthful component in Muslim societies will remain high and might decrease very gradually. The percentage of youth in the Muslim societies is likely to remain around 18 per cent in 2025 in a vastly increased Muslim population which is likely to touch 30 per cent or more, around that year.[7] As of now the Indian position appears to be not too bad. It is, however, almost certain that presently in India, too, the proportion of Muslim youth in the age group 15-24 is higher than youth component of the Hindus and allied faiths and it will continue to grow higher and higher in the coming decades, as revealed by the religious composition of India's population in 0-6 years age group.

As pointed out by Huntington, the implications of this mismatch of youthful component between the Islamic societies and other civilizations could be quite serious because the relatively larger proportion of youth amongst Muslims can lead to greater resurgence of global extremism. And perhaps the ageing western countries will not have enough young men to counter the threat. It should be remembered that youthful population is invariably more energetic, more productive, aggressive and violence prone, while an ageing population is slack, sedate, unproductive, and inclined towards introspection.

Apart from the strategic need for retaining a high percentage of youthful component, the motivation and orientation of population is equally important. An effete, luxury-seeking population, even though young, might not be able to vigorously defend the country and its people in difficult times. To that extent the rapid promotion of decadent moral values and promiscuous cultural mores among western and Hindu youth has the potential of destroying their vigour, vibrancy and capacity to defend themselves and their motherland.

Meanwhile, the growth rate of population has slowed down worldwide, as reported by the United States Census Bureau recently. Worldwide there was an addition of only 74 million people in the year 2002 — a figure well below the 87 million added in 1989.[8] The high rate of population growth had peaked out 40 years ago, when it stood at 2.2 per cent per annum.[9] Since then it has been declining sharply. It is therefore clear that the inadequately informed middle class activists shouting themselves hoarse about the need for family planning in India are trapped in a two decades old mindset.

By 2050, the population of 27 countries (members of the European Union) is likely to fall by 6 per cent, from 486 million to 454 million. In a thought-provoking article published in the *New York Times* in the first week of April 2004, Niall Ferguson, a Professor of International History at Harvard University, pointed out that a hundred years ago, when Europe's surplus population was crossing the oceans to populate America and Australasia, the countries that form today's European Union accounted for 14 per cent of the world population. But today that figure is down to a meagre 6 per cent.[10] And according to a United Nations forecast, by 2050 the Europeans will be reduced to just over 4 per cent.[11] The sharp decline is both absolute and relative. Even after taking into account the likely immigration, the United Nations estimates that the population of the current European Union members will fall by around 7.5 million over the next 45 years. In history of Europe such sharp reduction in population had never occurred since the outbreak of bubonic plague in the fourteenth century.[12] No wonder, the political dominance and economic clout of the European nations has substantially gone down in recent decades, largely due to their declining numbers and reduced work force, i.e. EAP (Economically Active Population). That is how demography acts as the arbiter of the destiny of nations. For running their factories, farms and transport systems almost all European countries have become dependent on immigrant labour, mostly Muslims, many of whom enter the continent illegally.

It was highlighted in a United Nations report in November 1997, that as many as 79 countries worldwide were at that time in serious difficulty because of their low birth rates. It is believed that by 2015 an estimated 67 per cent of the global population will live in demographically declining countries having fertility rates touching replacement level and many even sliding far below that benchmark. India could be one of them, especially the Hindus.

The only discordant note, however, comes from the Middle East and most Muslim countries. The 22 Arab countries of the region have a population of about 300 million. The region's annual population growth rate is 2.7 per cent, which is substantially higher compared to 1.5 per cent growth rate for the less developed world as a whole.[13] The average economic growth rate in the Arab region is the second lowest in the world. Additionally, bulk of the population of the Arab world is relatively young, with almost 39 per cent below the age of 15 and a median age of 20. At the same time, in recent years there has been a sizeable increase in the number of females entering the reproductive age group.[14]

According to one version, in the year 2025 while Christians might still be the largest religious group worldwide, Muslims will be the close second largest religious group constituting 30 per cent or more of the world population. According to another estimate, by 2025 A.D. the Muslims will be the largest religious group across the globe. Irrespective of whichever religious group happens to be the most numerous in 2025, the projection made in the United States National Intelligence Council Report on Global Trends 2020 about growth rates of various religious groups shows that even in the year 2025 A. D. the percentage growth of Muslims will be way ahead of all other religious communities. It estimates the growth rate of Muslims at more than 2 per cent in 2025 A.D., while the Hindus will be growing at 1.5 per cent and Christians still at a lower rate, anywhere between 1 and 1.5 per cent.

Till recently among all the nations across the globe, only the USA has been fully aware of the strategic dynamics of global demographics and its likely impact on the future of the world community. For more than a decade Pentagon has been quite concerned about the acute depopulation crisis facing the western civilization, especially the European countries, in contrast to the sharply rising population of developing nations, especially in Middle East and other Islamic societies. In late 1980s the United States Defence department had commissioned a number of studies to monitor the effects of the global population trends with the overall objective of assessing America's ability to influence the geopolitical events across the world. In one of the first reports on the likely demographic changes presented to the Commission on Integrated Long Term Strategy (published in a summary form in the Spring issue of *Washington Quarterly* (a research journal of the politically influential Center for Strategic and International Studies), an in-depth analysis of the implications of global population changes was presented.[15] An overview of the said demographic report compiled by Gregory D. Forester, an instructor at the National Defence University, Washington, highlighted the following significant conclusions :

(i) During the next two decades "demographic developments promise to have a material effect on the general complexion of the world". In other words, in the twenty-first century the growth and decline in the respective populations of various countries will substantially impact the geopolitical balance of power and thereby affect the destinies of many nations across the globe.

ii) An important issue in the coming decades will be the extent to which demographic developments will affect the size and composition of the military establishments of various countries. By and large, the emerging demographic changes will produce completely different concerns in developed countries when compared to developing countries. The declining fertility rates in western nations will make it difficult for the United States and its North Atlantic Treaty Organization (NATO) allies and the Soviet Union (now Russia) and its associate nations alike to maintain their defence forces at the current levels. But in sharp contrast, the exceptionally high fertility rates in many developing countries could lead to expanded military establishments as a "productive alternative" to counter the growing unemployment. It implies that where young manpower is significanly under-employed, the defence establishments will have a built-in momentum to expand their size by capitalizing on the unused manpower, for internal and external security functions.

(iii) While the changing demographics in various parts of the world may or may not alter the international balance of power over the next two decades, the types of conflicts likely to dominate the world in the years ahead will be manpower-intensive. This assessment has already come true and the general trend of growing manpower-intensive conflicts is already visible in many parts of the world, especially in a number of Islamic countries and even in Muslim societies of non-Muslim countries like Thailand, Philippines, Russia, India, etc.

iv) The population growth in the Middle East is likely to pose increased risks to the interests of United States in that region. The region's population, estimated at 233 million in 1987, was likely to reach the staggering figure of 418 million by 2010. Two large Muslim countries, Egypt and Iran, alone might add 35 million and 49 million numbers respectively by 2010. Similarly between 1988 and 2010, Africa's population will more than double to 1.3 billion. For instance, Nigeria which had an estimated population of 103 million in 1988, is expected to double in population size by 2009, triple by 2024, and quadruple by 2035 thus surpassing both the United States and Russia and might become third largest country in the world. Again Kenya's population of slightly over 20 million is expected to double in the next 17 years.[16]

The second military report on world demographics, was prepared in 1991 for the U.S. Army Conference on Long Range Planning by Nicholas Eberstadt of the Harvard University Center for Population Studies. In his critical analysis of the changing world demographics it was pointed out by Eberstadt, who is also a Visiting Scholar at the American Enterprise Institute, that the changing distribution of population in the world constitutes nothing less than a "mortal threat" to the western domination.[17]

Other things being equal, the size of Gross Domestic Product (GDP) of a country is directly proportionate to its work force, or "Economically Active Population" (EAP). That is how those countries which have a higher proportion of young and economically active population are able to achieve a higher rate of economic growth compared to the nations which have a higher proportion of ageing population. Every economist knows this basic truth. But there is a very important caveat to this broad principle : the economically active population must be educated and sufficiently skilled. An illiterate and unskilled population, incapable of earning livelihood through economically productive effort, is certainly a liability. That is the crux of the matter. While educated manpower is a solid asset and will surely add to the GDP, any growth in illiterate and unskilled numbers will act as a drag on development of a country, or civilizational group. Thus, the real culprit is not population increase, but illiteracy and lack of skill. It has been estimated that on average every human being is capable of producing in his life time more than four to five times of what he or she consumes during his or her life span. But so overpowering is the impact of knowledge and skill on a man's productivity that all those human beings who possess superior scientific knowledge or technical skill are capable of producing more than hundred times of what they use or consume in their entire life span. No one is better equipped to appreciate this fact than us, the Indian educated middle class, who are now in the vanguard of Information Technology revolution which has done India proud. Such indeed is the power of technology-soaked knowledge that it has the potential not only to change the fortunes of the tech-savvy individuals but even the fortunes of nations, nay the destiny of the entire mankind. That explains why many developed western nations like the USA have been welcoming bright educated and skilled youngmen from all over the world as immigrants. They know that tech-savvy immigrant youth will help them in accelerating economic development and increase their GDP. For example, the prosperous state of Singapore, our next door neighbour, has always kept its doors open for bright young scientists and technologists.

In the coming decades, large scale demographic changes in many parts of the globe will have a profound geopolitical influence in shaping the destinies of many countries, India included. Some of the major implications of the impending demographic changes are summarised below:-

- First, all those countries which are in a declining population mode will encounter serious economic difficulties, say after 10 to 20 years, unless they import migrant manpower — an option difficult to exercise in the present scenario of fear and suspicion about the intentions of Islamist groups who are hell bent on waging jihad against the civil society.
- Second, any substantial fall in the youthful component of a country or civilizational group will create large gaps in the ratio of working-age population and old-age population thereby restricting the size of its armed forces and undermining their vigour and resolve to defend their hearths and homes.
- Third, over a period of time, the population changes will lead to increased faultline conflicts due to competitive hostility for grabbing more land and the scarce livelihood resources between the numerically gaining and numerically losing civilizational groups. Historically such cultural conflicts invariably degenerate into civil wars for protecting or annihilating the cultural and civilizational values of the warring communities thereby causing bloodbath on the pattern of the events witnessed in Lebanon and the Balkans during the twentieth century. In India we are facing the disastrous socio-economic consequences of the massive silent invasion by Bangladeshi Muslims trying to usurp land and other livelihood resources of Assam, Nagaland, Meghalaya, Mizoram, West Bengal and Bihar. It is bound to cause large scale civilizational conflicts all around.
- Lastly, due to their shrinking size and ageing population the demographically declining countries or civilizations will have lesser say in the affairs of the world community, both politically and economically. Europe is a classic example of this consequence of decline in population and percentage of youth.

Unfortunately in India most people regard the population count, called census, as a routine statistical operation undertaken once in ten years. In reality there is much more to census than what is perceived by the educated middle class Indians (read Hindus). Demography is a deceptively decimating phenomenon. Initially it works slowly, almost invisibly, and then suddenly the population change gathers momentum and bursts upon the sky of the victim country or civilization, almost like a stealth bomber. That is how the fate of the Christians of Lebanon and the Balkans has been sealed, and that is what is going to happen to the Christians of Macedonia, where the percentage of Muslims has grown to 33 from a paltry 8.39 in 1900 A.D., while that of Christians has plummeted to 67 from 91.5 during the same period.

Till recently most European nations, overburdened with ageing populations, have been encouraging entry of young immigrants, mostly Muslims, to ensure smooth running of their factories and transport systems. It is only recently that the European nations have started entertaining existential doubts about the long term effect of immigrants from North Africa and West Asia flooding their continent because of the growing fear of being outnumbered and overwhelmed by an alien civilization.

2

Warnings from Census 2001

"It is not a problem that we have a problem. It is a problem if we don't deal with the problem."

Mary Utecht

The publication of religion-wise Census 2001 data in the first week of September 2004 created a wholly unwarranted controversy in political circles. Apparently, India has a surfeit of left-oriented politicians who are not only ill-informed, but also seized with an ostrich-like attitude. Piqued by the news of sharply increasing Muslim growth, many leftists started questioning the need for a headcount of the religious identity of the people. And not to be left behind in this cacophony, an important Minister of State announced that the government will ban the census headcount in terms of religion, as if that fiat alone will protect the country from the increased recurrence of faultline conflicts which might lead to another partition. As we shall presently analyse, a great deal of the noise being made by vote-bank supported politicians springs perhaps from their appalling ignorance, unless their intention is to mislead the gullible silent majority, mostly middle class Hindus.

During twentieth century demographic changes have played a major role in overturning the civilizational destinies of a number of countries. Unfortunately some of our political commentators have lately developed a tendency to view even major geopolitical events occurring in the country in abject isolation from the worldview by disregarding the global trends and developments. This irrational attitude, overstated both in the ongoing political theatre and the mainstream English media, is in sharp contrast to the rational and holistic approach of their distinguished peers of the previous generation. How can any political analyst forget that during twentieth century certain major demographic changes have taken place across the globe? Some of these changes were responsible for widespread religion-based civilizational conflicts leading to large scale killings, destruction of property, uprooting of millions of people and unspeakable crimes against innocent masses. It is difficult to comprehend how soon and why most of our political leaders and strategic thinkers have forgotten the tragic civil war of Lebanon in West Asia, and the gory strife in Bosnia and Kosovo in the Balkans, which were solely occasioned by the fast-paced demographic changes?

Historically, demographic changes have invariably led to escalation of religious and socio-economic tensions and consequential struggle for supremacy between the interacting but competing hostile communities, not only in the affected country, but often spilling beyond its borders into far away regions and continents. This broad principle tends to apply with greater validity where the demographically gaining community happens to be Muslims. It is common knowledge and world-wide experience that any increase in Muslim population of any country, or region, beyond the benchmark of 30 to 40 per cent invariably leads to a clamour for secession and culminates in a violent struggle for division of the parent country. That has been the unfortunate history of India, Cyprus, Lebanon, Bosnia, Kosovo, Chechenya, the Philippines and many other countries. Thailand is the latest addition to the long list of countries facing the secessionist threat by radical Muslim outfits buoyed by growth of population and worldwide jihadi fervour. In the endemic jihadi violence more than 1200 innocent lives of Thai citizens and security officers have been lost since January 2004.

What Does Census 2001 Reveal?

An objective analysis of the latest demographic trends in India, as revealed by the last five census operations, highlights the following two major incontrovertible facts:

- First, that during the last 120 years a regular trend of decline in the percentage of the members of Hindu and allied religions which includes the Hindus, Sikhs, Jains and Buddhists, all counted together (referred hereafter as Hindus and allied faiths, or "HF") has already been established; and
- Second, that during the last 50 years there has been a continuous steady increase in the percentage of growth of one single community, namely the Muslims, and as revealed by the last two decadal census enumerations this trend has now gathered considerable speed.

These two mutually complementary trends have gathered momentum after independence, as is evident from the census data of the last five decades. In percentage terms the population growth rate of all other communities, e.g., members of the "Hindu" and allied faiths, the Christians and the Parsis has been declining in every census, excepting the Muslims.

By way of clarification it may be mentioned that Explanation II of Article 25 of the Constitution specifically lays down that any reference to the term Hindu shall be construed to include, the Sikhs, the Jains and the Buddhists. In view of this lucid provision in our Constitution we have used the inclusive term "Hindus and allied faiths" to represent the Hindus, the Sikhs, Jains and Buddhists as one single group, throughout this book. This brotherhood of Indian-origin religions could also be called the "Omkar Parivar" because its members draw scriptural inspiration from the cosmic word 'Om' or "Omkar" which is common to the civilizational and scriptural ethos of all of them.

The religionwise break-up of the population of three major communities from 1951 to 2001, in line with the constitutionally inclusive definition mentioned above, is given below in Table 2.1.

Table 2.1 - Population of India (in thousands)

	1951	1961	1971	1981	1991	2001
Population	**361,088**	**439,235**	**548,160**	**683,329**	**846,303**	**1,028,737**
Hindu Faiths	315,001	381.567	472.517	586.681	720,100	866,351
	87.24%	86.87%	86.20%	85.86%	85.09%	84.21%
Muslims	37,661	46,940	61,418	80,0032	106,55	138,188
	10.43%	10.69%	11.20%	11.71%	12.59%	13.43%
Christians	8,426	10,728	14,225	16,645	19,651	24,198
	2.33%	2.44%	2.60%	2.44%	2.32%	2.35%

[Source: Compiled from *Religious Demography of India*, Summary Version, 2001, Appendix 2, p.112]

We find that after taking into account the changes resulting from partition during the 1941-51 decade, the Hindu percentage in Indian Union had gone up by 2.80% and that of Muslims went down by 2.95%, in the aftermath of cross-migration. Since then the percentage of Hindus and allied faiths has gone down substantially by as much as 5.2% during the last 50 years. It needs to be pointed out that after independence the decrease in the percentage of Hindus and allied faiths has been quite large, especially in the last two decades, as reflected in Appendix 2. As we shall analyse in the following pages, this ongoing decline is likely to accelerate in the coming decades. On the other hand, the Muslim population has been registering substantial increases in almost all states and will continue to increase rapidly at least for the next four decades, as is evident from the religious composition of the cohorts in the 0-6 years age group, as revealed by Census 2001.

The annual quantum of decline in the proportion of Hindus and allied faiths in Indian Union seems to have increased considerably since 1981. The decline of approximately one percentage point recorded in Census 2001 is the highest during any decade since independence.

As a result of the continuing sharp decline in the proportion of Hindus and allied faiths in the Indian Union, the increase in their proportion that took place after the traumatic events of the partition has been more than wiped out during the last five decades, and their proportion in the Indian Union in the year

2001 was less than what it was in 1951 after partition of the country. The Population changes have tremendous socio-political ramifications especially because of their concentration in a few regions. Unfortunately our demographers have never paid any attention to the likely consequences of this phenomenon.

Before proceeding further it will be useful to know the distribution pattern of Muslim population in Indian states. Table 2.2 below gives the population of Muslims from 1951 onwards till 2001 and their distribution and growth in different states across the country.

Table 2.2 - Distribution of Muslims in India (population in millions)

	1951 Total Population	**2001 Total Population**	**Absolute Increase No. of times**
India	**37.661**	**138.188**	**3.67 times**
Uttar Pradesh+ Uttaranchal	9.029	30.740	3.40 times
West Bengal	5.118	20.241	3.95 times
Bihar+Jharkhand	4.373	13.722	3.14 times
Maharashtra	2.436	10.270	4.22 times
Assam	1.982	8.241'	4.16 times
Kerala	2.375	7.864	3.31 times
Andhra Pradesh	2.418	6.987	2.89 times
Jammu & Kashmir	2.252	6.793	3.02 times
Karnataka	1.950	6.463	3.31 times
Rajasthan	0.991	4.788	4.83 times
Gujarat	1.451	4.593	3.17 times
Madhya Pradesh +Chhattisgarh	1.050	4.251	4.05 times
Jharkhand	N.A	3.731	N.A
Tamil Nadu	1.443	3.471	2.41 times
Delhi	0.100	1.624	16.24 times

[Source: Compiled from *Religious Demography of India,* Summary Version, Appendix 2, Table 2, p.112]

We have listed above only those 15 states where population of Muslims was more than one per cent of the total Indian Muslim population in 2001. These states have been arranged in a descending order and the last column shows how many times the Muslim population has multiplied during these fifty years (i.e. the ratios of 2001 and 1951 population). Certain important facts listed below emerge from this table:

- The total Muslim population has increased 3.67 times during the last 50 years as compared to a relatively lower increase of 2.75 times in Hindus and allied faiths. This means that in overall percentage terms the Muslims have grown 33 per cent faster than Hindus and allied faiths since 1951.
- The four states of Uttar Pradesh, Bihar, Jharkhand and West Bengal alone contain nearly half of the total Muslim population. Also the 5 contiguous states of Bihar, Jharkhand, Uttar Pradesh, West Bengal and Assam, along with far away Kashmir and Kerala constitute about 67% or two-thirds of the total Muslim population as revealed by Census 2001. It is well known that in most of these states the strategy of tactical voting (which is another name for communal voting) adopted by the Muslims has increased the communal divide and more or less institutionalized the obnoxious vote bank politics because of their growing numbers and percentage.
- The last column shows by how much the Muslim population has increased in the fifty years from 1951 till 2001. Prima facie a ratio of 4 or more tends to signify that there is considerable Muslim immigration taking place (e.g. Rajasthan, West Bengal, Assam, Maharashtra).
- It will also be noted that although prima facie the distribution pattern of population for 1951 and 2001 appears to be similar, according to Census 2001, the

Muslim percentage in states in which the Muslim ratio has been high has gone up further. It also shows how illegal immigration is affecting the distribution pattern of Muslim population. Evidently, the population changes in some parts of Rajasthan, an important border state, should be a matter of concern.

- Delhi State has witnessed a tremendous increase in the population of Muslims which has grown nearly ten-and-a-half times during the last forty years, rising from 155,453 in 1961 to 1,623,520 in 2001. It is believed that among them nearly 13 lakhs are Bangladeshi infiltrators.
- In Haryana, too, the population of Muslims has shown a quantum jump during the last 30 years, increasing from 405,723 in 1971 to 1,222,916 in 2001, i.e. more than threefold increase. The population of the predominantly Muslim enclave called Mewat (recently constituted into a Muslim majority district on the pattern of Mallapuram in Kerala) has registered heavy increase.

Based on the overall distribution of Muslims and Christians, the country can be demarcated into three zones showing differing religious composition, as is evident from the map below:

Map 2.1

INDIAN UNION

The three regions of differing religious composition

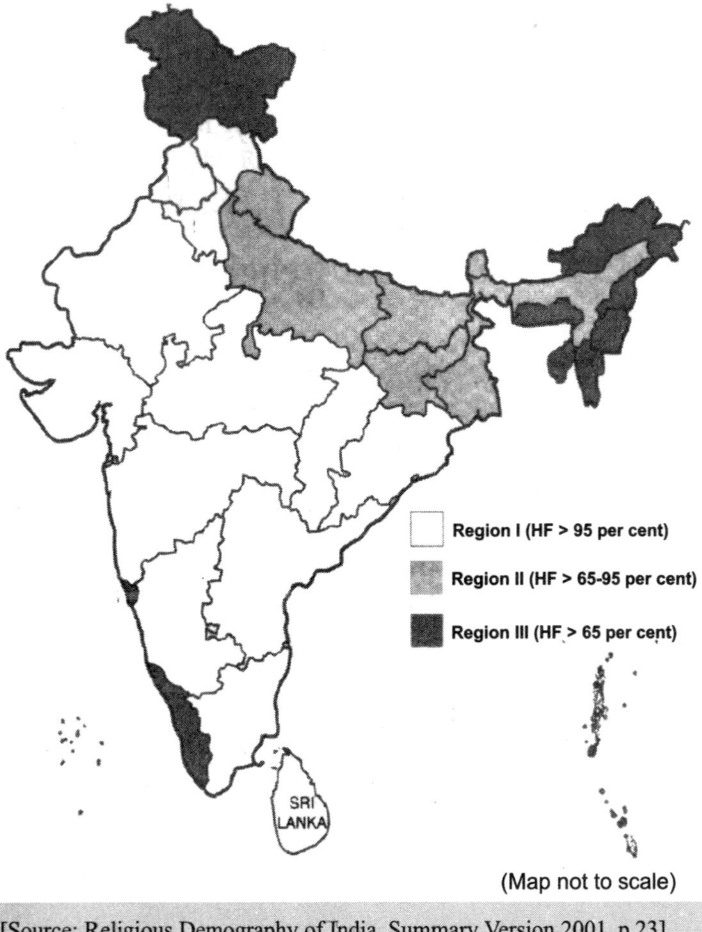

(Map not to scale)

[Source: Religious Demography of India, Summary Version 2001, p.23]

[Notes: 1. The term HF in the map denotes Hindus & allied faiths.]

2. In Region I Hindus and allied faiths hold predominant position.
3. In Region II Hindus and allied faiths are under pressure.
4. In Region III Hindus and allied faiths are already a minority or are fast approaching the minority status.

In the first region Hindus and allied faiths predominate because in this area the decline in Hindu percentage has not been too severe. In the second region due to sharp decline in their population percentage the identity of Hindus and allied faiths has come under pressure. The third region consists of states where members of the Hindus and allied faiths have already been reduced to minority, or are rapidly heading for minority status. Fortunately till now the first region is the largest and comprises most of the western, northwestern, central and southern states. Still all is not well because there are many pockets which can cause religion-based faultline conflicts in future. The second region has been the civilisational heartland of India comprising the states of Uttar Pradesh, Bihar and West Bengal. This region has come under great pressure because in these states the percentage of Hindus and allied faiths has declined between 1951 and 2001 by 3.8%, 4.6% and 5.7% respectively. The decline is much larger in certain areas of these states. As we shall see later on, these areas are mostly contiguous to the sensitive north-east. The third region comprising Assam and adjoining northeastern states, Kashmir and Kerala consists of three pockets — located in the north-east, the northern tip of India and along the southern coastal area. In this region as a whole the decline in the Hindu percentage has been more than 6.3% (from 57.1% to 50.8%) between 1951 and 2001. In fact we may say that there are only a few isolated pockets in these states where the Hindus continue to have some majority.

Unfortunately most Indian demographers caught in the sham-secular mindset have failed to recognise the core problem of relentless growth of only one community, i.e. the Muslims, leave alone studying its causes and suggesting remedial measures. After decades of denial, now a stage has been reached where even they cannot hide certain basic aspects of the growing demographic asymmetry reflected in Census 2001 and several surveys. We shall analyse in the following pages what these surveys reveal and whether any conclusion can be drawn from them warranting meaningful planning by the future governments.

Role of Fertility Differentials in Population Increase

Broadly the sharp growth in the population of any religious group vis a vis other groups is likely to result from the operation of the following three reasons:

1. Differences in the natural growth pattern of different communities. These arise due to differences in the fertility level caused by the acceptance or non-acceptance of contraceptives, differences in the age, sex and child mortality;
2. Immigration, mostly illegal and clandestine; and
3. Conversions.

As far as the sharp growth of Muslim population is concerned, it is caused mainly by the operation of the first two factors, whereas in the case of Christians the major cause is conversions resulting from proselytizing activities of the church. The havoc caused by illegal Bangladeshi immigration has been discussed separately in another chapter.

The International Institute of Population Studies, Mumbai (IIPS), conducted two important and comprehensive studies on family health and planning in the nineties. The first survey, NFHS-I (National Family Health Survey-I) was conducted in 1992-93 while the second one, i.e., NFHS-2 was done in 1998-99. The latter covered the behavioural pattern of more than 90,000 families spread all over the country. The two NFHS surveys revealed many important facts about the higher percentage growth of Muslim population, discussed in the following pages.

There are several ways of quantifying in statistical terms the total fertility of females. Here we shall consider the standard popular method which is called TFR or Total Fertility Rate. It is arrived at by calculating the weighted average of women in the age group 15 to 49 years (i.e. during the period in which children are born to them), of all the births occurring during the previous three or five years. In simple words, it indicates the number of births a married woman can currently expect during her child bearing years. In order to facilitate proper comparison the TFR of Muslims and that of Hindus and allied faiths pertaining to 15 large states is given below in terms of NFHS-2:

Table 2.3 - TFR of Large Indian States

Name of State	**TFR of Hindus**	**TFR of Muslims**	**Muslim-Hindu Ratio**
Madhya Pr.	3.35	3.39	1.01
J & K	2.68	2.72	1.01
Andhra Pr.	2.20	2.53	1.15
Gujarat	2.70	3.12	1.16
Tamil Nadu	2.16	2.57	1.19
Uttar Pr.	3.87	4.76	1.23
Orissa	2.45	3.01	1.23
Delhi	2.35	3.01	1.28
Bihar	3.36	4.44	1.32
Rajasthan	3.69	4.93	1:34
Maharashtra	2.45	3.30	1.35
Karnataka	2.04	2.84	1.39
Punjab	2.29	3.31	1.45
Kerala	1.64	2.46	1.50
Assam	2.00	3.05	1.53
W. Bengal	2.02	3.29	1.63
Haryana	2.77	5.98	2.16
India	**2.78**	**3.59**	**1.29**

It may be mentioned that we are comparing only 15 states having a population of 10 million or more. All of these were covered by NFHS-2. In this table the first column gives the name of the state, the second gives TFR of Hindus, the third gives TFR of Muslims, while the last column shows the ratio of Muslims/Hindu (i.e.M/H) or the ratio of Muslim TFR and Hindu TFR. The states have been arranged in an ascending order of this ratio. For the country as a whole this ratio is 1.29 which means the average Muslim TFR is about 30% higher than that of Hindu TFR. The four sensitive states of Assam, West Bengal, Kerala, and Haryana show values above 1.5. It means that in these states the Muslim growth rate is higher by 50 per cent or more.

TFR gives a fair assessment of live births. But all children born don't survive and many die young. Deaths occurring before the age of five years for every 1000 live births are referred to as 'child mortality'. According to NFHS-2 (1998-99), child mortality among Hindus is much higher than among Muslims, the ratio being 107 deaths among Hindus as against only 83 among Muslims, out of 1000 live births. Thus the incidence of child mortality among Muslims is lower than Hindus by a whopping 25 per cent. Similarly on the basis of NFHS-1 held in 1992, the crude death rate among Muslims was lower than Hindus by almost 13 per cent. It has been estimated by some demographers that in 1990s the life expectancy at birth for Muslims was 62.6 years compared with 61.4 for Hindus, giving Muslims a longevity advantage of 1.2 years. The higher incidence of child mortality and lower expectancy of life at birth among Hindus is often speciously ascribed to the fact that nearly 74 per cent of Hindus live in rural areas where medical facilities are relatively inadequate. But that alone cannot explain the huge difference in the child mortality of the two communities. It may be pointed out that while 36 per cent of Muslims live in urban areas, barely 26 per cent Hindu population is urbanized. Higher urbanization of Muslims shows they are socio-economically ahead of Hindus.

Incidentally, the incidence of child mortality, life expectancy at birth and degree of urbanization of a community are globally recognized determinants of socio-economic advancement or backwardness of a community, accepted both by economists and the World Health Organization. On all these counts, as the comparison above brings out, socio-economically the Muslims come out as more advanced than the Hindus. The three major human development indices clearly show that Muslims are socio-economically better placed than Hindus. This also clearly uncovers the so-called myth of Muslim backwardness is nothing more than a propagandist ploy.

It is well known that reduction in fertility is caused by adoption of family planning measures like contraceptive use and sterilisation. Table 4 below shows how effectively it has been implemented in some of these states. This table shows the percentage of couples adopting any contraceptive technique presently available. Sterilisation, both male and female, is the most effective measure of family planning; it is mostly reversible. Hence a comparison of this factor has also been made in the same manner. As done earlier, we have calculated the Muslims/Hindus ratios for contraceptive use and sterilisation. For India as a whole the percentage of Muslims adopting family planning is less than the Hindu faiths to the extent of 25 per cent. As regards sterilisation, the percentage of Muslims opting for it, is almost 50 per cent less than their Hindu counterparts. Even in a progressive state like Kerala where the literacy and prosperity levels of the two communities are almost equal, the percentage of Muslims opting for contraceptive use and sterilization is remarkably lower than that of Hindus. In percentage terms the difference is of the order of 35 per cent less in respect of Muslims. To be more precise, in Kerala while 71.6 per cent Hindus use contraceptives, the percentage of Muslim couples using contraceptives is barely 47.2. Similarly as against 58.7 per cent Hindus opting for sterilisation, the percentage of Muslims is a meagre 37.3. Only in two states of Tamil Nadu and Madhya Pradesh, the acceptance of family planning by Muslims is relatively good and the ratios of two communities are somewhat satisfactory.

Table 2.4 - Percentages of Couples using Contraceptives and those Sterilised

	Percentage Using Contraceptives		*Ratio*	Percentage Sterilised		*Ratio*
State	**Hindu**	**Muslim**	**% M/H**	**Hindu**	**Muslim**	**%M/H**
Bihar	27.3	9.1	0.33	22.9	5.5	0.24
Haryana	63.3	28.7	0.45	42.7	13.8	0.32
Rajasthan	41.4	25.4	0.61	33.7	17.1	0.51
Kerala	71.6	47.2	0.66	58.7	37.3	0.64
Assam	48.6	33.5	0.69	22.8	5.3	0.23
Uttar Pradesh	29.2	21.0	0.72	17.6	4.3	0.24
Karnataka	60.1	44.2	0.74	54.1	39.3	0.73
Punjab	68.2	50.2	0.74	29.6	17.2	0.58
Maharashtra	62.0	49.1	0.79	53.6	37.3	0.70
West Bengal	69.8	56.3	0.81	37.8	20.6	0.54
Tamil Nadu	52.3	48.9	0.93	47.2	37.6	0.80
Madhya Pradesh	44.0	45.3	1.03	38.5	30.0	0.78
India	**49.2**	**37.0**	**0.75**	**38.3**	**20.4**	**0.53**

A frequently flaunted argument is that the higher Muslim fertility and the lower acceptance of family planning by them is due to poor literacy amongs Muslim women. The Census 2001 has come out with detailed community-wise data on literacy levels, both of men and women. For entire India while the literacy rate for women amongst the Hindus is 53.2%, among Muslims it is marginally lower at 50.1%. Thus the Muslim/Hindu ratio (denoted hereafter as M/H ratio) for female literacy is 94% which means that the female literacy in both communities is almost the same. Again the literacy levels of Muslim women is higher than their Hindu counterparts in Maharashtra, Andhra

Pradesh, Karnataka, Orissa, Jharkhand and Gujarat, but their fertility levels, too are higher.[1] Interestingly in some states like Andhra Pradesh, Karnataka and Gujarat, the literacy levels of Muslims, both males and females, are higher than their Hindu counterparts, as is clear from the statement 8a of Census 2001 Report on Religion Data.[2] Prima facie, irrespective of the literacy levels of Muslim women, or for that matter even of Muslim men, there is a tendency in Muslim societies to abide by the diktats of their clergy and community leaders who regularly oppose family planning.

Some self-styled secular analysts often argue that the practice of family planning among Muslims is poor due to their largely backward status and poverty and that greater acceptance of small family norm will come with improvement in their literacy and economic betterment. But the example of Kerala gives a direct lie to all such apologist propaganda. According to the National Family Health Survey-2, conducted in 1998 in Kerala 17.9 per cent Hindus had low standard of living as compared to only 12.9 per cent Muslims. Yet the Muslim fertility is far higher than that of Hindus or even Christians. Perhaps it is because of this reason that Mari Bhat and Zavier in their research paper, published in *Economic and Political Weekly* issue of January 29, 2005, referred to the universal phenomenon of high Muslim fertility as the *'Muslim effect'*. Interestingly, when we compare the acceptance of family planning by Muslims with that of the scheduled castes and tribes (whose social status is even lower) as revealed by NFHS-2 the acceptance of family planning among the scheduled castes and tribes is higher than that of the Muslims and the former's TFR level, too, is lower than that of Muslims. The TFR level of scheduled castes and tribes is lower than that of Muslims; it closely approximates the average of Hindus and allied faiths. Similarly where the two communities have the same income level the TFR of Muslim is invariably higher than that of their Hindu counterparts. According to a survey-cum-study undertaken by Zoya Hasan and Ritu Menon conducted in the years 2000-2001 (almost at the same time when the latest census was conducted), the average family size of poor Muslim women was 3.5, while that of poor Hindu women was 2.8 which translates into 25% higher fertility of poor Muslim women.[3] After analysing socio-economic differentials of Hindus and Muslims, Mari Bhat and Francis Zavier have conclusively ruled out the possibility of poverty and illiteracy as major contributory factors for higher fertility of Muslims.[4] In terms of percentage more Muslims live in urban areas than the Hindus. Therefore, as a rule their fertility should have been lower, but that is not so. The assertion that higher fertility rate of Muslims is due to their educational backwardness is based on impressionist accounts about non-randomly selected groups.[5] According to the 50th round of National Sample Survey when urban and rural areas were taken together, female literacy was found to be 44 per cent for Hindus and 42 per cent for Muslims which was almost equal, while the male literacy was 67 and 61 per cent respectively — not revealing any great difference in literacy. Mari Bhat and Zavier have drawn attention to the fact that illiteracy of Muslims has been a long term legacy from the past. Commenting on this aspect a well known demographer, Davis Kingsley, had pointed out that even when ruling over India, the Muslims used to pay less attention to education and remained largely dependent on literate Hindus to do their secretarial work.[6]

Hence Mari Bhat and Zavier have concluded that when it comes to Hindu and Muslim fertility differentials, there appears to be no simple correlation between fertility and socio-economic factors like literacy and income levels. We can only generalise by saying that a higher Hindu TFR is the best guarantee against a skewed Muslim-Hindu ratio! This is best illustrated by Kerala where an especially low Hindu TFR of 1.64 has led to a high M/H TFR ratio of 1.5, although the Muslim TFR at 2.46 is the lowest among Muslims in all these states. On the other hand, this ratio is better balanced at 1.19 in the neighbouring Tamil Nadu because there while the Muslim TFR is similar to that of Kerala, the TFR of Hindus has not fallen as drastically as that of the Hindus of Kerala. We may also note that in Kerala which is touted as a model for other states to follow, in absolute numbers, Muslims have grown twice as fast as Hindus during the 1991-2001 decade, as is evident from statement 2 of Census

2001 report of Religion Data (page xxx of Report). On top of it, in the Muslim majority district of Mallapuram the population growth rate during 1991-2001 decade was a whopping 19 per cent which was more than twice the state growth rate of 9 per cent during the decade! It also gave Mallapuram 4 additional Assembly constituencies at the cost of some other districts during recent delimitation of the State Assembly's constituencies.[7] Though the report of NFHS-2 has maintained a studied silence on this issue, the NFHS-1 had made following significant observations about fertility of Kerala's Muslims which are self-explanatory:

1. Muslims have a considerably higher fertility than any other religious group. On average, Muslim women have 1.1 children more than Hindu women. However, even among Muslims, there has been a considerable decline in fertility over time. The lowest fertility levels (under three children per woman) are exhibited by Christians, Sikhs, and women from other religions (primarily Buddhists and Jains). ... Within each education group, Muslims have substantially higher fertility than Hindus. In the first three education groups, the Muslim TFR is 23-28% higher than the Hindu TFR. The differential is even larger (43%) for the relatively small number of women in the highest educational group. The differential between Hindu and Muslim fertility overall is 34%.........but religion is still strongly related to fertility even within education groups.[8]

The prevalence of female sterilisation does not differ much among most religious groups (e.g., the Hindus and Christians) except for the fact that it is very low among Muslims. .. ... the proportion of women and men who have been sterilized is twice as high for Hindus as for Muslims.[9]

The contraceptive prevalence rate is lowest amongst Muslims and highest amongst Sikhs for each educational category of women...The analysis suggests that educational differentials among different religious groups partly explains the religious differences in contraceptive use; however, the religious differentials persist even after controlling for education.[10]

The NFHS-1 Report for Kerala had made the following significant comments.[11]

- Knowledge of family planning is universal in Kerala.
- Approval of family planning is relatively low among Muslims.
- Differences by religion are the largest and have narrowed the least. Muslims have the highest current and cohort fertility of any group in the table. Current Muslim fertility, however, is higher than that of Hindus and Christians by more than one child, but cohort fertility of Muslims is higher than Hindus or Christians by two children. The average number of children ever born is higher for Muslims.
- The median age at first birth for Muslims is three years lower than that for Hindus and nearly five years lower than that of the Christians.
- The acceptance rate of contraceptives is the lowest among the Muslims.
- Hindus and Christians are more likely to want to stop childbearing at an earlier stage than the Muslims.
- The ideal family size of Muslims is one child higher than that of Hindus and Christians.

Age Distribution

Large changes in fertility level invariably alter the age distribution pattern as explained in chapter 1. Unfortunately in India we do not have the complete religionwise age distribution data. As a welcome change, the Census 2001 has for the first time provided the composition of 0-6 age group population from which certain conclusions about the dimensions of future changes in population can be reached. The child cohorts in the 0-6 age group will enter the reproductive age between 2011 and 2017 and thereafter continue to be reproductively active at least for the next 33 years. Other things being equal, the community having a higher percentage of 0-6 years old cohorts will give birth to more children. That provides the clue to the dynamics of future population growth in India during the next 40 years. And since among Muslims the percentage accepting family planning as a national goal is substantially lower than among members of Hindus and allied faiths, at least by 25 per cent, the cumulative impact of higher percentage of cohorts in 0-6 years age group plus the relatively much lower acceptance of family planning by Muslims is bound to speed up their percentage growth during the next 35 to 45 years. In short, that is going to be the overall big demographic picture for the next 40 to 50 years. Even if a concerted attempt is made by the Hindus and allied faiths to shore up their declining percentage, it will easily take nearly two generations of baby boomers, i.e., a span of 50 years, to prevent any further asymmetry in the religious composition of India's population. Even a cursory look at the religious composition of 0-6 age group will give an idea of the lasting damage already done to the demographic identity of Hindus and allied faiths. There is a lesson to be learnt from the comparable tragedy of Lebanon where the robust Christian majority was reduced to a helpless minority within 3 decades. By the time leaders of the Maronite Christian community woke up to the demographic disaster facing them it was all over. About Christians of Lebanon it was poignantly remarked that the owl of Minerva began its flight only after darkness had enveloped the sky ! Nearer home, the same verdict might also be pronounced by the next generation in respect of the tragedy facing the Hindus of Assam, and to some extent even those of West Bengal.

The table 2.5 below gives the religious composition of the 0-6 age group for the whole of India and the states having a total population of 10 million and more. The religionwise percentage of the 0-6 group is indicated in relation to the total population of two communities, namely the Hindus and the Muslims.

Table 2.5 - Composition of 0-6 Age Group Population in Major States

Name of State	Total Percentage	Hindu Percentage	Muslim Percentage	Muslim/ Hindu Ratio
Chhattisgarh	17.06	17.13	15.47	0.90
Madhya Pr.	17.87	17.88	17.86	1.00
Gujarat	14.87	14.79	15.75	1.07
Bihar	20.25	19.91	21.99	1.10
Tamil Nadu	11.59	11.54	12.90	1.12
Uttar Pr.	19.03	18.62	20.87	1.12
Andhra Pr.	13.35	13.21	14.87	1.13
Rajasthan	18.85	18.65	21.01	1.13
Orissa	14.56	14.43	16.49	1.14
Maharashtra	14.11	13.90	16.23	1.17
Jharkhand	18.40	18.04	21.18	1.17
Karnataka	13.59	13.29	16.10	1.21
Punjab	13.02	12.93	16.26	1.26
Delhi	14.56	14.06	18.54	1.32
Kerala	11.91	10.81	14.99	1.39
W. Bengal	14.24	12.72	18.70	1.47
Assam	16.87	14.49	21.82	1.51
Haryana	15.77	15.24	24.55	1.61
J&K	14.65	13.07	15.43	1.18
All India	**15.93**	**15.55**	**18.74**	**1.21**

[Source: Compiled for Census 2001 Religion Data Report.

Under ideal conditions the percentages of the two religious groups, i.e., the Hindus and allied faiths and Muslims, should be more or less equal as is the case in Madhya Pradesh. But when we look at India as a whole, we notice that although the 0-6 group (all communities) constitutes 15.93% of the total population, the percentage of Muslims is higher at 18.74%, i.e. roughly three percentage points more. The Hindu figure is substantially lower at 15.7% disclosing a difference of more than 3 per cent. The ratio of 0-6 age group Muslims and Hindus and allied faiths i.e. Muslim-Hindu ratio is given in the next column. It is 1.21 for the whole India (i.e., Bharat). In other words Muslims children in the 0-6 age group are higher by 21% as compared to Hindus and allied faiths. To get a feel of the big picture of the impending demographic changes we have just to take into account the fact of lower acceptance of family planning by Muslims. The Table 6 below has been arranged according to the ratio of the two communities in the 0-6 age group. The left side shows the states which have a lower Muslim/Hindu ratio as compared to the whole country and the right side shows states which have a higher value. We find that 12 out of 19 large states constituting 73% of the national population have a lower Muslim/Hindu ratio starting with 0.90 for Chhattisgarh. Seven states constituting 24% of the national population have a larger value with Haryana showing the highest ratio of 1.61, which means that Muslims have 61 per cent more 0-6 cohorts than Hindus. Logically therefore the state of Haryana will record the highest increases in the percentage of Muslim population during the next 40 years or so and the massive tilt will be reflected in the next 4 decadal censuses. Similarly another five states of Assam, West Bengal, Kerala, Jammu and Kashmir and Delhi will record sizeable increases in the Muslim population because of large differentials in the critical group of 0-6 years cohorts who will enter the reproductive age from 2011 onwards and will continue to procreate for the next 40 to 45 years. The macro picture about the impact of the 0-6 years cohorts on India's future population can be gauged from the table below.

Table 2.6 - Composition of Total and 0-6 Population

Name of State	Percentage of Total Population		Percent of 0-6 year Cohorts	
	Hindu	Muslims	Hindu Cohorts' Percentage	Muslim Cohorts' Percentage
Assam	65.38	30.92	56.16	39.97
W. Bengal	74.11	25.25	66.22	33.17
Kerala	56.28	24.70	51.05	31.08
J & K	32.83	66.97	29.30	70.54
Haryana	94.09	5.78	90.90	9.00
Delhi	87.34	11.72	84.34	14.92
Karnataka	85.86	12.23	83.95	14.49
Jharkhand	82.09	13.85	80.49	15.94
Uttar Pradesh	81.38	18.50	79.61	20.29
Maharashtra	88.31	10.60	87.00	12.20
Bihar	83.40	16.53	82.00	17.96
Andhra Pradesh	89.28	9.17	88.35	10.22
Rajasthan	91.40	8.47	90.45	9.45
India	**84.22**	**13.43**	**82.22**	**15.81**

[Source: Compiled from Census 2001 Religion Data Report]

A further analysis of Statement 7 (Appendix 1) reveals that out of India's 35 States and Union Territories the percentage of Muslim cohorts is higher than their Hindu counterparts in as many as 31 States and Union Territories. The percentage of Hindu cohorts is marginally higher than Muslim cohorts only in two States of Madhya Pradesh and Sikkim and two Union Territories of Andaman & Nicobar Islands and Diu and Daman.

Thus during the next 40-50 years population growth of Muslims will be even more fast paced, at least in 31 States out of a total of 35.

Comparisons are proverbially odious, but equally inevitable in the critical situation like the one facing the states of Assam, West Bengal and Kerala as revealed by 0-6 years age group populations. In these three states the threat of demographic changes leading to faultline conflicts is in no way different from what was witnessed in Lebanon in 1970s and in the Balkans in 1980s and the events presently unfolding in Macedonia where the Albanian guerrillas led by Ali Ahmeti have been trying to wrest more political power from the peace-loving but ageing Christian majority lacking the will to fight back the Albanian guerrillas.

Real Clue to Future Demographic Changes

As already explained, the religious composition of 0-6 age group provides the real clue to the pattern of population changes from 2011 A.D. onwards. It is this group which is going to increasingly reflect the religious composition of India's population in the coming decades, say between 2011 and 2051 when 0-6 years age group cohorts enumerated during Census 2001 will be reproductively active. That will give a big fillip to Muslim population during the coming five decades. Apparently this modus causing fast-paced Muslim growth has been in operation at least since 1981 or may be even from 1971 onwards. The 1991-2001 census has shown substantial decadal high increase in absolute numbers as well as in percentage terms of Muslims in states like Kerala, Assam and Haryana where the Muslim/Hindu ratios for 0-6 age group and the Muslim TFR are abnormally high.

As explained above, after 2011 the percentage of Muslim cohorts entering the reproductive age will be nearly 21 per cent higher than the Hindu faiths. Other things remaining the same, that translates into a headstart of 21 per cent higher reproduction rate for Muslims. And since the Muslim fertility is higher by at least 25-30 per cent, it will lead to their absolute growth rate of more than forty five per cent as compared to that of Hindus. Already the Muslim growth percentage has been higher in the 1991-2001 decade by about 36% (brought down to 29.5 per cent in terms of the "adjusted census data" by leaving out 3.6 crores Indians) which will further accelerate when 0-6 group cohorts enter reproductive age, say between 2011 and 2017. Prima facie that is what has been happening since independence, although the trend could have gathered a major momentum nearly three decades ago when members of Hindu faiths opted for family planning on large scale in response to the government's campaign. Evidently the Christians also opted for family planning in a big way. That is how the percentage of Muslims only grew and the overall population growth rate acquired a massive tilt in favour of the Muslim community vis-à-vis all other religious groups. It is well known that while all other communities have voluntarily adopted the small family norm, the Muslims have been persistently refusing to accept it, largely due to the edicts against family planning issued from time to time by the Muslim clergy on religious grounds. Very recently quite a few Maulanas and Islamic scholars have openly opposed the concept of family planning both by making statements to the press and by appearing on popular television channels, including an appearance made by a prominent leader of the All India Muslim Personal Law Board on the BBC channel in which he categorically declared that there was no place for family planning in Islam because it was against their scriptures.

Analysis by Professional Demographers

In *Economic and Political Weekly's* January 29, 2005 issue, a number of research studies and articles on Census 2001 and population trends were published. Though the tone and tenor of every article, excepting the one by Ashish Bose, was loaded against the so-called 'Hindu Right', the stark truth about the galloping Muslim growth could not be concealed by any demographer. At least the following 4 articles conceded not only that the fertility rate of Muslims was higher than that of Hindus, but also that the fertility difference has increased substantially after independence:

1. Role of Religion in Fertility Decline: The Case of Indian Muslims — by P.N. Mari Bhat, A.J. Francis Zavier;
2. Population Growth, Fertility and Religion in India — by P.M. Kulkarni, Manoj Alagarajan;
3. Hindu-Muslim Fertility Differentials — by R.B. Bhagat, Purujit Praharj ; and
4. Muslim-Hindu Fertility Differences — Evidence from National Health Survey-II — by A. Dharmalingam, K. Navaneetham and S. Philip Morgan.

The critical conclusions reached in the above four research papers were two. First, on an average every Muslim woman is giving birth to at least one child more than her Hindu counterpart. And second, the adoption of family planning methods is quite low among Muslims.

Of all the research papers published in the *Economic and Political Weekly*, the one authored by P.N. Mari Bhat and Francis Zavier contains the most comprehensive analysis of Census 2001 and the two National Family Health Surveys. Despite chiding the so-called Hindu right here and there, the article is refreshingly free from political rhetoric and cliches. In the beginning itself the authors conceded that the "fertility of Muslims, which was about 10 per cent higher than that of Hindus before independence is now 25 to 30 per cent higher than the Hindu rate, and that the difference according to religion is larger than the difference between the forward and depressed Hindu castes and tribes".[12] Some very significant conclusions arrived at by the two well known demographic researchers are discussed below.[13]

1. It is incorrect to say that the 2001 Census disclosed a higher reduction in the growth rate of Muslims than that of Hindus. Going solely by the fertility factor one finds that it is actually the Hindu growth rate which has declined faster. According to Census 2001 data adjusted for territorial changes the growth rate of Muslim population fell from 32.9 per cent in 1981-91 to 29.5 per cent in 1991-2001 while the growth rate of Hindus declined

from 22.7 to 19.9 per cent. Although in absolute terms the percentage decline in Muslims numbers appears to be marginally higher at 3.4 per cent vis-a-vis the fall in Hindus of 2.8 per cent, in real terms the decline in Hindu growth rate was higher at 12.2 per cent when compared to only 10.3 per cent decline in Muslim percentage. The researchers pointed out that the real pace of decline in percentage of population is measured "not in absolutes but in proportionate terms". That shows how a devious attempt was made in September 2004 by partisan political analysts, including some demographers and leading lights of print media and television channels to misguide the gullible Hindu middle class into believing that the speed of decline in the percentage of Muslim growth was higher than that of the Hindus. A fact not alluded to by Mari Bhat and Zavier is that the unadjusted census data showing the abnormally high growth in Muslim population during 1991-2001 reflected the truth, as revealed by 2001 Census.

2. The acceptance of sterilisation, the main method propagated for family planning in India, is particularly low among Muslims. The difference in the acceptance of sterilisation between Hindus and Muslims was 4 per cent in 1970. By the year 1998 it jumped to 18 per cent which was even higher than the difference in the overall use of contraceptives by the two communities.

3. The contention of some Muslim scholars and western analysts that discrimination in recruitment to public offices is the main cause of lack of interest among Muslims for acquiring higher education is totally incorrect. Some of these analysts often juggle with statistics to show that Muslims form only 3 per cent of those employed in administrative services, police, railways and nationalised banks. As analysed by Mari Bhat and Zavier, the foregoing figures do not indicate any high level of discrimination if one takes into account the fact that the Muslims constitute only about five per cent of those

graduating from colleges, and furthermore there could be some difference in the quality of education received. It may be pointed out that in his book, *Confessions of A Secular Fundamentalist* (Penguin Viking 2004), Mani Shankar Aiyar has harped quite laboriously on the grouse of Muslims about inadequate representation in administrative services. Being a diehard fundamentalist, Aiyar did not care to apply his mind to the basic issue of inadequate educational and scientific attainments of his constituents. But then Mani Aiyar is one of his kind and logic certainly is not his strong point. For instance, in *The Confessions of A Secular Fundamentalist* he has tried to prove by recourse to obfuscation and sheer non-logic that the growth rate of the Hindus and Muslims is the same. He has deliberately ignored the fact that according to the National Family Health Survey-I, held as early as 1992-93, on an average every Muslim woman was giving birth to 1.1 child more than her Hindu counterpart more than 12 years ago. It is difficult to guess why an intellectual like him must take recourse to obfuscation by suppressing the truth.

4. Many analysts ascribe the higher fertility of Muslims to higher poverty level and illiteracy. After analysing socio-economic differentials Mari Bhat and Zavier have ruled out the role of poverty and illiteracy as main contributory factors for higher fertility of Muslims. A higher percentage of Muslims live in urban areas than the Hindus, their proportion being 36 per cent and 26 per cent respectively. As a rule, therefore, the Muslim fertility should have been lower than that of Hindus. But that is not so.

5. There is no justification in blaming the state for low educational performance of Muslims. If the state alone could ensure higher levels of educational attainments by Muslims, then the community should have fared much better at least in Kerala and West Bengal, the two left-dominated states avowedly more favourably disposed

towards the Muslims. Unfortunately the educational performance of Muslims in these two states has been worse than their performance at the all India level. While the proportion of Muslim population is 21 per cent in Kerala and 27 per cent in West Bengal, the percentage of Muslim women graduating from colleges is abysmally low at 5 per cent in Kerala and 2 per cent in West Bengal.

6. According to the last National Sample Survey the incidence of poverty among Muslims was higher than among Hindus. But the real cause of this difference in poverty level was the bigger size of Muslim households. In urban areas the Muslim households have nearly one extra member than their Hindu counterparts. Similar difference in the size of households is present even among the poor households of the two communities.

7. According to the researchers, the higher fertility of Muslims, does not disappear completely even at higher educational levels. A significant quantum of Hindu-Muslim fertility difference remains even after a Muslim woman completes high school education. Interestingly the predicted fertility level of an illiterate Hindu woman is about the same as that of a Muslim woman having higher secondary or even better education. Mari Bhat and Zavier have described the phenomenon of higher fertility of the community as *"Muslim effect"*, a very apt though somewhat colourful description.

8. Mari Bhat and Zavier have tried to allay the fear that on the basis of their present growth rate the Muslims would outnumber the Hindus in India in the near future. They feel that such a transformation cannot take place in the foreseeable future. According to their projections, by 2101 India's population will stabilize around 1.70 billion of whom 1.27 billion will be Hindus and 320 million Muslims. The percentage of Muslims in the total population will, however, rapidly grow from 13.5 in 2001 to 19 in 2101, thus almost doubling from the post-independence level.

9. While the Hindu population would reach stabilisation in the sixth decade of this century (i.e. between 2051 and 2061), it will take four more decades for the Muslim population to stabilize. Thus, during the next 100 years, i.e., by 2101, the Muslim population will increase by 180 million and that of the Hindus by 440 million which addition will be more than twice in the number of Muslims added.

10. Before stabilization (i.e., reaching the replacement level of 2.1 children per women), the population of Muslims would have grown by 130 per cent, while that of Hindus will increase only by 50 per cent. One important implication pointed out by Mari Bhat and Xavier is that all those areas where Muslims were 35 per cent or more in 2001 will become Muslim majority areas by 2101. Though the fear that Muslims would outnumber Hindus in India as a whole is unwarranted, some new Muslim majority areas would certainly emerge. That could have a bearing on the local politics, so the researchers feel.

11. The role of religion in the development of an attitude towards fertility control as an act interfering with God's will in the matter of procreation should not be underestimated. During the two surveys, i.e., the NFHS-1 and NFHS -2, the religious difference in fertility was ascribed entirely to one single cause, namely opposition to family planning. Nine per cent of married Muslim women in both the surveys said that they had no intention to use contraceptives because it was against their religion. But among the Hindus and Christians less than one per cent married women gave that kind of response. Thus the effect of religion on fertility cannot be dismissed as inconsequential. What separates the Hindus and Christians on the one hand from Muslims on the other is that the latter's religious leaders give low priority to family planning. The Islamic clerics appear to be more dogmatic on this issue in countries where their

followers are in minority. For instance, Muslim minority communities in Thailand, Philippines, Nepal and Sri Lanka have higher fertility than other religious/ethnic groups.

Subsequent to the publication of the aforesaid collection of articles on India's demography in *Economic and Political Weekly* of January 29, 2005, P. N. Mari Bhat had to undertake the onerous task of clearing multiple cobwebs of doubt created by the divergent views expressed on the subject. In a highly lucid, though somewhat explanatory paper, 'Trivialising Religion: Causes of Higher Muslim Fertility', published on March 26, 2005, issue of *Economic and Political Weekly*, Mumbai, the author clarified the confusion created by partisan analysts. Rebutting the contention that the current difference in fertility between Hindus and Muslims was small and its scale was exaggerated by media, Mari Bhat pointed out that the decades of demographic research in India had shown that among the many fertility differences studied, the Hindu-Muslim differential is one of the "most enduring ones".[14] According to National Family Health Survey-2, the difference in the TFR between illiterate women and those who completed high school is 1.5 births (i.e. 3.5 and 2.0 respectively). It is a significant difference because a mere decrease of one birth per woman is needed to achieve the desired goal of stabilising India's population. Evidently therefore a difference of one birth per woman between the Hindus and Muslims which roughly comes to the order of 30 per cent cannot be dismissed as insignificant. By sheer logic of eclectic scientific analysis' the author systematically demolished, one by one, all flimsy arguments invented to justify the high Muslim fertility and the pleas advanced by the apologists for ignoring it as something inconsequential. Taking the discussion to the larger global plane, Mari Bhat has drawn attention to the higher fertility of Muslims throughout south-east Asia. Across the region the Muslim minority groups have higher fertility than the majority communities.[15] Even in countries where they are in majority, Muslims are not the forerunners in fertility transition. In Indonesia, Malaysia and Bangladesh, the Chinese and Indian ethnic groups have lower fertility than the Muslims. Clearly therefore the higher Muslim fertility has a religious basis. The percentage of women giving religious reasons for not wanting to use contraceptives is significantly higher among Muslims than among either Hindus or Christians. The use of sterilisation is particularly low among Muslims. Before concluding, the author has quoted the following interesting observations of Caldwell and Reddy, two well known demographers, highlighting the dogmatic Muslim opposition to use of sterilisation for family planning:

"The pressures within the Muslim population against sterilisation are often coercive. They range from refusal to eat with the sterilised, to accept food from them ..., to have them as servants, or to allow them to be buried in the Muslim burial ground. The majority of Muslims state the case against sterilisation in terms of religious morality, either that it is forbidden, or that Allah has committed himself to provide for children sent to this earth, while contemporary Hindu explanations are completely secular". [Caldwell *et al* 1982: 714].[16]

While giving full credit to Mari Bhat and Zavier for their illuminating research, it needs to be pointed out that in projecting the future demographic trends they have totally ignored two important factors of illegal immigration of Bangladeshis and conversions which have the potential of making the growing demographic asymmetry more adverse to the Hindus and allied faiths. These two factors are vitally important in the context of sharply growing imbalance in India's demography and must not be ignored. They have projected the dynamics of Hindu Muslim population by making some wobbly assumptions. According to them the Hindu population will reach the replacement level (i.e., TFR= 2.1) around 2021-26, while the Muslims will reach the replacement level a decade later.[17] But looking at the hostile attitude of Muslim clerics and scholars to the twin issues of mutiple wives and triple Talaq, it can be safely presumed that there is little possibility of the Muslim fertility reaching the replacement level of 2.1 by 2036, or even by 2051. It could as well turn out to be mere wishful thinking, because the projection looks palpably divorced from the ground reality of the community's dogged resistance to small family norm.

Another important omission is the failure of the two demographers to comprehend and correlate the impact of the geopolitical phenomenon of Islamist terror — a serious problem already confronting the Indian civilizational identity. They appear to be totally indifferent to repetitive attacks on Hindu temples, killing of unarmed pilgrims going to Amarnath and Vaishnodevi, the storming of the Indian Parliament and plans of terror groups to bomb the Indian Military Academy at Dehra Dun and destroy the hub of our sunrise IT industry in Bangalore. The number of such attacks may only increase if the recent incidents are any indication. It was amazing that most Indian demographers are not bothered about the attack by Lashkar's goons on Sri Ram temple in Ayodhya on July 5, 2005. Their indifference to the ghostly bomb blast at Sankatmochan Temple of Varansi on Tuesday March 7, 2006, and the likely repercussions of such attacks on Hindu identity is totally unacceptable. The gratuitous advice of Mari Bhat and Zavier to the Hindu community "to live and let live" tends to create the impression as if the Hindus were AK-47 carrying terrorists with bandoliers of RDX strapped to their bodies. They have totally ignored the truth that threats to the lives and property from terror attacks are being faced only by Hindus and no other community. Islamist terrorists are targeting only Hindu temples, and no mosque or church is or ever was on their hit list. Yet the researchers have passed a value judgement against Hindu community without stepping out to count how many Hindu pilgrims and worshippers have been killed by Muslim terrorists and how many temples are security protected against jihadi attacks all over the country, including scores of temples in metropolitan cities like Delhi and Mumbai. By ignoring depredations of terror groups most Indian demographers have displayed apathy towards the majority community. They appear to be a class apart, totally different from their western counterparts, who seldom fail to warn their countrymen of the impending demographic threats emanating from adverse population indicators and illegal immigration.

Future of Hindu Identity

It is nobody's case that the Hindus, now approaching one billion mark, will become a helpless minority all over India within the next 5 or 6 decades. No, that will not happen soon, certainly not in one go. What is most likely to happen is that in several parts of India, especially in states like Assam, Tripura, West Bengal and Bihar, the Hindu population will get drastically reduced and the community will come under increasing squeeze year after year. That will lead to flaring up of social tensions and cause sharper communal divide. This is already happening in Assam, some adjoining states of north-east, West Bengal and Bihar. The process of Hindu families relocating away from Muslim dominated border areas "in droves" after selling their property was highlighted by Bibhuti Bhusan Nandy in his two illuminating articles, one published in *The Hindustan Times*, New Delhi, in February 2003, and another published in *The Statesman*, New Delhi, in January 2005. It is anybody's guess how soon this trickle of Hindu outmigration, presently witnessed in Assam and West Bengal, will transform into a stream of moving refugees and then assume the shape of a turbulent torrent. Unfortunately no one cares to visualize when and how it will cause a countrywide commotion and civil strife — on a scale massively larger than what happened in 1947 at the time of partition.

It is extraordinary that most Indian demographers and political analysts tend to view the population changes as some kind of routine isolated statistical phenomenon wholly unrelated to the momentous geopolitical developments at national level and across the globe. They live cocooned lives, ignorantly engrossed in the microgroove of statistical analysis of population figures. They are indeed farthest removed from the ground reality. Not one of them has taken into account the far reaching effects of the huge Bangladeshi infiltration which is an earth-shaking event having the potential of causing faultline conflicts and socio-political upheavals across the sub-continent, if not tomorrow then certainly the day after. They are not bothered that unless we act now and here, multiple civil commotions replicating the blood-soaked events witnessed in Lebanon and the Balkans might grip the Indian sub-continent in the dangerous decades ahead. Perhaps they don't know that according to Niall Ferguson within next fifty years or so, Europe is likely to become a Muslim majority continent. Equally ignorant they are about the tragedy unfolding in Macedonia where Christians were 90.60 per cent in 1900 but are now reduced to 67 per cent. Buoyed by the fact that they constitute one-third of Macedonia's population, the Albanian Muslims have upped the ante for seeking greater autonomy in many municipal cantons where they have acquired majority or the near majority status. For Macedonians the year 2001 was quite troublesome because the jihadi militia led by Ali Ahmeti, a radical Albanian Muslim, spearheaded a violent campaign which nearly pushed the country into a bloody civil war. The threat of civil strife was avoided through a peace deal signed in 2001 between the Macedonian government and Ahmeti's guerrillas promising to decentralise the country's government by redrawing the borders of municipalities and giving them more powers.[18] Recently the Muslims mounted intense pressure by demanding delegation of more powers to municipal councils several of which are now like Muslim majority enclaves or cantons. The hostility between the two communities is rising at a fast clip. In villages inhabited by Albanians (read Muslims) a Macedonian flag is never seen; only Albanian flags are hoisted. In the last week of July 2004 more than 20 thousand Macedonian Christian demonstrators trooped into the capital Skopje to protest against the government's decision to give the Muslims more control over the municipal councils in which they have become a majority. While the government maintains that the proposed delegation of more autonomy to the Muslim-dominated municipal councils was crucial for maintaining peace in Macedonia, the critics argue that the plan will create "ethnic enclaves" thereby paving the way for future vivisection of the country. The problem of balancing the power share between the Macedonians and Albanian Muslims nearly drove Macedonia to the brink of civil war in 2001.[19] When Macedonians asked for a referendum on November 7, 2004, on the issue of redrawing municipal boundaries, the former Muslim guerrilla leader, Ali Ahmeti, remarked menacingly that he could not remain "indifferent" if the proposed referendum put the 2001 peace agreement in jeopardy. Many Macedonians are leaving the areas inhabited by Albanians. Those Macedonians Christians who have the requisite financial means are migrating out, with New Zealand as the destination of choice.[20] Mercifully no referendum was held in November 2004 because of the call for its boycott given by some partisan groups. Otherwise Macedonia would have surely plunged into political strife. To cut the long story short, the Christian numbers are declining fast all over the Balkans — an event totally comparable to the demise of Christian majority in Lebanon in early 1970s. By now for all practical purposes the fate of the Orthodox Christian civilization in the Balkans appears to have been sealed. The outmigration of Christians from Muslim dominated areas of Macedonia is not something new. Nearer home its echoes can be heard in the border districts of Assam and West Bengal from where an exodus of Hindus has already started. The fate of the paranoid Christians of Oslo and those residing in its suburb Aksherus in the far away Norway is no different where the phenomenon of non-Muslims being forced to move out is termed as "the ousting effect".[21] In Norway, the Muslim population has quantum jumped 75 times during 23 years, i.e., between 1980 and 2003.

Equally surprising is the tendency of our political analysts and demographers to ignore the warnings issued by international agencies about the threat posed by Islamist terror groups to civil societies worldwide. Sometime ago the National Intelligence Council of the USA, a strategic think tank, in their report, *"Mapping the Global Future"*, projected that the world economy in 2020 will be 80 per cent larger than its size in 2000 A.D. and that the average per capita income, too, will be fifty per cent higher thereby making the world much more prosperous. While painting a rosy picture about the future of China and India, they forecast the likely "emergence of China and India as new major political powers — similar to the rise of Germany in the 19th century and the US in the early 20th century."[22] According to the NIC report, vis a vis China, India has in its favour the advantage of a rising working age population, democratic institutions, capital markets and many world class high-tech firms. At the same time, the report sets their happy forecast about a more prosperous world against the backdrop of the fear of an increasingly uncertain era in which globalisation might be seen as less benign "due to politics being more influenced by religion". The National Intelligence Council warns about the impact of increased activism and spread of radical Islam. It foresees the risk of an Islamic caliphate emerging to unite radical Muslims across ethnic and national boundaries and expects "a more pervasive sense of insecurity, which may be as much based on psychological perceptions as physical threats". People will be better off, but will feel less safe.[23] This telling comment about the likely emergence of a caliphate in the near future is not a prophesy made by the neo-conservative group (often referred to as a cabal), but an assessment by an independent think tank of pragmatic experts, wholly unrelated to US government. It is well known that Islamist ideologues, supported by Al Qaeda and ISI, have a long term grand design to establish a caliphate extending from Indonesia to Europe by sweeping across the entire Indian sub-continent in which India is the sole large-sized non-Muslim country. It needs no great geopolitical vision to know that the soft and submissive Indian republic is likely to be the most fertile ground where the proposed South-Asian caliphate could strike roots.

All these threats and security concerns have been totally ignored by Indian demographers and political analysts. They pretend to be ignorant of the fact that India is sandwiched between two radical Muslim countries, both intent upon establishing a South-Asian caliphate which has been the subject of intense discussion and planning among Islamist groups nurtured by the ISI and Al Qaeda. Like ostriches they refuse to see the far reaching consequences of the fast growing asymmetry in the religious demography of India in the context of geopolitical developments in the Indian sub-continent and across the globe. Hopefully one day, some day, the wisdom of correlating the population changes with the political developments, within and beyond our borders, will dawn on our demographers and strategic analysts. But that may be too late. The Indian nation must overcome the fatal attraction of ignoring the "ousting effect" which has been causing the Hindus to relocate from the areas in which the Muslim population races beyond the benchmark of 30-40 per cent and then makes life difficult for non-Muslims—a squeeze now being experienced by the Norwegians of Oslo also. This trend is not something new; it has been the common experience of non-Muslims of many countries at different points of history. In the aftermath of Paris riots of October-November 2005 several Muslim dominated localities of Stockholm (Sweden) and some towns of Denmark have experienced the emergence of "No Go" areas for local police. They have to reinforce police teams before entering Muslim areas.

In view of the factors recounted above and the fast growing gap between the 0-6 age group population of the two communities, it should surprise no one if the Muslims become 20 per cent of India's population by 2061 or even earlier. This strong possibility should be kept in view along with likelihood of Hindus and allied faiths becoming a minority between 2061 and 2101 A.D. in the total population of the sub-continent, i.e., India, Pakistan and Bangladesh all counted together.[24] Unless the demographic imbalance is corrected soon, the territorial space for Hindus and allied faiths and the size of the Indian Union, i.e., Bharat, will progressively shrink. Ultimately, India could become a relatively smaller entity, say by the end of this century, or a little later.

India's political leadership and slumbering middle class has failed to realize that the demographic crisis is a furiously ticking timer. On reaching the critical flashpoint in next few decades it could destroy the nation's unity and obliterate its secular identity, just as it did in Lebanon and the Balkans.

The demographic picture is far from reassuring and should be the cause for concern to all right thinking people. It seems that the Hindu moorings of India are changing fast. In several areas, these moorings have already been lost, in some others these are being erased quite rapidly. And the adverse transformation seems to be taking place even in areas like

Haryana and Maharashtra which were free from such changes earlier. The state in India has complete access to enough data and strategic information to pinpoint the scale and magnitude of the problem. And the government surely has the means to ensure that the problem does not reach the point of no return by radically altering the delicate population balance essential for peaceful co-existence between different communities and for maintaining communal peace. Yet the central government and the Indian elite and opinion makers have shown no will to effectively respond to the menacing problem so far.

As far as central government is concerned, it is not a matter of not knowing, or not having the competence to act. No, there is something more to it. It is perhaps a matter of not being concerned. It seems that the state in India and a large proportion of educated articulate Indians, including opinion makers, believe that the fast-paced changes in the relative proportion of different religious communities in India are not a matter of legitimate concern. Apparently the leftist groups have convinced the government and the Indian middle class of city dwellers that even if Hindu identity is altogether erased from the whole of India, or from certain specific parts of India, it will not be a matter of legitimate concern. Perhaps in their opinion, the Hindu identity and heritage of India is not something which merits to be valued or preserved.

3

Doctoring Population Data

"Facts don't cease to exist because they are ignored."

Aldous Huxley

We have seen how a wholly unwarranted controversy was created in political circles as well as English media by the publication of religionwise data of Census 2001 in the first week of September 2004. It was amusing to see in the Saturday Special of a leading national daily on October 2, 2004, two interesting articles on Census 2001 authored by Muslim columnists — both based on the false premise that the decadal population growth of Muslims according to Census 2001 was declining faster than that of Hindus and not rising, as revealed by Census 2001.[1] One of these was by the well known political commentator, late Dr. Rafiq Zakaria, while the other was by Abusaleh Shariff, a demographer associated with the NCAER (National Council of Applied Economic Research). It is well known that the census figures initially announced by the Registrar General in the first week of September 2004 had revealed that the population of Muslims was growing at a fast pace, way ahead of all other religious groups, which led to multiple howls of protests by the leftists and self-styled secularists who started baying for the blood of the Registrar. Bowing to the intense pressure mounted by the government, the Registrar decided to present the census data under two heads, namely the "unadjusted" and the "adjusted". The "adjusted data" which was manufactured by deleting more than 3.6 crore Indians living in Assam and Jammu & Kashmir from 1961 onwards, showed that in percentage terms the Muslim population was growing at 29.5 per cent (as against 36 per cent in terms of the "unadjusted" data). And to achieve the desired political objective on the eve of Maharashtra state elections, the entire census headcount in respect of Assam and Jammu & Kashmir was deleted with retrospective effect from the last five census operations from 1961 onwards. It is difficult to comprehend how and why these two gentlemen accepted the doctored Census 2001 data without going into even elementary details. For instance, in the asterix marked footnote to the Statement 1-a of the Religionwise Data of Census 2001 which gives the proportion and growth rate of the respective population of religious communities for the last four decades from 1961 to 2001, it has been clearly stated that it "excludes Jammu & Kashmir and Assam for all decades from 1961 to 2001".[2] Clearly, therefore, the so-called "adjusted data" was nothing but fudged census data manufactured by a kind of sleight of hand.

Indeed most surprising is the fact that both these columnists used the doctored census data for arriving at highly contestable conclusions by ignoring the truth. Surely neither Dr. Rafiq Zakaria nor Abusaleh Shariff could be so naïve as not to comprehend that the revised figures labelled "adjusted" were nothing short of statistical manipulation intended to bluff the gullible Indian people, primarily the English-knowing Hindu middle class. They totally ignored the salience of deleting with retrospective effect the census figures pertaining to the two demographically sensitive states of Jammu & Kashmir and Assam from 1961 onwards — something never done before either in India or anywhere else. Much greater commitment to truth, however, was shown by a former civil servant turned politician, Syed Shahabuddin, who had the sagacity to question in one of his articles that "why the Census Commissioner did not choose to fill up the Assam gap of 1981 and J & K gap of 1991 by intrapolation" and leave the figures pertaining to the previous decades untouched.[3] Although the methodology suggested by Syed Shahbuddin would have been ethically correct and quite in conformity with the internationally accepted best practices, that could not have produced the politically desirable goal. Recourse to that standard methodology would have only reinforced the analytical assessment originally made in the Census 2001 Report on Religion showing a high increase in the growth rate of Muslims. If the NCAER associated demographer, Abusaleh, tries his hands at the proposed mode of interpolation, suggested by Syed Shahabuddin, he will discover that without omitting the census data pertaining to the last four decades in respect of Jammu & Kashmir and Assam, comprising more than 3.6 crore Indians from Census 2001, the politically desirable goal could not have been achieved.

I remained in touch with the office of the Registrar General of Census for updating two chapters of my book, *Long March of Islam,* since May 2004. My personal visits to the Census Office in that connection unwittingly gave me an insight into the questionable process of fudging the Census 2001 by deleting with retrospective effect the total headcount pertaining to Assam and Jammu & Kashmir pertaining to last five enumerations undertaken in 1961, 1971, 1981, 1991 and 2001 — an unparalleled attempt to deceive and disinform the Indian people. It involved deletion of 3.6 crore Indians from Census 2001.

In conformity with the globally recognised best practice of maintaining purity of statistical analysis and for the sake of truth, it will be desirable to rely on the "unadjusted" census data released by the Registrar in the first week of September 2004. As we shall presently understand, the fudged data, euphemestically labelled as "adjusted", is nothing more than clumsy mutilation of census figures.

As explained in the previous chapter, for the last fifty years the population of Muslims alone has been racing ahead at a fast pace, way ahead of all other religious groups. It may be recalled that the Census 1991 had recorded that the Muslim growth rate during 1981-91 decade had risen to 32.76 per cent as against the declining Hindu growth rate of 22.78 per cent.[4]

Unfortunately the Census 2001 showed a further sharp acceleration in the growth rate of Muslims, while recording a sharper decline in the growth rate of Hindu faiths. It showed that in percentage terms the growth rate of the Muslims during the decade remained very high, while that of the Hindus had fallen to a new low of 20 per cent.

In percentage terms the growth rate of the Sikh community, an integral component of Hindus and allied faiths, has been going down very rapidly. Their growth rate had sharply declined from 32.2 per cent during the decade 1961-71 to 24.3 in 1981-91. According to Census 2001 it has hit a new low of merely 18.2 per cent (unadjusted data). In other words, during the last four decades the growth rate of Sikh population has gone down quite fast, i.e., by nearly 14 percentage points. What is more important is that this declining trend is likely to be maintained, even gather speed, for the next 30 to 40 years because of the disproportionately lower percentage of Sikh cohorts in the age-group 0-6 years, as revealed by Census 2001. Interestingly, according to the adjusted data (contrived by omitting 3.6 per cent of India's population from 2001 census figures) the percentage decline in growth of Sikh population comes to 16.9 which translates into nearly 50 per cent decline in their growth rate during the last four decades. It is, however, gratifying to note that the Sikh community has taken prompt notice of this disturbing trend and the matter was deliberated upon by Sikh Sangats in a number of Gurudwaras in Punjab and west Delhi to devise remedial measures. More importantly, perturbed by the sharply declining Sikh growth rate, Sardar Tarlochan Singh, a former Chairman of the National Minorities Commission, summoned top Sikh religious leaders and intellectuals to deliberate on the problem. He even requisitioned the services of Ashish Bose, a well known demographer, for making a presentation before prominent leaders of the Sikh community in the first week of November 2004.[5]

The demographic threat to the Hindus is nearly as serious as to the Sikhs, perhaps much graver in the eastern region, especially Assam and West Bengal. Unfortunately there is very little awakening among the Hindu masses spread over the vast rural countryside about the impending demographic crisis likely to confront the Indian nation during the next few decades. In sharp contrast to the somnolent attitude of Hindus, numerous Muslim scholars, community leaders and some members of the All India Muslim Personal Law Board have been openly exhorting the Muslims to reject family planning and continue to opt for larger families. The cold facts about the rapid changes in demography of India in favour of Muslims have already been discussed.

Though the sharp increase in Muslim growth rate, revealed by the Census 2001, is an established fact, truth is a red rag to politicians of our country trying to usurp power by recourse to vote bank strategy. All hell broke loose in the so-called 'secular' political circles as soon as the census data was released by the Registrar, J.K. Banthia. Although the officer had performed his official duty in an upright manner, unseemly attempts were made to haul him over coals. A leading English daily labelled him a "saffronite". Quite a few newspapers reported that he was given a dressing down by the Home Minister himself, though God alone knows why. Ultimately the Registrar was pressurised by the powers-that-be into making certain unwarranted changes in the Census 2001 data by deleting retrospectively more than 3.6 crore Indians from Census 2001 headcount to make the findings politically acceptable on the eve of Maharashtra elections. This huge deletion of all census enumerations pertaining to Assam and Jammu & Kashmir from 1961 onward with retrospective effect was done, after attempting all sorts of permutations and combinations, solely for scaling down the percentage growth of Muslims just to show that their growth rate, too, was declining like that of Hindus and Sikhs. The desired objective of projecting a declining trend of Muslim growth rate could not have been achieved even by leaving out of calculations the entire 2001 census data pertaining to the State of Jammu & Kashmir which showed a total population of only 101,43,700 comprising 67,93,240 Muslims, 30,05,349 Hindus and 3,45,111 'others'. In the huge headcount of more than one billion people, it was too small a figure and its deletion alone could not have achieved "the politically desired" result.

While grappling with the problem created by political diktat suddenly a bright statistician in the Registrar's office recalled that no census had taken place in Assam in the year of grace 1981. Why not exclude that State as well, having a total headcount of 2,66,55,528 which included a high percentage of Muslims ? Luckily for the beleaguered Registrar the census figures of Assam did fit the bill when added to those of Jammu & Kashmir, but there was a difficult proviso. To project the desired downtrend in Muslim growth rate, it was necessary to delete the entire census data pertaining to these 2 states from 1961 onwards with retrospective effect — *something never done before*. More importantly, it was totally violative of the spirit of the Census Act 1948, and the then pending Right To Information Bill. But ultimately the 'pseudo-secular' politics triumphed over truth and the growth rate of Muslims was brought down by omitting 1,50,33,851 Muslims, 2,03,01, 794 Hindus and 14,63,573 'others' belonging to the two States of Jammu & Kashmir and Assam from Census 2001. The peremptory deletion of the combined population of these two States was able to take care of nearly 43 per cent Muslims along with the Hindus and 'others' constituting the remaining 57 per cent population. The peculiar demographic mosaic of the two States, both having a high percentage of Muslims, provided the necessary scope for doctoring the census data for achieving the politically desirable goal. Thus the politically motivated fudging, though uniquely unprecedented, was accomplished by deleting from the Census analysis nearly 3 crore 67 lakhs residents of two States (including Muslims, Hindus, Sikhs and others) constituting more than 3.6 per cent of India's population on the frivolous plea that no comparable data was available for Jammu & Kashmir in respect of Census 1991 and that similarly no actual headcount took place in Assam during 1981 census. Simultaneously the census data pertaining to 4 decades, from 1961 to 2001, in respect of the 2 states of Jammu & Kashmir and Assam was deleted with retrospective effect in an arbitrary manner just to achieve the desired politically acceptable result.

To call this mutilitated data as "adjusted" is an insult to the I.Q. of average Indian. Frankly, it is something fit to be labelled as "maladjusted" census data, because there could be no legal or moral justification for omitting more than 3.6 per cent of India's population pertaining to two important States having high concentration of Muslims. What has been done has no parallel in the history of India's census operations, nor in the annals of census in any other democratic country! This unprecedented doctoring of Census 2001 data has left several important questions unanswered.

First, why was not the same dubiously ingenious method of arriving at the "adjusted" data applied at the time of analysing the Census 1991 figures? At that time, too, there was a similar problem in relation to one State, that is Assam, where no census could take place in 1981. The truth is that at that time no one questioned the census results because there was no political compulsion. To put it more bluntly, in 1991 no one felt the political need to fudge the census data because it was not a hot potato then, nor were the figures of 1991 census released on the eve of any State elections. In any case, there appears to be absolutely no justification for deleting from record the census data of Jammu & Kashmir and Assam for the years 1961 and 1971 because no controversy had ever erupted about the census figures of those two decades. While the census data of Jammu & Kashmir and Assam for the decades 1981 and 1991 have been deleted from the Registrar's revised analysis on the specious ground that in 1981 there was no census in Assam and similarly in 1991 no census operations could take place in Jammu & Kashmir, the unstated opaque reasons for deletion of census data of 1961 and 1971 in respect of these two States retrospectively are shrouded in mystery. The government owes an explanation, and a convincing one at that, for resorting to this unwarranted and unprecedented malpractice which amounts to deliberate tinkering with the data of previous census operations undertaken 30 - 40 years ago, the findings of which had remained incontrovertible all along.

Second, what is the legal and moral justification for omitting the headcount of Jammu & Kashmir and Assam, forming more than 3.6 per cent of country's population, from the analysis of

2001 census? Are the two States of Jammu & Kashmir and Assam not part of India ? Are more than 3.6 crore people living in the two States not Indians ? How dare the Indian government arbitrarily omit more than 3.6 per cent of the country's population from the census after the actual headcount had already been done ? What has been done by the government is a clear violation of the letter and spirit of the Indian Constitution as well as the law of the land. To take recourse to such deception simply to please the leftists and a particular communal constituency amounts to grossness of the highest order.

Third, will not this dangerous step of excluding the census data of the two strife-torn States from 1961 onwards send a wrong signal to the ISI-sponsored separatist forces operating in the two vulnerable states? Will it not strengthen their case for breaking away from the Indian Union? As a result of this shortsighted move, devised solely to garner communal votes in the elections in Maharashtra and other States, the insurgent groups of J&K and Assam will be able to convince their local supporters, and even proclaim at the international fora, that the Government of India has no case to prevent them from seceding because of the deletion of all residents of J&K and Assam from India's census data for the last 40 years ! They might convincingly argue that the Indian government does not consider them Indian nationals.

Fourth, what will be the methodology of analysing the next census due in the year 2011 and thereafter in the subsequent decades? It looks inevitable that the two States of Jammu and Kashmir and Assam will have to be similarly excluded from the Census 2011 and all successive censuses scheduled to be held in future. Without a similar 'maladjustment', (outrageously called as "adjustment"), there is a strong possibility of the 2011 census springing a more shocking surprise by recording another unprecedented quantum jump in the Muslim growth rate, now that it has been artificially brought down in the year 2001 to meet the political requirements. What will be the mode of analysing India's population statistics in the coming decades now that a novel precedent of omitting certain States from census headcount has been established?

Fifth, was the government of the day legally empowered to play ducks and drakes with the census data, by deleting retrospectively nearly 3.6 per cent of India's population after the actual headcount had been conducted ? If so, under which law can such a large number of Indian citizens be ignored and left out, particularly when the census operations are conducted under a special statute, that is the Census Act passed in 1948?

Sixth, has the government any legal powers to modify, amend and delete with retrospective effect the census data pertaining to the last 40 years in such a cavalier and contrived manner, especially when there was absolutely no complaint from any quarter about the census data analysed and published in the years 1961 to 1991? If this manipulative procedure is not challenged, it could lead to a situation in which every political dispensation coming to power in future will invent similar questionable methods for distorting the census findings to meet their political aims. There is absolutely no enabling provision in the Census Act, 1948, for making retrospective changes in the census data, especially after the headcount had been conducted and published ten, twenty, thirty, or forty years ago.

Seventh, is not the government bound by the ethical norm of good governance in the matter of dissemination of correct and truthful information to the public ? In a peculiar situation like the present one, what is the sanctity of the recently passed and much-hyped Right To Information Act, which received Presidential accent sometime ago for being placed on the statute book, especially when the government itself fudges facts? Can the government palm off the so-called "adjusted" census data as truthful information, if someone makes a formal request for religionwise census data? Will not the government's action in deliberately excluding the population of the two States showing high percentage growth of Muslims constitute a deliberate and wanton act of concealment of truth and thus seen to be violative of the Right To Information Act?

Lastly, this manipulative episode did not show the Election Commission in good light either. This wanton manipulation of the census data on the eve of State elections was a clear violation of the model code of conduct and suo motto notice of government's malfeasance should have been taken by the Election Commission. It is difficult to accept that the Commission has really fulfilled its statutory responsibility to act as a wide awake and effective watchdog, especially on the eve of Maharashtra elections. How is it that the Election Commission took no notice of this gross fudging of the census by deviously deleting with retrospective effect the census figures of the two States since 1961?

As a footnote it may be added that this unprecedented manipulation of population data took place when an economist of international acclaim, Dr. Manmohan Singh, happened to be the Prime Minister of India. As a rule, all economists are acutely conscious of the need for maintaining purity of statistical data and our Prime Minister could be no exception. Yet the fudging was done in an unabashed manner. There are, however, reasons to believe that the Prime Minister was kept out of the political loop which decided to doctor the population data.

It is time that the government as well as the Indian people, especially the top politicians and educated classes, started viewing the phenomenon of the skewed population growth of India's religious groups in the global context. Let us not turn our back on truth. Galloping Muslim population is a global problem, including India. It is already worrying many democratic countries and strategic thinkers. Time has come when the broad spectrum of our political leadership and the Indian people should know that the Muslims were only 12 per cent of the world population in the year 1900, they grew to 18 per cent in 1980-90, and now the Muslim population is likely to quantum jump to 30 per cent of world population by 2025 — barely 19 years away from now.[6] Meanwhile the incidence of jihads being waged across the globe has risen in tandem with growth of Muslim population. It is difficult to guess how many decades more the Muslims will take to reach the benchmark of 40 per cent of the world population. Should the Muslims reach that magic percentage, say even after the next 100 or 120 years, it could change the course of mankind's history.

Not many TV anchors, nor many political leaders, know that within the next 50-60 years, the 'Christian' Europe is likely to become a Muslim majority continent. A warning about that possibility was given by Niall Fergusson (a contemporary historian and strategic analyst teaching at Harvard University) in an article published in the *Sunday Times*, London, in April 2004. Some enterprising futurologists have proposed that Europe could be called "Eurabia" after 50 years or so. Most of the Muslim societies have exceptionally high fertility rates — higher by wide margins when compared to non-Muslim societies. Saudi Arabia is multiplying at a fertility rate of 5.7 per woman, Yemen at 7, Afghanistan at 5.6, Palestinian territories at 5.6, Nigeria at 5.4 and Pakistan at 4.1 and so on. Fertility rates of most European countries range between 1.1 and 1.6 per woman, far below the population replacement level of 2.1 children per woman. Till a few years ago India was at a declining fertility rate of 2.9. Now it could be far less, at least in respect of the Hindus and allied faiths who have adopted the small family norm in a big way. For instance in Kolkata district (West Bengal) the fertility rate of Hindus was only 1– far lower than that of Christian Europe.

Without taking a global view of the fast changing demography, the Indian nation cannot prepare itself for handling the impact of skewed population changes on country's secular and pluralistic ethos and the consequential challenge of the growing jihadist campaigns. Europe is almost paranoid by the fear of the fast-paced growth of Muslim population overtaking the declining Christian numbers. Do our centre-stage political leaders know that the Prime Minister of UK, Tony Blair, has already started advising the British couples to opt for a 5 children norm? And fearful of the growing population of jihad-infested Indonesia the Australian government has advised all couples to make more babies — at least 3, preferably many more. A cash bonus of $2,083 for every baby born after June 2004 has been promised to every couple by Australia's Chancellor of the Exchequer, Peter Costello, in the budget allocation for the year.[7] Some demographers, associated with the United Nations Development Programme (UNDP), have warned that once an anti-natal ethos gets entrenched in a society it tends to become almost irreversible. Russia and Germany, both trapped in a serious depopulation crisis, are two typical victims of this growing anti-natal ethos in western societies. In all probability, apart from some other factors, e.g., the despicable gender discrimination, spread of anti-natal ethos appears to have adversely impacted the growth rate of Sikhs during the last two decades, as revealed by the Census 2001.

It is time for a rational, cool-headed and objective analysis of the census data in the context of national as well as global developments. Recourse to acerbic remarks and rabble rousing invectives like 'malice-mongers', used by late Dr. Zakaria, are poor substitutes for a dispassionate discourse. Perhaps a great deal of noise being made by partisan politicians appears deliberate, unless it stems from their appalling ignorance.

Both in Lebanon and the Balkans the demographic change had a kind of terminator effect on the pluralistic civilizational moorings of the once-upon-a-time Christian territories. For instance, due to adverse demographics the Maronite Christians who constituted an overwhelming majority of Lebanon's population were reduced to a minority within a short span of four decades. By 1932 the Christian majority in Lebanon had gone down to a mere 55 per cent, while the proportion of Muslims rose to nearly 45 per cent. The changed demographics accelerated the long-standing hostility between the two communities and soon the Muslims started clamoring for a greater say in the affairs of the country on the basis of their increased population. Ultimately according to an agreement reached in 1943 between Maronite Christians and the Muslims, known as the National Pact of Lebanon, the two hostile groups decided to share power in proportion to their ratio in the country's population. The posts of top ministers in the government were apportioned between the Christians and the Muslims in the ratio of six to five respectively, based on 1932 census figures. Lebanese Christians were better educated and more enlightened than their Muslim counterparts whose lives were dominated and controlled by Mullahs and religious scholars. While Christians restricted the size of their families, the Muslims did not, perhaps owing to the diktats of their clerics and religious preachers. By 1970 the Maronite Christians had landed themselves in a declining fertility rate of 4 children per woman, while the Muslims maintained a steady fertility rate of 6 children per woman. The result was that between 1970 and 1975 Lebanon became a Muslim majority country in a raging civil war. In the ensuing bloodbath and mayhem nearly four to five million Christians outmigrated within two years, mostly to Europe and America. Even the intervention of the USA and belated attempts of Israel to provide succour to the beleagured Christians could not save them from ignominous rout at the hands of jihadi militias. Luckily most of the Christians were well educated and enterprising and have many Christian lands to migrate to. By now the percentage of Christians in Lebanon is believed to have come down to 30 per cent or less. Yet the trend of well-to-do Christians migrating out of Lebanon continues till date.

The foregoing facts speak for themselves, even though they defy the prevalent culture of political correctness, deeply ingrained in a section of our country's westernised middle class and inattentive English media. It is difficult to fathom how can they fail to understand that the growing asymmetry in the religious composition of population will surely and seriously undermine the secular and multicultural character of Indian nation in not-too-distant future. Apparently these busybodies have developed a myopic vision. Nearer home, they refuse to see the frightening consequences of sharp demographic changes taking place in the north-eastern region, West Bengal and Bihar on unity and territorial integrity of our motherland in the context of growing jihadi threat worldwide and in our immediate neighbourhood.

4

Terminator Tsunami

"The question is not whether we will die, but how we will live."

Joan Borysenko

During last three decades the problem of continuous influx of Bangladeshis into Assam, West Bengal, Bihar, Orissa and almost all north-eastern States has taken a weird shape. The alien infiltrators are now swarming all over the country and their massive presence is writ large across dozens of cities including Delhi and Mumbai. They have spread out to many far away states like Punjab, Haryana, Maharashtra and even to the textile town Coimbatore in Tamil Nadu. The mind-boggling invasion from Bangladesh since 1970s has come to constitute by far the most formidable threat to the integrity and sovereignty of India. For the last five decades the successive central governments have remained focussed solely on the Jammu & Kashmir imbroglio, and in the process wilfully ignored our eastern flank. Unfortunately throughout the last three decades India's, political leadership has failed to realise that much more than Kashmir, the Bangladeshi influx has the potential to tear asunder the socio-political fabric of India and thereby pave the way for another vivisection of the country.

After considering the overall concentration of various religious groups in different parts of India we can easily identify the areas where the impact of massive Bangladeshi infiltration will be felt first and foremost. It is crystal clear that the north-eastern region will be the first victim of this silent tsunami the reverbrations of which are being felt all over the country, including the far from border metropolitan cities of Delhi and Mumbai.

On a conservative estimate, the total number of Bangladeshi infiltrators and their progeny presently living in India could be anything between 2.5 to 3 crores. At a national convention on demography held at New Delhi in April 2005, however, quite a few participants held the view that by now the total number of Bangladeshi infiltrators and their progeny could be as high as 5 crores. The mind-boggling dimensions of the problem were lucidly presented by Bibhuti Bhusan Nandy (a retired senior officer of the Cabinet Secretariat) in a research study titled *'Space Invaders'* published in the *Hindustan Times,* New Delhi of February 14, 2003. In his well researched article, Nandy highlighted the fact that an analysis of Bangladesh's 1991 census data undertaken by Sarifa Begum (of the Bangladesh Institute of Development Studies, Dhaka) revealed that the 1991 census figure of 104.7 million population of Bangladesh initially disclosed a clear shortfall of more than 10 million people. The actual headcount during that census was at enormous variance with the estimate of 116-117 million for the decade projected by the UNDP (United Nations Development Programme). Thus there was a huge shortfall of nearly 13 million people revealed by the census enumeration for the decade 1981-1991. The actual headcount was found to be lower than even Bangladesh government's own moderate estimate of 112-113 million population for 1991 census. After a detailed study, Sarifa Begum attributed the "missing millions" to the unregistered 'outmigration'. Through her well researched analysis of the 1991 census data of Bangladesh, Sarifa Begum established that between 1981-1991 nearly 14 to 15 million Bangladeshis had entered India.[1] In another context she further estimated that nearly 3.5 million people had "disappeared" from East Pakistan between 1951 and 1961, while another 1.5 million had possibly entered India between 1961 and 1974.[2] Thus as per Sarifa Begum's estimate the total number of outmigrated or missing Bangladeshis comes to 19 million to which must be added another 2 million Bangladeshi citizens, mostly residents of the districts bordering India, whose names were removed from that country's electoral rolls between 1995-96. Obviously those two million Bangladeshis whose names were struck off the electoral rolls had managed to enter India. Surely they could not have migrated to China or Australia. That makes a grand total of 21 million people who had managed to infiltrate into India till 1996. And since then the silent invasion has continued unabated for the last 10 years during which millions more must have infiltrated into India. These figures based on analytical studies conducted by Sarifa Begum, a Bangladeshi Muslim demographer, highlight the magnitude of the massive illegal influx. And if we take into account the progeny of the illegal immigrants, by now their numbers could be anything close to 30 to 50 millions. After all, Delhi alone is reported to have 1.3 million Bangladeshi infiltrators, while their numbers in Kolkata and Mumbai are substantially higher.

Let Facts Speak

The frequent denials of illegal infiltration by Bangladesh authorities stand fully rebutted by the research carried out by one of their own demographers, Sarifa Begum. It has been rightly pointed out by Bibhuti Bhusan Nandy that between 1981-91 the much higher growth rates of population in Indian districts bordering Bangladesh when compared to the significantly lower growth in the adjoining areas of Bangladesh clearly establishes that there has been a massive influx from Bangladesh into India's border districts. The conclusion is further strengthened by the fact that in the decade 1981-1991 there was very low population growth in Hindu-concentrated districts of West Bengal, while the urban towns of the State experienced an explosive growth in population. Cold statistics tellingly illustrate this point.[3] Greater Jessore and Greater Khulna districts in Bangladesh registered 1.97 and 1.58 per cent growth respectively as against 3.16 per cent in the adjoining West Bengal district of North 24 Parganas. Similarly Greater Mymensingh in Bangladesh showed a paltry growth rate of 1.82 per cent as against a population growth of 3.84 per cent in the adjacent Garo Hills district of Meghalaya. Greater Comilla district of Bangladesh showed an increase of 1.89 per cent as against a growth rate of 3.36 per cent in the adjoining Tripura. Just sample how several semi-urban areas of West Bengal located close to Bangladesh border witnessed a virtual population explosion during the decade 1981-1991: Gobardanga (8.64 per cent), Khardah (9.5 per cent), Raiganj (13.93 per cent), Ashoknagar (7.45 per cent), Mekhliganj (7.98 per cent) and Tufanganj (22.45 per cent). All these towns have witnessed a fast paced growth of Muslim numbers. Interestingly, the average growth rate of urban and semi-urban population for West Bengal during the decade 1981-1991 was barely 2.45 per cent.[4]

Census 2001 has revealed many more far reaching and worrisome population changes, especially in the north-eastern region and the Marxist-ruled state of West Bengal — even in the Hindi heartland state of Bihar. For instance, in the geographically crucial state of Assam, the Muslims have already attained the majority status in six districts, i.e., Dhubri (Muslims 12,16,455; Hindus 4,05,065), Goalpara (Muslims 4,41,516; Hindus 3,14,157), Barpeta (Muslims 9,77,943; Hindus 6,62,066), Nagaon (Muslims 11,80,267; Hindus 11,06,354), Karimganj (Muslims 5,27,214; Hindus 4,70,708) and Hailakandi (Muslims 3,12,844; Hindus 2,23,191). As nearly five years have elapsed since the census enumeration took place in 2001, by now another district, Marigaon, is believed to have become a Muslim majority district, thereby taking the tally to seven districts. It looks certain that the Hindus and allied faiths will be reduced to minority status in most districts of Assam within the next two or three decades. A comparative study of the last two census reports of 1991 and 2001 reveals that a formidable demographic tragedy is unfolding in Assam, West Bengal and the adjoining areas.

Troublesome Decades Ahead

The problem appears to have reached almost an irremediable stage solely due to the complicity of self-seeking politicians who have persistently denied the mammoth silent invasion of Bangladeshis not only into Assam and West Bengal, but all over the country. A brief analysis of the data given below in Table 4.X indicates the high percentage of growth in Muslim population in border districts of Assam and gives a clear idea of the massive deluge of infiltrators which is surreptitiously inching forward to overwhelm the entire north-eastern India, and even West Bengal in the near future.

Table 4.X - Growth of Muslim Population in Border Districts of Assam

No.	District	Percentage in 2001	Percentage in 1991	Decadal Growth		Ratio of Muslims to Hindus Faiths
				H Faiths	Muslims	
	Assam	30.92	28.43	13.9	29.3	2.10
1.	Kokrajhar	20.40	19.33	5.2	19.1	3.65
2.	Dhubri	74.30	70.48	5.9	29.6	5.01
3.	Goalpara	53.70	50.19	12.8	31.7	2.48
4.	Bongaigaon	38.50	32.74	2.3	31.8	13.57
5.	Barpeta	59.40	56.06	9.7	25.9	2.67
6.	Kamrup	24.80	23.38	23.5	33.7	1.43
7.	Nalbari	22.10	19.94	9.2	25.2	2.75
8.	Darrang	35.50	31.97	8.8	28.7	3.26
9.	Marigaon	47.60	45.30	16.1	27.5	1.70
10.	Nagaon	51.00	47.19	13.1	32.1	2.45
11.	Cachar	36.10	34.50	15.4	24.5	1.60
12.	Karimganj	52.30	49.17	13.6	29.6	2.16
13.	Hailakandi	57.60	54.79	13.8	27.2	1.97
Average		**46.87**	**43.32**	**12.97**	**28.56**	**2.20**

Source: Compiled from Census 2001 and Census 1991 Reports.

The third column gives the percentage of Muslims according to 2001 census, while column 4 shows their percentage in 1991. Columns 5 and 6 show the respective percentages of decadal growth of Hindus and allied faiths and that of Muslims during the 1991-2001 decade. Column 7 compares these growths in terms of the ratio of Muslims to the Hindus and allied faiths. The following important conclusions are self-evident from Table 4.1.

- The percentage of Muslims in border districts of Assam has risen substantially during the last decade, by well over 3 percentage points, from 43.32 per cent in 1991 to 46.87 in 2001. It is significantly higher than the average Muslim presence of 30.9 per cent in Assam and their 13.4 per cent share in the population at all India level. Similarly the ratio of Muslims to Hindus and allied faiths is much higher in border districts — a natural corollary of the former's fast paced growth, both by infiltration and procreation.
- It looks extraordinary that Bongaigaon district, located near the strategic 'chicken neck' area, has recorded a phenomenal increase of nearly 31.8 per cent in Muslim population during the last decade, i.e., 1991-2001 while Hindus grew only 2.3 per cent. As mentioned elsewhere, a well known ULFA leader, Mithinga Daimary, who was arrested during the December 2003 joint operations by the Royal Bhutanese Army and Indian security forces, had revealed that arms were being supplied to them through a conduit running through Bongaigaon district. Daimary further confirmed that the weapons used to be smuggled from Bangladesh via porous border of Meghalaya. In the context of that revelation there is a pressing need for assessing the likely geopolitical impact of high Muslim growth in Bongaigaon district on country's defence and internal security scenario because chicken neck is the lifeline sustaining our strategic link with north- eastern states. According to Onkareshwar Pandey, after the Kargil failure, Pakistan has now enlisted the services of Muslim fundamentalists of Assam to tear away the "entire north-east from the rest of India by cutting off the chicken neck

area between North Bengal and Assam".[5] In the interests of national security, the reasons for the Bongaigaon region around 'chicken neck' developing into a Bangladeshi-Muslim dominated area need to be investigated and analysed threadbare. Frankly, just now no one can say for sure whether this dangerous demographic change is happening by sheer coincidence or by ISI's nefarious design. At the same time, the causes of steep decline in Hindu population in Bongaigaon district during the last decade need to be probed thoroughly and a determined effort made to halt it. Perhaps the peace-loving but hard pressed Hindu community has been outmigrating from this area because of aggressive forays by Bangladeshi Muslims — at least that is what some Hindus of the area have been saying.

- During the last decade in six important districts of Bongaigaon, Kokrajhar, Dhubri, Barpeta, Nalbari and Darrang the decadal growth rate of Hindus was abnormally low, the lowest being in Bongaigaon district where the Hindus grew barely 2.3 per cent during the decade. In terms of absolute numbers the Muslims have grown 13.5 times faster than the Hindus in Bongaigaon. This trend has far-reaching implications because it clearly shows that members of Hindus and allied faiths are migrating out in large numbers from Bongaigaon. There have been persistent reports that many Hindus have sent away their womenfolk and children from several predominantly Muslim-dominated towns and villages of Assam and West Bengal. While leaving Muslim-dominated areas a sizeable number have sold their land and property virtually at throw-away prices. The population statistics of these six districts of Assam, reflecting abysmally low Hindu growth rate, have confirmed what Bibhuti Bhusan Nandy had written more than two years ago in his article in The *Hindustan Times*, New Delhi, in February 2003 and recently in January 2005 in *The Statesman*, New Delhi, about the plight of Hindus living in border districts.

- The abnormally high decadal increase of 3.54 per cent in Muslim population in border districts translates into a Muslim/ Hindu ratio of 2.20 which shows that the Muslims have grown more than twice as fast as Hindus and allied faiths. It vividly spells out the contours of the coming troublesome decades for the Indian nation in general and the Hindus in particular.

An equally disquieting scenario is writ large across as many as seven districts of West Bengal, as would be noticed from the Table 4.XI below.

Table 4.XI - Growth of Muslim Population in Border Districts of West Bengal

No. Distt.	Percentage in 2001	Percentage in 2001	Decadal Growth		Ratio of Muslims To H.Faiths
			H Faiths	Muslims	
W. Bengal	25.3	23.6	15.1	25.9	1.71
1. Kooch Behar	24.2	23.3	12.8	18.6	1.45
2. Dinajpur (composite)	38.5	36.8	22.2	32.0	1.44
3. Maldah	49.7	47.5	19.3	30.7	1.59
4. Murshidabad	63.7	61.4	16.1	28.4	1.76
5. Haora	24.4	22.2	11.2	26.0	2.32
6. Kolkata	20.3	17.7	0.7	18.9	29.09
7. S.Paraganas	33.2	29.9	15.2	34.2	2.24
Average	**37.5**	**34.5**	**12.5**	**28.7**	**2.29**

Source: Compiled from Census Reports.

The growth rate of Muslims in the border districts of West Bengal is also very high, though somewhat lower than that of Assam. Two border districts of Murshidabad (Muslim population 63.7 per cent in 2001, i.e. 4 years ago) and Malda (Muslim population 47.5 per cent in 2001, i.e., 5 years ago) have already become Muslim majority areas. The demographic change in the new district of North Dinajpur (part of the former composite

Dinajpur) where the Muslim percentage has risen to 47.4 per cent appears to be equally worrisome. From the data given in Table 4.XI the following facts are established:

- The average decadal growth of 3.07 per cent in Muslim population of border districts of West Bengal is much higher than the state average of 1.64 recorded during the last decade. Evidently the Muslims are growing at a much higher rate in border districts largely due to infiltration through porous border and also perhaps due to higher procreation rate of the community, especially the Bangladeshis.
- Muslim growth is significantly higher in southern districts of South Parganas and Kolkata. The decadal Muslim growth rate was 34.2 per cent in South Parganas during 1991-2001 which is more than twice that of the Hindus at 15.2 per cent. The Muslim growth rate was 18.9 per cent in Kolkata as against a measly 0.7 per cent growth rate of Hindus.[6] This phenomenon is partly explained by the abysmally low Hindu TFR of 1 in Kolkata which is far below the replacement level of 2.1. The TFR of the Hindus of Kolkata is thus lower than even the TFR of demographically dying nations of Europe. It raises the vital question of the likely over-acceptance of family planning by Hindus of West Bengal in general and by Kolkata Hindus in particular. Perhaps one reason for the pathetically poor Hindu growth rate in Kolkata could be the sharp increase in popularity of condom-cum-abortion culture among the "bhadralok" urban Hindus on the pattern of Communist Russia, and other demographically dying countries of Europe like Italy and Germany. The malaise might be more prevalent in Kolkata than in other areas of West Bengal. Yet another possible reason for the steep decline in Hindu growth rate could be that slowly and steadily the Hindus have started migrating out of the city, as was darkly hinted by Prafull Goradia in a thought-provoking article published in *The Pioneer*, New Delhi, in June 2005. Whatever may be the cause, at this rate Kolkata

could transform into a Muslim majority metropolis within the next two decades or so!

- The Hindu growth rate is also quite low in the border districts of Kooch Behar and Haora. It could be due to the outmigration caused by the fear psychosis unleashed by the Bangladeshi invasion. The modus operandi used by the Bangladeshi Muslims to oust the Hindus from border areas was described in a very perceptive research paper presented by Prof. Jayanta Kumar Ray (formerly Centenary Professor of International Research, Calcutta University) in a seminar on 'Illegal Migration from Bangladesh' organised by Astha Bharati on November 27-28, 2001, in New Delhi. According to Prof. Ray, the infiltrators initially take recourse to committing thefts, dacoities, murders and molestation of women. Eventually they don't hesitate even to stage large scale riots. Unfortunately the ruling politicians, preoccupied with using the infiltrators as vote bank, turn a blind eye to the depredations of the latter.[7] The adverse circumstances leave the indigenous people, mostly Hindus, with no option but to move out from the area. That might explain how most Hindu residents of border districts of Assam and West Bengal have moved out from vulnerable border areas in search of safety and security.

Nearly five years have elapsed since Census 2001 and by now two more districts of West Bengal, i.e. Malda and Uttar Dinajpur are believed to have become Muslim majority areas. Between 1951 and 2001 the Hindu population in the state has declined by 5.7 percentage points, from 79.8 to 74.1 per cent despite huge influx of persistently persecuted Bangladeshi Hindus into West Bengal. During the same period the share of Muslims has galloped ahead by whopping 5.7 percentage points. As revealed by Census 2001, during the last decade the Muslim growth rate in the state has quantum jumped to 28.7 per cent as compared to 12.5 per cent growth rate of Hindus. In other words, the percentage of Muslim growth is more than twice that of the Hindus.

Bibhuti Bhusan Nandy has been saying now for more than two years that due to massive infiltration from across the border, more and more Hindu families are moving out from border areas virtually "in droves" after selling their property. In this context a welcome development, though grossly belated one, is the admission of the gravity of the situation by the Chief Minister of West Bengal, Buddhadev Bhattacharjee. He has gone on record that illegal immigrants are spreading "the message of Islamic fundamentalism". On June 23, 2005, while inaugurating a BSF seminar he admitted that there "is a serious problem with some of our neighbours". "Bangladesh says there are no Bangladeshis in India whereas the entire demography of certain parts of the country and West Bengal is being changed due to infiltration. In many places there are more Bangladeshi settlers than Indians."[8] According to Mr. Bhattacharjee, three types of illegal immigrants were coming from Bangladesh. First, there are groups who spread the message of Islamic fundamentalism and campaign for Muslim rights in Kashmir. Second, there are groups which are directly involved in subversive activities. The third group is of north-Bengal based KLO (Kamtapur Liberation Organisation) militants who have found shelter in Bangladesh after being driven out of Bhutan in December 2003. All the three groups are being supported by the Bangladesh government.[9] And the situation has become so critical that the Governor of the state, Shri Gopalkrishna Gandhi described the relentless infiltration as a "time bomb" — which indeed it is. Many people are calling the influx as 'the Bangla bomb'. The Chief Minister's concern was supported by Bimal Pramanik, Director, Centre for Research in Indo-Bangladesh Relations, Kolkata, who after analysing the Census 2001 data came to the conclusion that unabated illegal infiltration through porous eastern border was responsible for sharp changes in the demographic pattern.[10]

Close on the heels of the candid admission made by the beleagured West Bengal Chief Minister came the revelation made by Mamta Banerjee, the fiery Trinamool Congress Member of Parliament, that many Bangladeshi immigrants have voting rights both in West Bengal and Bangladesh. If that revelation is true, then the successive Marxist governments of West Bengal will have to do lots of explaining. The demographic disaster unfolding in Assam and West Bengal is nothing short of a massive political racket about which the Indian middle class and opinion-makers have been kept in dark for decades by the fundamentalist secular lobby, including the Marxist rulers of West Bengal.

Plight of Non-Muslims in Bangladesh

Apart from the huge immigration of Bangladeshi Muslims into India, the situation has another disturbing aspect hitherto totally ignored by successive Indian governments. That is the problem of forcing out of that country all minorities, including the Hindus, the Buddhists and even Christians in large numbers — a phenomenon common to most Islam-dominated countries. Bangladesh has an area of 147,570 sq. kilometers with an approximate population of 140.6 million out of which Muslims constitute 126.1 million (89.7 per cent), Hindus and allied faiths (including Buddhists and ethnic tribals) form 14.1 million (10 per cent) and Christians are 0.41 million (0.29 per cent). It is interesting to note the gradual decline in the percentage of Hindus and allied faiths, decade after decade, starting from 33 per cent in 1901 and then coming down to 29.6 per cent in 1941. After partition it fell to 22.9 per cent in 1951 and thereafter it steeply went down to less than 10 per cent in 2001. The Hindu Muslim data, based on 7 censuses conducted in Bangladesh, is given below:[11]

Data Relating to the Percentage of Muslims and Hindus in Bangladesh.

Census Year	Muslim Percentage	Hindu Percentage
1941	70.30	28.3
1951	76.9	22.0
1961	80.4	18.5
1974	85.4	13.5
1981	86.7	12.1
1991	87.4	12.1
2001	89.5	10.5 (includes all non-Muslims)

The proportion of Hindu community now stands reduced to 9.1 per cent as per Census 2001 of Bangladesh. The persecution of Hindus and Buddhists in Bangladesh is nothing short of systematic and extensive ethnic cleansing which has continued for decades. Its colossal dimensions are graphically reflected in the census statistics of that country which recorded a decline of 20 percentage points in Hindu population during the last 50 years, down to 9.1 from 29 per cent. Yet the world community has maintained a disturbingly studied silence in the matter. Prima facie the persecution of minorities in Bangladesh is in no way less serious than the ethnic cleansing of the Jews by Hitler and his Nazi goons in the last century. Its scale is certainly bigger than what had been witnessed in Bosnia, and more recently in Darfur region of Africa. Yet the world has remained a silent spectator. But why blame the international community, when the successive slumbering governments in India have persistently failed to seek justice for Bangladeshi Hindus. According to Salam Azad, a well known Bangladeshi author of the book, *Contribution of India in the War of Liberation of Bangladesh,* lately the killings, rape and forcible annexation of properties have resulted in the average daily outmigration of nearly 475 persons belonging to minority communities. He says that now minorities have only three options:

a. To change their religion and embrace Islam ;

b. To leave the country bare handed ; or

c. To seek external support to combat the atrocities.

In a candid interview given to V.K. Shashikumar of *Tehelka,* a New Delhi based weekly, Salam Azad pointed out that in numerous madarasas flourishing in Bangladesh, covertly patronized by the fundamentalist regime of Khalida Zia, children are taught that the Muslims are the most superior community in the world. They are also brain-washed that converting a non-Muslim to Islam is an act of faith. Salam also drew attention to the fact that at the time of graduating from madarasas the youth are told that "if you kill a non-Muslim then the doors of paradise are open to you".[12] Furthermore, the madarasa students are also taught that by marrying non-Muslim women they will be serving the cause of Islam. In the circumstances, the Hindu women often become easy targets of Muslim lust. Unlike Muslim women, the Hindu women go out in large numbers to work and do not wear burka, i.e., veil. They are subjected to unimagineable atrocities. The conditions are so bad that "if a Hindu woman is raped, no police station in Bangladesh will take cognizance of the crime." Neither will courts entertain such complaints.[13] Bangladesh still has a large chunk of Hindu population and they are the ones who face the brunt of fundamentalist attacks. The Hindus are also targeted because they still own large properties. By and large the Christians manage to escape intense persecution because Bangladesh continues to get non-governmental aid from some Christian nations. Most attacks on Hindus are organized at the behest of government in a "pre-planned" manner by using the network of fundamentalist outfits.[14] The fanatic youth coming out of thousands of madarasas invariably target modern educated women most of whom are Hindus. It may be recalled that in February 2002, at the time of releasing the Hindi version of his Bengali book, *Hindu Sampraday Keno Bangladesh Tyag Korechhe* (Why Hindu Community Is Leaving Bangladesh), in Kolkata, the author had predicted that the agenda of Khaleda Zia's Bangladesh Nationalist Party (BNP) was to talibanize the country. He had forewarned about large scale persecution of the Hindu minority by the armed cadres of the BNP in association with other militant groups[15] Viewed in the poignant backdrop of ethnic cleansing of minorities in Bangladesh the relentless invasion of infiltrators into India suggests the existence of a well-planned conspiracy.

According to the 1991 census, the percentage of Assamese speaking population had fallen below 40 per cent in Assam during that decade, while the percentage of Bengali speaking people has been steadily rising.[16] On a conservative estimate it could be presumed that nearly 90 per cent of Assam's Muslims are immigrants from Bangladesh. When that figure is added to those who have been declaring themselves as Bengali speaking (mostly Hindus) the overall percentage of Bangladeshi Muslims might add up to 40 to 45 per cent of Assam's population.[17] According to the Census 2001, the total population of Assam was 23,216,288 and 40 per cent of that figure comes to 9,286,512 and that should be the number of Bangladeshis hosted by Assam. In other words, there are likely to be more than 92 lakh Bangladeshis in Assam alone. And that number is growing fast because the fertility rate of Bangladeshi Muslims is far higher than that of the Assamese Hindus, or for that matter even higher than the Hindus of West Bengal or any other Indian State. The reasons are mainly three. First, non-acceptance of the small family norm by Bangladeshis in deference to the diktats of their ulema. The second reason is the Islamic scriptural sanction allowing them to have multiple wives, though not more than four at one time. The third reason, and an important one for higher fertility of Muslim women, is the higher incidence of divorce in Muslim societies because of the religious privilege allowed to men for having more than one wife, often practised by divorcing the older wives in preference to younger ones. The result is that a higher proportion of Muslim women are divorced and get re-married. And since most new mates opt to have a child from their new partner, the reproduction rate tends to be higher among Muslims than other communities. Prima facie that should explain why the fertility of Muslim women is universally higher than all other religious groups, it being more or less a global phenomenon.

Due to fast changing demography, the Indian nation has already entered a critical phase of existential crisis. It is amazing how our political leadership has been constantly denying the mind-boggling dimensions of Bangladeshi invasion and openly misleading the people by recourse to repetitive lying. There is no sense in blaming the Bangladesh government alone for denying the truth established so painstakingly by one of their own researchers about outmigration of 14 million Bangladeshis to India in one single decade of 1981-1991, when our own political leaders are taking recourse to blatant lying about the gravity of the problem. In a detailed report submitted to the central government not so long ago by the Governor of Assam, it was categorically stated that at least 6 thousand Bangladeshi infiltrators were entering the State every day which adds to nearly 22 lakhs infiltrators every year. It means that more than 2 crore infiltrators must have entered Assam alone within the last 10 years. True to his fundamentalist secular commitment to the politics of minority vote-bank the Chief Minister, Tarun Gogoi, promptly joined the issue with the Governor by denying that there was any large scale influx of illegal immigrants. Interestingly, if Sarifa Begum's figure of 14 million illegal immigrants entering India within one single decade of 1981-91 is juxtaposed with the figure given out by Assam Governor, it looks quite logical that by now there could be nearly 5 crore illegal Bangladeshi immigrants in India — a figure mentioned by more than one participant in the national convention on Census 2001 held in Delhi in the last week of April 2005. Yet there is no dearth of leftists and sham secularist Hindus decrying the Supreme Court's July 2005 judgement striking down the IMDT Act and terming the infiltration as invasion of India. Strangely enough, even without going through the voluminous irrefutable data available about massive illegal immigration, including the testimony of a Bangladeshi demographer Sarifa Begum, the erudite Lok Sabha Speaker, Somnath Chatterjee, too, has questioned the wisdom of the apex court in striking down the IMDT Act.

This dirty vote-bank politics of suicidal proportions is not confined to the political leadership of Assam or similarly threatened states like West Bengal and Bihar. It is practised and perfected right here in the capital of our troubled nation. For instance, the Minister of State for Home, Sriprakash Jaiswal informed the Rajya Sabha on July 14, 2004, that the illegal infiltration from Bangladesh was of "explosive proportions with illegal immigrants estimated at 1.2 crores."[18]. While replying to a question by Datta Meghe, a Member of Parliament belonging to NCP (Nationalist Congress Party), he admitted that the number of infiltrators in Assam alone stood at 50 lakhs while in the neighbouring West Bengal it was a staggering 57 lakhs. Astonishingly within two weeks the Minister made an abrupt about turn and declared in the House that the figures given in his earlier reply were "hearsay". But political observers were quick to point out that soon after his July 14 statement the Minister had visited Assam where the State Chief Minister, Tarun Gogoi, remonstrated with him for admitting the existence of the problem. That made the Minister renege on his previous statement within a few weeks by saying that the earlier figures were based on hearsay and that too from "the interested parties".

In a detailed report submitted in August 2000 by the Working Group on Border Management, headed by Madhav Godbole (a former Union Home Secretary having impeccable credentials), it was clearly stated that the number of illegal Bangladeshi immigrants was 1.5 crores at that time. It was further stated in the Working Group's detailed report that on an average at least 3 lakh illegal immigrants were entering India every year. That adds upto a minimum of 1.62 crore Bangladeshis in the year 2004 on the assumption of at least 3 lakhs illegals entering India every year. The Working Group on Border was an officially constituted body and its report is packed with facts and figures collected from reliable official sources. Therefore the figures of illegal Bangladeshis calculated by the Working Group could not have been dismissed as ' hearsay'. It is a mystery that when an authentic, well documented, official report was readily available in Home Ministry, from where did the Minister of State for Home obtain the "hearsay" figure of 1.2 crore illegal Bangladeshis. Furthermore, when an official estimate confirming presence of 1.5 crore illegal immigrants in the year 2000 was on the record of central government, what made the Minister of State resort to lying in the Parliament on the specious plea that the earlier figure of 1.2 crore was nothing more than hearsay? It is a pity that the two mutually contradictory replies of the Minister remained unchallenged in the Parliament and such patent falsehood was swallowed hook, line and sinker by our legislators.

The worst fears about the long suspected intentions of Pakistan's ISI (Inter Services Intelligence) trying to infiltrate Bangladeshis for destabilizing the north-eastern region came true when three Bangladeshi infiltrators caught by Dibrugarh police in the first week of March 2005 confessed that they were taught to speak Assamese in Bangladesh before being smuggled into Assam. A more disturbing aspect revealed during interrogation was that the prospective infiltrators were told in Bangladesh that they would secure political patronage in Assam as long as they voted for a particular national political party.[19] The infiltrators were working as masons at a private campus in Jiban Phukan Nagar locality of Dibrugarh. Of the three infiltrators one was a juvenile. He was the first to break down and confessed that he was from Rongpur area of North Bangladesh and that he along with some others had been pushed into Assam three months ago. The two other infiltrators, both in late twenties continued to tell the police that they were from Goalpara. But the cat was out of the bag when the juvenile infiltrator told the police that those two were also from Bangladesh. During the recent months there has been a spurt in the influx of illegal immigrants. Most of them possess a smattering knowledge of Assamese and they tell the people that they are from Barpeta or Goalpara or some other town of lower Assam. Most of them are engaged in manual labour or rickshaw pulling or some similar profession. The police authorities find it difficult to deport them as infiltrators often manage to get some kind of documents to prove their Indian identity.[20]

The debate about the problem of illegal Bangladeshis has some very important constitutional and legal aspects centred around the ill-conceived and discriminatory legislation called Illegal Migrants (Detection by Tribunals) Act (IMDT Act) which was declared *ultra vires* by the Supreme Court in July 2005. In January 1980 when elections to the Seventh Lok Sabha were held Assam was in the grip of a mass agitation launched against illegal influx of Bangladeshis. A call had been given by the All Assam Students Union (AASU) and Assam Gana Parishad (AGP) to boycott the general election. Consequently no elections could be held in 12 constituencies out of a total of 14. In the entire state elections could take place only for 2 constituencies, i.e, Karimganj (Reserved SC) and Silchar both of which were located in Barak valley where there was practically no impact of the agitation against Bangladeshi infiltrators, because of their preponderance in the region. Subsequently in 1983 the Election Commission decided to complete the electoral process in the remaining 12 constituencies, despite continuing unrest and tension in various parts of the state. Even then elections could not be completed in seven out of the twelve constituencies due to the call for boycott. Despite an all-out effort by the government, no election could be held in Brahamaputra valley because of highly disturbed law and order situation. In this manner nearly half the constituencies of Assam remained unrepresented throughout the tenure of Seventh Lok Sabha. Unfortunately the "black law", as IMDT Act was known in Assam, was passed by a Lok Sabha in which more than half of the Assamese electorate, concentrated in Brahamputra valley, were not represented at all. It is an enigma that when a nationally applicable law, known as the Foreigners Act, was available in the statute book for detecting and deporting illegal immigrants, why did the government decide to pass another law for the same purpose and chose to restrict its promulgation to one State, i.e., Assam alone.

The IMDT Act which came into force on October 15, 1983, was a patently infiltrator-friendly legislation. In flagrant violation of the universally accepted norms, it put the onus of proving that the newly arrived foreigner was an illegal immigrant on the complainant. To add insult to the injury it stipulated that complainant should pay a token fee while lodging a complaint. Additionally it entailed that only those who resided within a radius of 3 kms from the place where an illegal immigrant was staying were entitled to make a complaint — a grotesque disability which was removed later on in 1988 by amending the IMDT Act. The widespread Assam agitation was called off after the signing of the Assam Accord in August 1985 between the central government, the All Assam Students Union and their allies, including the AGP, and the government of Assam. The tripartite agreement fixed March 25, 1971 (the day Bangladesh came into existence as an independent nation) as the mutually agreed date for detection and deportation of Bangladeshi infiltrators. It was accepted that those Bangladeshis who entered Assam before that date shall not be expelled and will become entitled for Indian citizenship in due course of time. It was also decided to update the National Register of Citizens right upto the cut-off date. But that part of the Accord was never implemented because of manifest dishonesty on the part of powers-that-be who were hell-bent on capturing political power through recourse to vote-bank politics. Evidently the law was conceived in political deception and conceit; it was nothing less than a fraud on the gullible people of Assam. Though crores of rupees were spent on setting up and sustaining a number of Tribunals under the Act, the end result was pathetic; less than 1500 illegal immigrants were identified and deported by the government during two decades of enforcement of the new law. Soon widespread disaffection erupted among various sections of the indigenous population against the IMDT Act because of its inefficacy in deporting illegal immigrants. As resentment against the continued infiltration mounted and intentions of the government became suspect, the All India Lawyers Forum for Civil Liberties filed a public interest litigation in the Supreme Court seeking deportation of illegal immigrants. It was followed by another PIL filed in year 2000 by the AGP Member Parliament from Dibrugarh, Sarbananda Sonowal (a former AASU President), praying that the IMDT Act be quashed because it was discriminatory and unconstitutional. After prolonged legal battle in the Supreme Court finally Sonowal won; it was indeed a historic win. The Supreme Court gave its verdict on July 12, 2005, declaring the IMDT Act unconstitutional and ultra vires. In a stinging indictment of the government the Supreme Court made the following observations:

"A deep analysis of the IMDT Act and the Rules made thereunder would reveal that they have been purposely so enacted or made so as to give shelter or protection to illegal migrants who came to Assam from Bangladesh on or before 25 March 1971, rather than to identify or deport them."

Drawing heavily upon the report sent by the then Governor of Assam to the President on November 8, 1998, which stated that Assam was facing "external aggression and internal disturbance" because of the silent invasion by illegal immigrants the apex court proclaimed in its judgement that the "provisions of the IMDT Act and the Rules made thereunder clearly negate the constitutional mandate contained in Article 355 of the Constitution, where a duty has been cast upon the Union of India to protect every State against external aggression and internal disturbance. The IMDT Act which contravenes Article 355 of the Constitution is, therefore, wholly unconstitutional and must be struck down." Among other things the Supreme Court in its 114 page long judgement made the following important observations:

- By enacting the impugned law the Parliament divested the central government of the legal authority to deport illegal Bangladeshi immigrants whose growing numbers were creating a serious law and order problem in Assam.
- All over the world the onus of proving that he or she was a bonafide national of the country of his or her domicile lies on the accused, while the IMDT Act shifted the burden of proof unfairly to the complainant and the State government.
- Illegal immigration was tantamount to "external aggression" on the State of Assam and therefore in terms of Article 355 of the Constitution, the central government had a duty to protect Assam from external aggression and internal disturbances.
- The continuing immigration was responsible for impeding the economic growth of Assam despite immense natural resources possessed by the State.

The Supreme Court judgment has raised political temperature in the State. The All Assam Minorities Students Union (AAMSU) gave a call for a state-wide strike on July 13, 2005, which elicited good response in Muslim-dominated districts of the State. It accused the Assam government of failure to defend the enactment of IMDT Act and threatened to withdraw support to the ruling dispensation. Meanwhile, on July 14, 2005, in a meeting chaired by the Prime Minister, the central government decided to set up a Group of Ministers to study the implications of the Supreme Court judgment, hear the viewpoints of various groups and then recommend further action in the matter.

The verdict of the apex court was hailed by the majority of Assamese people across the State, especially the students and the youth groups. There were mass celebrations and Sarbananda Sonowal became an icon and was given a tumultous welcome befitting a 'national hero' when he returned to Guwahati on July 13, 2005. Rapturous crowds of thousands of Assamese lined up on both sides of the road when he came out of airport and proceeded to the city where a grand reception was held to felicitate him. Next day when Sonowal visited Dibrugarh, the constituency he represents in the Lok Sabha, he was hailed as "Jatiya Bir", a historic title associated with the legendary Ahom army general, Lachit Barphukan, famous for his indomitable courage, military prowess and chivalry.

The IMDT Act has been a source of legal battles for quite some time. Most legal experts had questioned its constitutional or legal justification because of its discriminatory and anti-national nature. Yet the Home Minister, Shivraj Patil categorically refused to repeal it. When Prime Minister, Dr. Manmohan Singh, visited Assam in November 2004, he too, refused to repeal the obnoxious law on the ground that it was needed for protection of minority community. The gratuitous plea advanced by the Home Minister and the Prime Minister to retain the Act ran contrary to the reasons given for passing the legislation in the Statement of Objects and Reasons for placing it on the statute book which categorically stated that the Act was to be used only for detecting and deporting illegal immigrants for protecting "the integrity and security" of the region. For facility of reference and clarity of purpose the relevant Statement of Objects and Reasons is reproduced below:

1. "The influx of foreigners who illegally migrated into India across the borders of the sensitive eastern and north-eastern regions of the country and remained in the country poses a threat to the integrity and security of the said regions. A substantial number of such foreigners who migrated into India after the 25th day of March

1971 have, by taking advantage of the circumstances of such migration and their ethnic similarities and other connections with the people of India, illegally remained in India without having in their possession lawful authority so to do. The continuance of these persons in India has given rise to serious problems. The clandestine manner in which these persons have been trying to pass off as citizens of India has rendered their detection difficult. After taking into account the need for their speedy detection the need for protection of genuine citizens of India and the interests of the general public, the President promulgated, on the 15th October, 1983, the Illegal Migrants (Determination by Tribunals) Ordinance, 1983, to provide for the establishment of Tribunals.

2. The Ordinance provided for the establishment of Tribunals for determination in a fair manner of question whether a person is an illegal migrant. The definition of "illegal migrant", as provided in the Ordinance, recognized 25th March, 1971, as the cut-off date. The Ordinance also empowered the central government to make a reference to the Tribunal and also enabled private citizens to make applications to the Tribunal for determining the question whether any person is an illegal migrant as defined in the Ordinance. The Ordinance also made suitable provisions for appeal, barring the jurisdiction of civil courts, and expulsion of persons found to be illegal migrants.

3. The Bill seeks to replace the Ordinance."

The most important aspect of the Statement of Objects and Reasons was that it clearly spelt that the purport of the new enactment was to protect the integrity and security of the country from the threat posed by the illegal infiltration which should be done through "speedy detection", and nothing more, nothing less. There was no mention in it that the law was meant to be used for protecting the interests of minorities, as was sought to be misrepresented in the unbecoming stand taken by the Prime Minister and the Home Minister. It is clear that in order to please their minority vote-bank the government had turned the

IMDT Act on its head, virtually upside down. The sole raison d'etre for passing the Act was to protect the interests of the people of Assam and no one else's. While the Statement of Objects and Reasons was goal oriented and quite lucid, the mischief was done during drafting of the law, perhaps purposely, by the author of the Act, Abdul Muhib Mazumdar, formerly a Minister in Saikia's cabinet, way back in 1983. When the obnoxious legislation was struck down by the Supreme Court, he lamented that his baby had been killed. The partisan law was his brainchild. It was nothing short of a fraud on the Assamese people.

In supporting the IMDT Act the Home Minister, Shivraj Patil totally forgot that at the time of taking oath of office he had legally bound himself to protect the integrity and sovereignty of India (of which Assam is an integral part). That responsibility was legally enjoined on him by a specific mention in the statement of Objects and Reasons of the Act which highlighted that the illegal migrants posed a threat to "the integrity and security" of the north-eastern region. By abdicating that solemn responsibility cast on him both constitutionally and legally by virtue of oath of his office, and instead openly pleading the cause of a particular community (read illegal immigrants) and acquiescing in the retention of Bangladeshi infiltrators, the Union Home Minister wantonly violated the sacred oath of his office. It is extraordinary that this simple wisdom did not dawn on the Home Minister at all. The second aspect of the contentious law was much more damaging and disturbing. How was it that the central government chose only one State, that is Assam, for promulgating this obnoxious legislation? Apart from entering into India in large numbers, illegal Bangladeshis are now present in a number of States, virtually all over the country, including Assam, West Bengal, Bihar, Uttar Pradesh and Maharashtra. For instance, in a sealed affidavit sworn in the High Court on behalf of the Delhi Police Commissioner in September 2003 an admission was reportedly made that Delhi state had a swarming population of approximately 13 lakh illegal Bangladeshis.[21] Without such a massive illegal influx the Muslim population of Delhi could not have multiplied more than ten-and-a half-times during the last 40 years, as revealed by Census

2001. Thus detection and deportation of illegal immigrants is a national problem, though Assam happened to be the worst affected state by this predatory invasion. Then why was the IMDT Act made applicable only to Assam ? Action of the central government in promulgating and enforcing this law only in the state of Assam was patently illegal. Therefore judgment of the apex court and its stinging strictures on the central government were perfectly in order. By no stretch of legal propriety could the central government dare single out one state, the state of Assam alone, for applying a law which is repugnant to the spirit of Indian Constitution.

While discussing the silent invasion of north-east by Bangladeshi infiltrators and consequential alienation of the ethnic groups, it will be useful to know the intensity of the feelings of local population. During an informal and frank interaction on the subject a retired para-military officer, belonging to the north-east, bluntly asked a question which foxed everyone. He asked point-blank whether the central government would have the daring to ignore the problem by looking the other way if millions of Pakistanis had illegally entered north India through Punjab and Rajasthan? His question remained unanswered, but it exposed the duplicity of the central government, and at the same time highlighted the strong feelings of the neglected region. The people of north-east have developed a feeling of having been abandoned and thrown to wolves by the central government! No wonder, the entire population of north-east has been alienated and the region sucked into the vortex of unending turmoil.

In any case, time has come for hard introspection by all mainstream political parties, opinion-makers and genuinely secular groups (sham secularists excluded) to find an urgent solution to the problem of adverse demography precariously accentuated by the unremitting invasion by illegal immigrants. They must realise that the continuous influx of Bangladeshis into India has already taken the shape of a terminator tsunami which can destroy and subsume the entire north-east, even parts of eastern India, including West Bengal and Bihar. This ill wind has assumed the proportions of a raging maelstrom which has the potential of wrecking the Indian nation by setting in motion the ISI inspired process of balkanization. Even states like West Bengal, Bihar, Delhi, Tripura, Nagaland and Maharashtra have been badly affected by this silent invasion. Among other things, most disturbing is the fact that 85 per cent of the total encroached forest land in Assam is reported to be in the hands of illegal Bangladeshi immigrants who have now acquired a major say at least in elections to 43 seats of Assam State Assembly out of a total of 126 constituencies.

In view of the high presence of Bangladeshis in Delhi, the matter was also agitated in Delhi High Court through a writ petition to seek expulsion and deportation of infiltrators. In February 2005 the division bench of Chief Justice B.C. Patel and Justice S.K. Kaul directed the government to fulfil its specified target of at least 1000 deportations of infiltrators every month. Attention was specifically drawn to the fact that though the High Court had recommended the proposed action as early as 2003, the progress was very tardy. During the last three years (i.e., from 2002 to 2005) the Delhi Police had managed to deport only 15,461 Bangladeshis whereas their number ran into lakhs.[22] An ingenious, though wicked, plea was taken by the central government that the proposed deportation will infringe upon the bilateral relations with Bangladesh in the light of Vienna Convention. It was argued that the matter has to be pursued diplomatically at the level of Home Secretaries of the two countries. The High Court pulled up the government and described the plea as "absurd" and accused the authorities of delaying the "whole process of deportation of Bangladeshi migrants". It was for the second time that the High Court snubbed the central government.[23] A submission was made by Delhi Police that they were facing considerable difficulties in deporting Bangladeshis. In one instance, to dodge the police the infiltrators took shelter in a mosque. Sometime they take shelter in the house of some influential family of the minority community. On February 21 2005, a team from Lodhi Road Police Station was attacked and the mob pelted stones at them and broke windowpanes of the police vehicle. That did not impress the High Court which regretted that during the last 14 years there had been no worthwhile progress to remove the Bangladeshi infiltrators. The government was directed to deport at least 100 aliens every day.

Interestingly, the issue of Bangladeshi infiltrators also dominated the Chief Ministers conference held in New Delhi in April 2005 to discuss matters concerning internal security where the Chief Ministers of seven non-BJP states described it as a grave threat to national security. They entreated the government to tackle the problem fast and firmly. Several Chief Ministers of the region, especially the Christian-dominated states like Nagaland, Meghalaya and Mizoram, squarely blamed the Assam government for failing to perform its legal duty and even facilitating the movement of infiltrators via Assam into other north-eastern states. Some of them have openly started admitting that because of their very small populations (e.g., Nagaland with a population of less than 2 millions, Meghalaya 2.32 millions and Mizoram less than 1 million) vis-a-vis the huge population of Bangladesh totaling more than 14 crores, today the threat to the relatively small Christian population of north-east is much more acute than that to the Hindus of Assam or West Bengal. No wonder a strong undercurrent of resentment against Bangladeshi infiltrators has emerged in all these Christian-dominated States and student groups of Nagaland and Meghalaya have joined hands with the students of Assam for launching a "throw out Bangladeshi" campaign.

Many opportunistic political parties, swearing by sham secularism, but deeply mired in vote-bank politics, have been regularly trying to underplay this growing threat to the nation's security. These left-oriented political outfits are not bothered by the defiant stance taken by several Bangladeshi thinkers, economists and former diplomats who have been openly justifying the ongoing migration by advocating the concept of "lebensraum" (a German word meaning "living space") for space-squeezed Bangladeshis. They have been openly trying to legitimise the migration. Sometime ago Professor Amena Mohsin of Dhaka University, had candidly proclaimed her country's intentions when she wrote that "the migration was a normal and natural phenomenon" which cannot be stopped and therefore ways and means must be found to legalise it. In an article titled *"The Question of Lebensraum",* published in a weekly periodical, *Holiday,* Sadeq Khan, a former Bangladeshi diplomat, not only justified the continuing influx, but openly advocated the provision of living space for the surplus millions of that overpopulated country by blaming the crisis on "the colonial devastation" of East Bengal in the eighteenth and nineteenth centuries. Incidentally India, too, has a big tribe of sermonising secularists who see nothing wrong in the massive influx of more than 3 crore illegal Bangladeshis.

Interestingly despite strictures of the Supreme Court the last word on the subject has not been said. Recently in second week of February 2006 a decision was taken to amend the Foreigners Act by adding a provision for setting up tribunals for determining whether or not a person was an illegal immigrant - a provision comparable to the obnoxious legal protection incorporated to help infilltrators in the IMDT Act repealed by the apex court. Surprise of surprises, this decision has been taken by the GOM (Group of Ministers) presided by the Prime Minister himself. It will surely lead to more turmoil and agitation in Assam, the state from which he was elected as Member of Rajya Sabha.

Jihadi Warriors of Bangladesh

It is well known that the four party ruling dispensation led by the BNP (Bangladesh Nationalist Party) in Bangladesh has been guilty of systematic harassment, persecution and ethnic cleansing of religious minorities, especially the Hindus and the Buddhists. Prime Minister Khaleda Zia and her alliance partners came to power in October 2001 with the backing of two notorious fundamentalist outfits, namely the Jamaat-e-Islami and Islamic Oikya Jote. It may be recalled that the Jamaat-e-Islami had emerged as the third largest party in 2001 elections. Since then it has grown from strength to strength. It has been targetting for enlistment impressionable young students graduating from madarasas funded by West Asian charitable trusts like Darul

Ansar al Khairia and Al Fujairia of Dubai and Al Harmain and Al Yamama trusts of Saudi Arabia. According to a well known Bangladeshi newspaper, dozens of madarasas functioning in hilly terrain of Naikhangchari have been imparting weapons training to jihadi youth. Most of the terror groups have been training their cadres in the inaccessible terrain of Cox Bazar and Chittagong hills, close to Burma border which are ineffectively administered. They have a number of training camps in the Arakans, across the Myanmar border. The two radical parties, Jamaat-e-Islami and Islamic Oikya Jote who share political power with the BNP have been calling shots for pushing forward the goal of talibanisation of Bangladesh. Many leading lights of the BNP, too, have close links with Pakistan's Jamaat-e-Islami. Due to growth of fundamentalist ideology Bangladesh has become almost like Afghanistan, a haven for jihadi groups swearing by Bin Laden's cult of murder and mayhem. In fact, there are reasons to believe that Al Qaeda is now firmly entrenched in Bangladesh from where it has been trying to move ahead into India on the one hand and to south-east Asian countries through the Arakans hills on the other. It is well known that the Islamists have an ambitious plan to extend their area of operation in south-east Asia via Myanmar to Thailand, Malayasia and Singapore for ultimately joining the jihadi groups of Indonesia and the Philippines. There has been a sharp growth in the number of madarasas in Bangladesh and in the border areas close to India. It is well known that more than 3,000 trained Bangladeshi jihadis had gone to Pakistan and Afghanistan for participating in Afghan Jihad against Russian army and nearly 34 of them had been killed in action. Subsequently a large number of Bangla jihadis returned home and organised a number of militant groups, including Harkat-ul-Jihad-al-Islami (Bangladesh). In the first week of December 2004, this rabid fundamentalist organisation hit banner headlines, both in India and Bangladesh, when it threatened to assassinate members of the Indian cricket team, during their scheduled tour of Bangladesh to play test matches in Dhaka and Chittagong. The close links between the ISI, the Bangladeshi terror outfits and Al Qaeda are well known. The conduit for this tripartite liaison was Fazlur Rahman, a notorious radical leader of the 'Jihadi Movement in Bangladesh' (of which HUJI-B is a constituent). It may be recalled that Fazlur Rahman was one of the signatories to the notorious declaration of jihad against the United States and all Christians and Jews, issued on February 23, 1998. Among other signatories to the declaration of jihad were Osama Bin Laden, Ayman Al Zwahiri (of Egyptian Jihad group), Rifa'i Ahmad Taha alias Abu Yasir (of Egyptian Islamic group) and Sheikh Mir Hamzah (of Jamaat -ul-Ulema-e Pakistan). For all practical purposes, HUJI-B, set up in 1992, is a branch of the notorious Harkat-ul-Jihad-al-Islami of Pakistan. Just like its parent body, it has an agenda of spreading terror and its leadership owes allegiance to Al Qaeda. Jihadi activities of HUJI -B have been on upswing since the year 2000.

Over the years Harkat-ul-Jihad-al-Islami has built a strong and committed cadre of thousands of Jihadis in Bangladesh. It may be recalled that in a statement issued in May 2002 the State Department of America had described HUJI-B as a terrorist organisation having ties with jihadi outfits of Pakistan. Subsequently the US State Department in their annual report *"Patterns of Global Terrorism 2003"* had listed HUJI-B under the leading 'Forty Other Terrorist Groups', in addition to the 37 designated terrorist organisations. It had been linked to a number of terror crimes including the attempt made to assassinate the former Bangladesh Prime Minster, Sheikh Hasina Wajid, in August 2004 and the murderous knife attack on the liberal Bangladeshi scholar Professor Humayun Azad in February 2004. Prof. Azad had been a staunch opponent of the growing fundamentalist ideology. Though he survived the February attempt on his life, later on he died in Germany under mysterious circumstances. Yet the Finance Minister of Bangladesh, Saifur Rahman, who happened to be in Delhi in the first week of December 2004, had the temerity to proclaim that there was no such militant outfit in Bangladesh. Surely Saifur Rahman must be aware of the contents of five investigative articles on growth of radical Islam in Bangladesh published in the widely circulated Bangladesh daily *Pratham Alo.* In the third article published on August 16, 2004, in *Pratham Alo,* it was specifically mentioned that HUJI-

B, an outfit established in 1992, was actively involved in running training camps for jihadis in the Chittagong hill areas.

Pakistan's involvement in promoting terror network in Bangladesh can be ignored by India only at its peril. As pointed out by Brig. (Retd) Subhash Kapila, Pakistan has certain strategic imperatives for using Bangladesh as a convenient alternative base for activities against India.[24] Some important reasons analysed by Brig. Kapila are as follows :

1. Post 9/11 the presence of US intelligence agencies in Pakistan has made it difficult for the ISI to openly carry out anti-India activities through western border;
2. Extensive fencing along the international border and Line of Control has significantly reduced the scope for sponsoring terrorism in Jammu & Kashmir and waging proxy war against India from western front ; and
3. With the changing international political equations, the Pakistan-based jihadis are now unable to make much headway in Kashmir, except operating from some safe havens set up earlier.

That explains why Pakistan has changed its strategy by shifting ISI's major operational theatre to Bangladesh which offers an attractive route for its decades old aggression against India for waging the avowed war of a thousand cuts, as is often boasted by jihadi warriors and their mentors. Though the ISI sponsored terror tap running into Kashmir is yet to be fully turned off, the ISI has drafted a new blueprint codenamed "Operation Pincode" to step up the heat against the Indian nation. This nefarious operation against India has already been launched through Bangladesh border. The avowed aim of Operation Pincode is to destabilize India's eastern flank by Islamisation of Assam and adjoining north-eastern states, including West Bengal and Bihar. The long term objective is to create a Greater Bangladesh as the first step in the direction of carving out the proposed caliphate. A multipronged strategy has been devised by the ISI in concert with fundamentalist elements safely ensconsed in Khalida Zia's BNP led alliance. According to intelligence reports, the top leadership of ULFA has already been bought over by the ISI to lend full support to the Islamist cause. Most top leaders of ULFA like Paresh Baruah, Arvind Rajkhowa and others are living in great luxury in Bangladesh virtually as guests of the Bangladesh government which has persistently refused to hand them over to India despite repeated requests. For sometime past the Bangladesh-based ULFA leadership has been carrying on a charade of negotiating with Indian government a peaceful settlement of their demands through Mamoni Raisom Goswami (a Jnanpeeth award winner of Assam). But recently the cat was out of bag when BSF Inspector General, S.C. Srivastava, disclosed at a Press Conference held in first week of June 2005 at Shillong that ULFA was operating seven hotels of international standard in Dacca, Chittagong and Sylhet. It is believed that the organisation is operating three bank accounts in Bangladesh traced to Arab Bangladesh Bank's Farm Gate branch in Dhaka, Zinda Bazar branch in Sylhet and Al-Barak Bank's Pahartali branch in Chittagong.[26] Three hotels in Dacca were being managed by Subal Barua alias Ahmed, Satish Sharma alias Kamal, and Ashish Deka alias Hossain, while another two hotels in Sylhet were run by Dulal Roy alias Saidul and Anil Dey alias Sohail. In all probability, these managers of ULFA run hotels had converted to Islam, as is clear from their newly acquired Muslim names. All of them belong to the regular cadres of the banned outfit presently hosted by Bangladesh and are hand in glove with ISI and some functionaries of the Bangladesh government. A top ULFA leader, Deepak Baruah, had reportedly attended a meeting held sometime in February or March 2005 at an undisclosed location in Bangladesh to discuss the modalities of carrying forward "Operation Pincode" for achieving the long term goal of overrunning a major portion of Assam along with some other strategic areas.[27] Additionally a number of covert and overt outfits have been positioned in Bangladesh and fifth columnist cells organized in Assam, West Bengal and adjoining states with ISI's massive financial support, including millions of 'Takas' (Bangladesh currency) bankrolled by the international terrorist, Dawood Ibrahim, to implement the strategy. For imparting training to jihadi warriors a number of camps have been set up in Chittagong hills and other districts like Sylhet and Rajshahi the details of which are known to Indian intelligence agencies and the Border Security Force. As explained above, dozens of veteran Al Qaeda operators have lately shifted to Bangladesh to promote the fundamentalist Wahabi ideology in the adjoining states of India. One such organization, Jagrata Muslim Janata Bangladesh, is headed by Banglabhai alias Siddiqui Islam, alias Azizur Rahman, who commands a jihadi group of approximately ten thousand committed youth. They have been spearheading a violent campaign in several districts bordering India and the infection seems to be spreading to certain sensitive districts of Assam where echoes of Banglabhai's fundamentalist ideology can be heard. There are reports of a radical change in the attitude of many illegal immigrants residing in India. Needless to mention the objective of the ISI operators acting in tandem with certain elements of Khalida Zia's regime is to establish an Islamic Caliphate based on the model practiced by Taliban in Afghanistan. The octopus-like grip of Islamic terrorists on Bangladesh and the wide sweep of their organizational network was displayed when on August 17, 2005, the banned Jamiat-ul Mujahideen and Banglabhai's JMJB (Jagrata Muslim Janata Bangladesh) carried out 459 serial bomb blasts in 63 out of 64 districts of that country with remarkable precision and within a short span of 30 minutes or so, leaving 2 persons dead and 38 injured. The spectacularly staged blasts demonstrated the long reach and resolve of emboldened jihadi groups to implement their agenda for total Islamisation of the country. Handbills demanding enforcement of Islamic laws and threatening anti-Islamic NGOs, issued in the name of Jamiat-e Mujahideen Bangladesh were found at the sites of bomb blasts. The leaflets warned the US President, George Bush and British Prime Minister, Tony Blair, of retaliation unless they "get out of Muslim countries". It goes without saying that the terror groups of Bangladesh have full support of Pakistan's ISI and ultimately most of these bomb-savvy cells will be infiltrated into India to stage bomb attacks. According to the Dhaka-based Bengali daily *Ittefaq*, the terrorist groups were planning attacks on non-Muslim religious leaders and their places of worship including Dhakeshwari temple of

Hindus, the church at Tejgaon and the Buddhist temple at Kamiapur.[29] In recent months activities of Jihadi groups have gathered enormous momentum.

The strategic parameters of the ISI's brainchild, "Operation Pincode", have many tactical strands. The first step is to flood Assam, West Bengal, Bihar and north-eastern states with infiltrators many of whom are trained in militancy and terror tactics. This is already being done vigorously — almost viciously. The second step is to establish a number of Islamic spy-modules throughout the region and even in far away parts of India like Maharashtra, Gujarat, Delhi, Haryana and even in the farthest states of Tamil Nadu, Karnataka and Kerala, both for intelligence collection and promoting communal trouble by capitalizing on friction-fomenting issues. It is widely believed that in this mission, too, the Islamists have achieved considerable success. Indian intelligence agencies know this fact quite well. The third important strand is to subvert the loyalty of discontented regional and local groups, including casteist outfits by financing them and espousing their causes by agitating in press and public so that they turn against the Indian state and ancient civilizational values. There are a number of instances of such subversion, including the winning over of ULFA and the support being extended by Bangladesh government to Bodo and Tripura militants. The recent bloody clashes between the *Karbis* and the *Dimasas,* two Hindu ethnic tribes, bear the stamp of a typical ISI covert operation. As revealed by three Bangladeshi infiltrators caught by Dibrugarh police in the first week of March 2005, before pushing them into India the infiltrators were taught elementary Assamese and perhaps some other regional dialects spoken by Nagas, Mizos and Manipuris, etc. One hears rumours about the infiltrators being taught even Marathi, Gujarati and Tamil too during pre-infiltration training in Bangladesh. Even far away Coimbatore in Tamil Nadu is reported to have quite a few thousand Bangladeshis — many of them possess rudimentary knowledge of Tamil language.

The strategy of using Bangladesh for launching repetitive jihadi attacks on targets in India bears the unmistakable stamp of the ISI of Pakistan. One recent instance of the perfidy of

Bangladesh based terrorists was the attack on Ramjanambhoomi temple on July 5, 2005, which was planned in Bangladesh. One of the masterminds of Ayodhya conspiracy was Maqbool Hussain, a Dhubri born Jaish-e-Mohammed terrorist and a close confidante of Maulana Azhar Masood, chief of JeM. Maqbool was arrested by Delhi Police on October 29, 2005, along with his associate Adnan, a Pakistani national and seasoned terrorist. Originally from Assam, Maqbool had taken up residence in Dhaka and used to operate under different identities. The code name assigned to him by Jaish was Zahid, while in Bangladesh he was known as Anwar. He had travelled to Karachi on forged documents and even met Masood Azhar at Bahawalpur. A diehard Islamic terrorist, Maqbool, had studied for five years at Deoband in India from 1992 to 1997. The mastermind of bombing of Sankatmochan temple in Varanasi in March 2006, too, was an Indian, Pash Imam of a mosque in Allahabad (U.P.) who also studied at Dar-ul-Uloom in Deoband.

Another important tool being used to destabilize India is the endless printing of fake Indian currency both in Bangladesh and Pakistan which is regularly smuggled into India with the help of spy-modules and then widely circulated to destabilize the Indian economy. The proceeds are being regularly used to financially support the spy-modules and furthering subversive activities in various parts of the country. It is well known that a number of anti-India secessionist outfits are being financed and sheltered in Bangladesh for staging bomb blasts, random killings and other terrorist activities.

It may be recalled that sometime ago Seraj-ul Alam Khan, a well known Bangladeshi intellectual, had brought out a cleverly contrived plan for establishing the hegemony of Bangladesh in the entire region. The document titled *Democracy and Economic Development of Bangladesh* envisages a long term strategy for overrunning and appropriating the north-eastern region and forming Greater Bangladesh by segregating the north-eastern states from India by tempting them to have access to Bay of Bengal through Bangladesh's seaports for economic prosperity through enhanced export opportunities. The plan is a simple ruse, a bait to subvert loyalty of north-eastern states to India. It even tries to lure Bhutan and Nepal into a composite regional entity called "Eastern Zone" and promises to set up a two-tier Zonal Parliament of the region under the tutelage of Greater Bangladesh. There is practically little difference between the objectives of "Operation Pincode" and Alam Khan's vision of a new Bangladesh-centric zonal entity sought to be constituted by weaning away Assam and adjoining states from India along with two independent nations of Nepal and Bhutan. Alam Khan's plan is indeed more diabolical in its conceptual framework and long reach.

It is sometime argued that the influx from Bangladesh is largely motivated by economic considerations because of acute economic distress in that country. That is farthest from truth. It is a complex problem in which our two neighbours on either flank are deeply involved. The sheer enormity of the problem has serious political and civilizational overtones. The evil designs of dozens of fundamentalist outfits, sponsored by the ISI, active all over Bangladesh and north-eastern region are self evident. Several million Takas (Bangladeshi equivalent of Indian rupee) have been bankrolled to terror groups by several Arab and Pakistan-based Islamic charities. Thousands of madarasas have been set up in Bangladesh and along Indo-Nepal and Indo-Bangladesh border. More than 50 extremist Islamic groups are functioning in Bangladesh, some with the avowed aim of establishing an Islamic Caliphate starting from southern Philippines running through Indonesia, Singapore, Malaysia, Thailand to Bangladesh and thence extending via India to Pakistan and beyond, right upto West Asia.

Although the Assam Gana Parishad (AGP) came to power in 1985 on the promise of detecting and deporting illegal immigrants, it soon forgot the commitment made to the electorate. Apparently in their desire to retain political power, the AGP leaders made no direct reference to the problem of illegal influx, nor did the National Democratic Alliance include it in their manifesto of the 1999 general elections. Clearly the problem of detecting and deporting the immigrants is now heavily overshadowed by the formation of a strong vote-bank of Bangladeshis which our self-seeking politicians are not prepared to ignore. There are sharp differences on the subject and the Assamese society is already in a turmoil. The conflict of political interest between the state government and the central government was highly visible when the National Democratic Alliance (NDA) was in power at New Delhi. But even now difference of opinion persists between the Congress Chief Minister Tarun Gogoi and the present Governor, Gen. Ajai Singh, the latter being more concerned about safeguarding integrity of the nation, as is evident from his well documented and candid report to the central government submitted recently.

In order to tackle this menacing problem political analysts have, from time to time, suggested the following measures :

1. All Indian nationals should be issued Photo Identity Cards;
2. No ID cards should be issued to illegal immigrants/ foreigners, nor should they be given the right to vote ;
3. A quota system may be evolved for those coming into India from Bangladesh or even Myanmar to work in Assam, north-eastern States, or any other part of India, and Work Permits issued to them.
4. Work Permits could be issued initially to a limited number of persons, in groups of 20 or more, in the first year and subsequently increased depending upon the availability of jobs.
5. The employers should be held responsible both for the well being of the permit-holding employees and must ensure their non-disappearance — a clumsy paper commitment almost impossible to fulfil.

Some of these suggestions could be tried after careful deliberations and consultations with the concerned citizen groups and political parties. It is also being advocated that a general amnesty could be granted to all those who came, say before 1981 or 1991 and they could be allowed to stay on provided they acknowledged their illegal status. But recourse to such general amnesty will harm the national interest. It might also set a bad precedent in the years to come. Looking to the widespread political corruption and the deeply ingrained malaise of vote-bank politics in future some state or central governments might try to make use of the strategem of amnesty for retaining the infiltrators in a bid to ride back to political power. The proposal for issuing work permits too does not make much sense especially when Assam has an abnormally high proportion of unemployed youth — presently numbering more than 20 lakhs or nearly 10 per cent of population. This suggestion, too, could be misused for building a vote-bank of aliens by promising them jobs through Work Permits at the cost of Indian nationals who will remain unemployed and hungry. The first right to employment or access to livelihood resource belongs to the deprived and hungry youth of Assam — and never never to the infiltrators!

The government should undertake the following steps for effectively dealing with the menace :

1. Now that the IMDT Act has been struck down by the apex court, the first major step should be to identify and deport all infiltrators in accordance with the provisions of the Foreigners Act in an expeditious manner. There should be no let up in this campaign.
2. It is time for doing some out-of-box thinking. Along our north-eastern border a crash programme of resettling ex-servicemen and retired personnel of para-military forces belonging to the concerned state, or region, should be launched. These 'Sentinel Settlements' of ex-servicemen should be financially supported by the government to buy land and keep licensed weapons for defending their farms and border areas. For better results a chain of sentinel cooperatives on the pattern of Israeli-style 'Kibbutz' need to be established all along the Indo-Bangladesh border as well as in equally vulnerable border areas of Gujarat and Rajasthan. In the north-east the situation has now become so volatile that nothing short of this strategy will be able to protect the local people and ensure unity and integrity of the nation.

3. The deployment of Border Security Force along the Indo-Bangladesh border should be augmented by establishing more outposts and provision for additional manpower made to ensure intensive vigil. It will be useful to introduce trained dogs for strengthening border patrolling.

4. The entire border with Bangladesh should be protected by a high-tech fortified security barrier with electronic sensors, double concertina fencing and machine-gun mounted watch-towers as add-ons, just as Israelis have done to keep away Palestinian terrorists. In this task it would be useful to seek technical advice of Israeli engineers who have developed an effective technique for ensuring trans-border security through high-tech fencing and barriers. These measures should be implemented as crash programme.

5. The long overdue task of compulsory registration of all Indian nationals must be completed at the earliest, first and foremost in Assam and then in other sensitive north-eastern states including West Bengal and Bihar. Every citizen should be issued a multi-purpose photo ID card, and there should be full documentation of all foreigners and non-citizens. The process should start first from Indo-Bangladesh border and adjoining states of north-east and then cover West Bengal, Bihar, Uttar Pradesh and Delhi. It will have to cover all States, especially the major cities.

6. On the pattern of the United Kingdom a law should be passed by the Government of India forbidding employment of illegal immigrants by imposing on-the- spot heavy financial penalty of Rs fifty thousand for infringement on defaulting employers, whether individuals or businessmen. Just like the U.K., the Government of India must make public its firm resolve to implement "zero tolerance" of illegal immigrants. Under the new British law, the Immigration, Asylum and Nationality Act, the employers will be fined 2000 pounds on the spot every time they hire an illegal immigrant. Also fingerprinting of all visa applicants will become mandatory within next three years. All skilled workers legally

entering Great Britain must have qualifications equal to 'A' level and above. Even so they will be allowed to settle down in the United Kingdom with their families only after they have worked for five years and passed a fairly comprehensive English language and citizenship test.[30] To make the anti-immigration law more stringent, India should also incorporate a legal provision whereby the acts of both the employer and the illegal immigrant taking up or giving an unauthorized employment would be a cognizable offence.

7. A concerted drive must be launched throughout the country to detect all illegal immigrants, delete their names from electoral rolls and deport them. If necessary, for completing this task, a joint working group of representatives of India and Bangladesh may be constituted and the latter country persuaded to accept repatriation of their nationals.

8. All those Bangladeshis and other foreigners who have entered India illegally should be deprived of the right to vote through a special legislation passed for the purpose and their ration cards annulled. Simultaneously action should be taken to cancel all fraudulently obtained identity documents of infiltrators.

9. All madarasas and newly built mosques in border districts and even in the interior where Bangladeshi immigrants are concentrated should be enumerated, registered and watched for subversive and anti-national activities, especially where the doctrine of *jihad* is propagated.

Even though it may not be possible to identify and deport millions of immigrants back to Bangladesh, a bold no-holds barred attempt must be made both by the central and state governments to identify and deport quite a few million Bangladeshi — out of more than 30 million infiltrators that we are hosting presently. Thereafter, in the entire north-eastern region, including Assam, Manipur, Tripura, Meghalya and Mizoram a concerted programme of promoting national integration at grassroots level should be launched. In due course of time the project should be extended to West Bengal, Bihar,

Uttar Pradesh, Delhi and other States where Bangladeshis have come to constitute a sizeable proportion of the total population. If necessary, certain select voluntary organisations may be co-opted to make the programme successful. Perhaps Ramakrishna Mission could be involved in promoting national integration. Intensive efforts need to be made in the States of Assam and West Bengal to identify those Bangladeshis who have managed to acquire Indian citizenship and attempts made through NGOs to bring them into national mainstream.

In view of the threat posed by fundamentalist teachings in thousands of new madarasas set up at the instance of the ISI, it may be worthwhile to organise sociological surveys by circulating well-designed questionnaires to ascertain and assess the politico-religious attitude of the left-over Bangladeshi immigrants and thereafter concerted efforts made to integrate them into national mainstream by seeking help of their community leaders.

Not only Members of Parliament and State legislators, but even prominent journalists and editors should be briefed from time to time about the problems of security and national integration in border regions, with special reference to the influx of Bangladeshis. That would ensure greater public support for the proposed task and also ensure transparency in operations.

Exasperated by the pathetic indifference of the central and state governments towards this growing menace, midway through the celebrations of Rongali Bihu on April 12, 2005, a determined Bihutoli of Dibrugarh youth constituted a proactive outfit, Chiring Chapori Yuva Mancha, named after an obscure locality of the town. This ginger group of young activists decided to launch an economic boycott of Bangladeshis through a peaceful campaign. Ostensibly the provocation was provided by the capture of three Bangladeshi infiltrators by Dibrugarh police in the first week of March 2005 who confessed that they had been taught a smattering of Assamese language before being pushed into India. In the last week of April the Yuva Mancha gave a call to the people for implementing the following four point agenda:

1. No one should employ any illegal Bangladeshi immigrant;
2. No one should travel in a vehicle driven or plied by an illegal immigrant;
3. No one should transact any business with illegal immigrants; and
4. No one should provide any shelter or accommodation to illegal immigrants.

The call given by the Dibrugarh youth was a sort of a people-powered action programme which gave fright to illegal immigrants and thousands of them fled from Dibrugarh and some other districts of Assam, including Sibsagar, Jorhat, Golaghat and Nalbari, etc. The activists of Chiring Chapori Yuva Mancha, mostly educated youngmen in their twenties, addressed a press conference in Dibrugarh on May 14 2005 and said that their chief objective was to make the Assamese people aware of the dangers involved in allowing the infiltrators to settle down in the state for which default the future generations will never forgive them.[31] All over northern Assam it came to be known as "Dibrugarh modus" for dealing with illegal influx. Soon thousands of SMS messages were buzzing across the state saying "Save nation, save identity. Let us take an oath .... no food, no job, no shelter to a Bangladeshi. Start a complete economic blockade to illegal immigrants". The boycott call had an escalating effect on what most people in Assam describe as the "Bangladeshi problem". Without any overt violence but perhaps overawed by an element of intimidation, busloads of suspected Bangladeshis left Dibrugarh town and Jorhat district without a clear destination. The youth who forced their departure were sure that they were illegals. The local media went ballistic: the Assamese language papers came out with photos and press reporters occupying vantage points talked about the exodus of infiltrators with undisguised glee. Litterateurs, lawyers and scholars lent their support to the campaign. The district administration and state government were nonplussed. There was no violence; so no action could be taken against the organizers of peaceful campaign. The objective too was unexceptionable: it involved strengthening citizen's rights.[32]

Seeking Public Support

Now that the Dibrugarh youth have blazed a new dynamic trail, the next step should be to give a wake-up call to all Indians, especially the 'identity threatened' citizens of Assam, West Bengal, Arunachal Pradesh, Meghalaya, Mizoram, Nagaland, Tripura and Sikkim to boycott all Bangladeshis thereby setting the tone for a sustained peaceful campaign of non-cooperation, reminiscent of our freedom movement. For this purpose a strategic plan should be devised by organising self-help groups at grassroots level by involving the masses to implement the following "peaceful action programme" :

1. The already launched campaign of "Dibrugarh modus" involving total economic and social boycott of illegal immigrants should be rigorously sustained and spread far and wide, even if it causes some hardship and suffering to certain segments of Indian society. Well publicised awareness meetings should be held in all major cities, especially in commercial and industrial centres, highlighting the threat to the nation's unity and integrity. Special attention may be drawn to the fact that Assam, West Bengal, north-eastern states and even Orissa, Bihar, U.P. and Maharashtra have millions of jobless hungry Indians who have a prior claim on the country's livelihood resources. We cannot afford to ignore our own countrymen and leave them to starve at the cost of giving jobs to illegal immigrants. As a rule, resolution of the hunger pangs of our own countrymen must take priority over foreigners. Later on the momentum of 'awareness meetings' should be extended to smaller town and rural areas. In due course, the proposed peaceful 'Dibrugarh modus' campaign should take the shape of a mass national movement which must be peaceful and orderly.

2. The "Dibrugarh modus" action groups should actively motivate all Indian householders and businessmen to refuse to give any employment, not even part-time jobs to any illegal immigrant, not only in Assam but all over India.

Our people must be reminded that while illegal Bangladeshis infiltrators are having a good time after usurping jobs and livelihood resources in our country, thousands of Indians, including marginal farmers, are dying of hunger and many are committing suicide. Just like the Swadeshi movement of yore, the campaign should emphasise that Indian enterpreneurs and citizens must employ only Indian labourers, and not foreigners, even if it means some monetary loss and physical inconvenience. Any greedy businessman or individual employing illegal immigrant should face boycott and social ostracization.

3. People should be dissuaded from selling their lands, shops and houses to illegal immigrants, no matter howsoever high price might be offered. In the event of any threat of violence, *vigilante* groups of patriotic youth should be organised to protect the interests of Indian citizens, just as is being done by the voluntary groups of *vigilantes* keeping a hawk-like watch along the open border between the USA and Mexico.

4. All state and national level leaders and political parties should be asked to publicly clarify their stand on the issue of relentless illegal influx of Bangladeshis. This may be done by writing open letters, presenting memoranda and recourse to verbal communications to political leaders and parties. All public meetings and functions organised by those public figures who don't reply, or fail to favourably respond to the appeals made by the 'Dibrugarh modus' groups should be boycotted.

5. In every constituency the elected representatives, both Members of Parliament and MLAs, should be requested to keep effective track of the detection, disqualification and deportation of illegal immigrants. They must publicly apprise their constituents at regular intervals of the efforts made in this direction and report progress of the process of identification and deportation of illegal immigrants.

5

Growing Ungovernability of North-East

"During times of universal deceit, telling the truth becomes a revolutionary act".

George Orwell

For more than two decades alarming signals have been emanating from north-eastern India which important region continues to slide towards a state of total ungovernability. In recent years the incidence of unremitting violence in the region has grown phenomenally despite extensive deployment of security forces. A sudden outburst of violence gripped north-east in the first week of October 2004 in which 45 people were killed in a series of bomb blasts and terror attacks unleashed by terror-spewing militants in Nagaland and Assam.[1] On 2nd October 2004 twin explosions, caused by landmine blasts, rocked Dimapur, a prosperous and bustling city of Nagaland in which 30 persons, including many children, were killed and 100 injured. Immediately thereafter, despite a high alert sounded all over the north-eastern region and extensive combing of the vulnerable areas by security forces, different militant groups managed to strike in several towns of Assam including Dhubri, Bongaigaon, Kokrajhar, Darrang, Morigaon, Chirang, Udalgiri,

Shonitpur, Sibsagar, Karbi Anglong, Kamrup, Nalbari and Tinsukia, raising the overall toll to 70 or more deaths in less than 24 hours.[2] Earlier on 15th August 2004, the Independence Day celebrations were marred by a powerful explosion in Dhemaji causing gruesome death of 16 innocent school children. Lately many insurgent groups have developed the capability to hit anyone anywhere and at any time. In many parts of the north-east such attacks and indiscriminate killings have become commonplace occurrences. It is no use denying the fact that the situation in the region has been slipping out of control quite fast.

No Law, No Public Order

The gravity of the widespread disorder can be assessed from the fact that in the first week of October 2004 in Talap area of Tinsukia, a group of suspected militants belonging to the United Liberation Front of Assam (ULFA) wiped out an entire Army patrol of four soldiers in a grenade attack. In another blast, allegedly carried out by the NDFB (National Democratic Front of Bodoland) militants at Bijni fish market in Bongaigaon district one person was killed and 17 injured, while in a similar incident at Gauripur weekly 'haat' in Dhubri district 16 persons were injured. Subsequently there were a number of killings by bomb attacks all over Assam. And after widespread serial bombings the United Liberation Front of Assam served extortion notices to more than 50 business houses, apart from asking many doctors to pay up ransom. The quantum of extortion sums demanded varied from Rs ten lakhs to 25 lakhs. For instance, a businessman of Sibsagar had been directed to shell out Rs 25 lakhs, while a doctor of Tinsukia ran away from town after receiving an extortion demand of Rs. one crore. Businessmen also got phone calls by militants asking them to pay up within a fortnight and quite a few agreed to make some payments. Prosperous commercial centres like Dibrugarh, Sibsagar and Tinsukia are among the major towns targeted for extortion drive. One of the extortion notices was purported to have been signed by one Achinta Saikia, a man who claims to be the Finance Secretary of ULFA's Eastern Zone.[3] Businessmen openly say that they have little confidence in the local police which are unable to check the movement of ULFA cadres, leave alone nabbing them. Though the Inspector General of Police (Special Branch) tried to underplay the extortion racket by saying that majority of extortion notices were fake, he admitted that such extortion attempts were commonplace.[4] Meanwhile on December 13, 2004, Kanglei Yawol Kanna Lup (KYKL), a banned Metei militant outfit, managed to abduct the Vice Chancellor of Manipur University, N. Bijoy Singh, along with the University Registrar, R.K. Ranjan. Later on they were released on the morning of December 18, 2004, after being allegedly punished for their so-called involvement in a recruitment scam relating to the University's Audio-Visual Research Centre (AVRC). The outfit claimed that the Vice Chancellor and the Registrar were summoned by them for chastisement because they had flouted the recruitment rules in connection with the appointment of Director, AVRC.[5] It was further claimed that this was done as part of "Operation New Kangleipak" launched sometime ago. Kangleipak was the traditional ancient kingdom of Manipur. Subsequently the same group had shot six male teachers in their legs on charges of aiding students who were found cheating during an examination, besides parading a school teacher before journalists and then debarring him from teaching for life, saying that he was neglecting his profession.[6] It may be mentioned that although Hindus constitute majority in the turbulent state of Manipur, they are concentrated in a small area located in the centre of the state. From June 20, 2005 onwards, for 54 days, the Manipur Valley was totally blockaded, call it a hostile siege if you will, by ANSAM (All Naga Students Association of Manipur). The blockade created acute shortages of food and medicines in the valley because no supplies were allowed to reach Manipur valley despite all efforts of the government. The successful blockade was enforced by an estimated five lakhs Nagas living in the hilly areas around the valley who did not allow any truck to reach Manipur. Three districts of Manipur, Ukhrul, Senapati and Tamenglong have large Naga population and Naga student groups want the Naga-inhabited areas to be merged with "Greater Nagaland" or

'Nagalim'', a political concept propagated by the National Socialist Council of Nagalim (Isaac-Muivah group). To put it across bluntly, for almost two months there was practically no government in and around Manipur. Ultimately the siege was lifted only when the Prime Minister Dr. Manmohan Singh, himself spoke to some interlocuters of Naga leadership. That shows how precariously poised is the writ of the Indian government in the north-eastern India.

There were numerous bomb attacks in Assam in the months of November and December 2004. By now the ULFA is reported to have formed an alliance with the Maoists of Nepal. And according to Assam Police, the ULFA has hired the services of some ultras of Harkat-ul-Mujahideen for carrying out subversive activities. It claimed that 50 militants of the Harkat outfit were hired or commissioned by the ULFA in the second week of December 2004 to carry out terror attacks.[7]

Without fail every year the residents of Assam and many other north-eastern states face the threat of terror attacks on innocent civilians and vital installations in the run up to the Independence Day and Republic Day. These attacks are mostly engineered by the ISI through multiple terrorist organizations like the ULFA, MULTA, All Tripura Tiger Force and similar other outfits which have training camps in Bangladesh and whose leaders find shelter there. The month of August 2005 witnessed a number of bomb blasts across Assam targeting the oil pipelines and other vital installations. The situation was so grim that the Indian Railways had to suspend a number of night trains to Assam and its neighbourhood due to fear of threat to the lives of passengers.

In the circumstances, it will be an understatement to say that there is practically no government in many parts of north-eastern India. Scores of insurgencies are being waged in the region by numerous militant outfits, some known, others unknown – each militant group has been operating against the State, innocent civilians and sometimes even against mutually hostile partisan armed outfits. The latest fraternal strife between Karbis and Dimasas is one more instance of ungovernability.

Involvement of Two Hostile Neighbours

While the great guessing game was on about the possible linkages of the National Socialist Council of Nagalim (Isak Muivah group) and the ULFA-NDFB combine in the ghastly Dimapur blasts in the year 2004 on Gandhi Jayanti (2nd October 2004), a new militant group, Al Jihad-e-Islam, came forward on October 15, 2004, to claim responsibility for the twin ghastly explosions at Dimapur. A vernacular newspaper of Guwahati, *Janasadharan*, reportedly received an e-mail from one Mohammed Salim Khan, who claimed to be the self-styled "North-east Chief" of the aforesaid Jihadist outfit. He owned the responsibility for Dimapur attacks.[8] Though Nagaland Police discounted the possibility of involvement of the so-called nondescript militant organisation, most security experts believe that it will be dangerous to ignore the claim of Mohammed Salim Khan. It may be recalled that Dimapur is the stronghold of the NSCN (Nationalist Socialist Council of Nagalim), a known militant Naga group, which had till then scrupulously kept its word for maintaining peace with the Government of India since the cease-fire agreement reached in 1977. Therefore any suspicion of the complicity of NSCN in Dimapur blasts could be straightaway ruled out. The twin bomb blasts were therefore staged by some non-Naga insurgent outfit. The needle of suspicion thus pointed clearly towards ULFA which has its Central Command headquarters in Bangladesh and whose senior leaders have taken shelter in that country, especially after the successful operations by the Bhutanese army in December 2003.

Preliminary investigations into Dimapur twin blasts revealed that approximately 4 to 5 kilograms of RDX was used in the explosions and the cost of staging the dastardly crime might run into million of rupees. Excepting the ULFA, no other militant group of north-east could meet that kind of heavy financial burden. Even ULFA would be unwilling to spend so much money on one or two strikes, unless the cost was underwritten by the Pakistan-Bangladesh intelligence combine.[9] Many districts of Assam, including Karimganj, Cachar, Hailakandi, Nagaon and Dhubri, where illegal immigrants are now in majority, have witnessed a big upsurge in Islamist mobilization and activity.[10] According to the latest intelligence inputs, the ISI was planning to utilise the services of the MULTA (Muslim United Liberation Tigers of Assam) to stage subversive acts in Cachar district where the CRPF personnel recovered 50 foreign-made detonators from Bagheor village on September 2, 2004, and arrested an insurgent suspect. Reports indicate that in districts like Cachar where ULFA lacks an organisational base, they are trying to use MULTA.[11]

Thus the lengthening shadow of Islamist terror in the north-east now threatens to engulf Nagaland. For sometime past, the government of Nagaland has been complaining about the growing influx of Bangladeshis into areas like Niuland and Dimapur. In September 2004 the Naga Students Federation (NSF) had launched an "oust Bangladeshis" campaign targeting the immigrants after two Bangladeshis had allegedly raped a minor Naga girl.[12] Nagaland is full of tough hilly terrain with large pockets of uninhabited tracts now being seized by Bangladeshis. Little is known to the New Delhi chatterati about the vulnerability of vast isolated areas of the north-east, including Nagaland in which state Bangladeshi immigrants, now believed to be around 4 lakhs, seem to have occupied vast tracts of hilly lands. It may be pointed out that according to the 2001 census, Nagaland has a total population of only 20 lakhs. Army intelligence sources suggest that Bangladeshis "trained in ISI camps are now moving deep into Kohima, Peren and Wokha, besides Dimapur".[13] Thanks to the decades of monumental neglect by the ever somnolent central government, the Islamist threat is now a reality in the north-east. It is a fact that a large number of ISI-sponsored moles among Bangladeshi immigrants have set up a number of cells in the region. According to an intelligence officer overseeing the investigations of Dimapur blasts, in August-September 2004 an information was received that a group of 20 trained Bangladeshi Jihadis were trying to sneak into Nagaland through the Karimganj border with an agenda of carrying out large-scale violence in the north-east. Unfortunately nobody realised that they could launch such a devastating attack in Dimapur.[14] In the circumstances, any casual or dismissive attitude towards the claim of Al Jihad-e-Islam might prove costly for security of the region which offers immense potential for significant manipulation in promoting multiple patterns of terrorism because of the growing interest of two foreign powers, both our neighbours on either side, in fomenting violence in the area.[15] In May and June 2005, there were many serious bomb blasts including the one which was staged fairly close to the State Assembly in Guwahati.

According to 2001 Census of Bangladesh, between 50 years from 1951 to 2001 that country's population galloped from 44.166 million to 131.40 millions, registering a whopping addition of 87.23 millions which translated into a three-fold increase. And this increase was inspite of the massive ethnic cleansing of the Hindus, Buddhists and other minority groups since 1947. Between 1951 and 2001 the population of Hindus and Buddhists in Bangladesh was drastically reduced from 22.89 per cent to a mere 10.03 per cent palpably by forcing them to migrate. By now the Hindu percentage is believed to be around 9 per cent. The sole reason for this sharp decline of Hindus and Buddhists has been widespread ethnic cleansing which continues till date. Interestingly in 1901 the population of the region now constituting Bangladesh was 28.927 million, but during the next 70 years, i.e. between 1901 and 1971 it rose to 70.885 million – barely a little more than twice. During the previous fifty years, i.e., from 1901 to 1951, population of that country had increased only one and half times. Clearly the last three decades have seen a huge growth in population of Bangladesh of which a substantial portion numbering at least 3 crore are now in India, though some estimates place the figure at around 5 crore. The estimated figure of 3 crore infiltrators has been arrived at by taking into account detailed calculations made by Sarifa Begum, a well-known Bangladeshi demographer, plus authentic statistical inputs from reliable sources.

More than seven years ago, the present Governor of Jammu & Kashmir, Lt. General (Retd) S.K. Sinha, during his tenure as Governor of Assam, had sent a 42-page detailed report to the President about the menacing ramifications of rampant immigration from Bangladesh. It drew pointed attention to the fact that the demographic invasion had created widespread societal schisms endangering the social, cultural and political harmony of the State, apart from constituting a grave danger to the security of the nation.[16] Among other things he drew specific attention to the following facts:

i) The population of Muslims had recorded a mammoth increase of 77.42 per cent since 1971 (No census could take place in 1981 in Assam due to disturbed conditions);

ii) Four districts of the state, i.e., Dhubri, Goalpara, Barpeta and Hailakandi, had already acquired the Muslim majority status (now their number is seven) ;

iii) Between 1994 and 1997 in 57 of Assam's 126 Assembly constituencies the number of voters had increased by more than 20 per cent, as against the all India average of nearabout 7.4 per cent; and

iv) The number of illegal Bangladeshis in India at that time was estimated at 13.2 million including 5.4 million in West Bengal, 4 millions in Assam and 1.5 million in Delhi.

The estimated figure of illegal Bangladeshis is reported to be more than 30 million (or 3 crore) at present and their silent invasion continues unabated. Sometime ago the military intelligence had unearthed an ISI plot of pushing Bangladeshis into India with a view to swelling their numbers in the border districts of Assam and West Bengal.[17]

It is well known that ULFA (United Liberation Front of Assam) had initially started as a wayward child of the Assam agitation. But later on this rebel child turned a fifth columnist primarily due to the greed for filthy lucre offered by the Inter Services Intelligence of Pakistan. It has been operating hand in glove with the government of Bangladesh and has become the 'B' team of Jihadists operating from across the border. In December 2003, responding to Indian government's request, the Bhutanese government had undertaken a major campaign to destroy and drive out ULFA militants from the forest areas of Bhutan where they had set up a number of training camps and communication centres. The military operation, executed with precision and boldly by the Royal Bhutanese Army, gave a body blow to ULFA militants many of whom were killed and captured. Their interrogation revealed that ULFA has very intimate links with Bangladesh authorities and through them with the ISI (Inter Services Intelligence) of Pakistan. On being questioned by Bhutanese authorities, a senior ULFA leader, Mithinga Daimary alias Deepak Cachari, confirmed the close links of insurgents with Pakistani intelligence operatives. He disclosed that in mid-2002 a group of ULFA cadres, including some members of their central committee had visited Pakistan for receiving training in PTDs (Programmed Timing Devices) and other explosives. Among them were ULFA Organising Secretary, Ashanta Baghphukan, Raju Baruah and other leaders like Biju Deka, Prasanto Rajguru, Merin Das and Pradyut Buragohain.[18] It was learnt that a consignment of PTDs (Programmed Timing Devices) was expected to reach them in January or February 2004, but before that the Bhutanese army swung into action. The interrogation corroborated the information already collected by Indian intelligence agencies that the ISI has been providing both funds and armaments for training to ULFA and other militant organisations of the north-east. According to Daimary, the ULFA had 8 major camps and 5 small camps, 4 wireless sets and 5 satellite phones in Bhutan which had nearly 400 insurgents spread out in various locations. The major camps included the General Headquarters at Sukuni, CHQ (Central Headquarters) at Wangpho, their West Zone camp, or 709 Battalion camp near Kalikhola, 7th Battalion camp on the way to GHQ, Morang Camp behind CHQ, Nelang camp near Deothang and so on. He disclosed that the last consignment of arms in Bhutan was received from Bangladesh in December 2002, through Meghalaya-Bongaigaon corridor.[19] According to the information gleaned from various sources by Indian intelligence agencies, the insurgency spearheaded by the NDFB leadership was being supported in a similar manner by Bangladesh government and the ISI.

It is well known that for more than one decade the ISI has been hyperactive in Nepal. Apart from facilitating hijacking of Indian Airlines flight IC-814 in November 1999, the ISI operators worked overtime to establish a chain of hundreds of mosques and madrasas along Indo-Nepal border. According to unconfimed reports most of these mosques were used as transit facilities for bringing in weapons from Bangladesh which were transferred to Maoists through handpicked members of the Islamic Yuva Sangh, a fundamentalist outfit floated by the ISI through late Mirza Dilshad Beg, who was a minister in an earlier Nepalese regime. Dilshad Beg was a close associate of the notorious international terrorist. Dawood Ibrahim, who used him as a conduit for bankrolling funds for anti-Indian activities and subverting governance in Nepal. Though later on Dilshad Beg was killed, perhaps by the notorious gangster Chhota Rajan's men, an effective network of ISI spies was successfully established in Nepal with his active support.

According to a former European envoy to Nepal (name withheld) Kathmandu and many important towns of Nepal were swarming with thousands of ISI agents. He estimated their strength to be around twenty thousand which appears to be an exaggeration. But no one can deny ISI's massive presence in Nepal and their substantial political clout all around. It may be recalled that in the first week of April 2004 a huge consignment of sophisticated weapons, including some heavy armaments, coming by sea was seized at Cox's Bazar in Bangladesh which was large enough to arm one battalion of insurgents. According to informed intelligence sources that consignment of weapons, mistakenly seized by Bangladesh police, was meant to be delivered to the Maoist rebels of Nepal via the contraband corridor running through Bangladesh; Meghalaya and North Bengal. At least one prominent member of the Young Communist League (YCL), a pro-Maoist outfit, was widely known to be on the payroll of the ISI. Some cadres of the YCL were often seen hobonobbing with the activists of Islamic Yuva Sangh whose many members reportedly participated actively in the Maoist rebellion. Prima facie the active association of the Islamic Yuva Sangh with the armed Maoist rebels and the financial clout of the ISI, could have prompted the hasty erasing of Nepal's Hindu identity by delcaring it as a secular state. The sudden declaration of Nepal as a secular state, even before a new

Constitution could be written, came as a shocking surprise to a large majority of Nepalese citizens some of whom even took to streets in Birganj and many other towns to lodge their protests. The fact that removal of the Hindu identity of Nepal became the first priority of the Maoists appeared to be somewhat mysterious to most Nepal watchers in India. It looks like a pay back gesture towards those who have been helping the Maoist insurgency. Possibly there is much more to the turn of political developments in Nepal than what meets the eye.

It may be recalled that according to reports received in September 2004, the ULFA had decided to join hands with the Muttahida Jihad Council (i.e., United Jihad Council), an umbrella organisation of various Islamic militant groups operating in Jammu & Kashmir. This was confirmed sometime ago during seizure of grenades from the hideouts of a slain ULFA militant, Lachit Rabha, killed in an encounter at Jerdoba in East Garo Hills district of Meghalaya. The recovered grenades were similar to those used by the Pakistani army and resembled the ones hurled at the policemen by Jaish-e-Mohammed terrorists during attack on the Indian Parliament in December 2001.[20] After successful dismantling of terrorist infrastructure in Afghanistan by the USA, Bangladesh now has emerged as the new haven for Pakistan trained terrorist outfits of different hues, including Al Qaeda.

The rapidly dwindling population of minorities, especially the Hindus, which came down from 23 per cent in 1951 to less than 10 per cent in 2001, was the subject of a one-day conference organized by European Human Rights Conference on Bangladesh on June 17, 2005. A seminar was organized to discuss the worsening law and order situation, violation of human rights and persistent attacks on minority religious groups including the Hindus, Christians, Buddhists and Ahmediyas. Among others it was attended by I.K. Gujral, a former Indian Prime Minister and P.A. Sangma, former Speaker of Lok Sabha. Putting across the viewpoint of persecuted minorities of Bangladesh, Sangma drew attention to the spectacular decline in their population. He also highlighted the fact that an obnoxious legislation called Vested Property Act has been used as a tool "for robbing the Hindu community of its property".[21]

What Ails North-East?

What ails the north-east is a million dollar question. Different experts sitting in New Delhi continue to proffer different kinds of solutions, mostly run-of-the-mill recipes, for solving problems of the region. While the State-level politicians have always used political power for feathering their nests, the successive central governments largely viewed the problem of unremitting violence and disorder through the bifocal lens of inadequate security forces and lack of economic development. In accordance with their tunnel-vision understanding of the situation they treated it either as a law and order problem, or remained focussed on economic development by making grandiose announcements of financial packages. But neither prescription has worked, nor will ever work unless the real cause of the malady was diagnosed. Meanwhile the situation continues to deteriorate. By now the entire north-east has become almost ungovernable. In rural areas and far away hamlets there is no reassuring feeling of safety among local residents, unless security forces are located in immediate neighbourhood. Multiple militant groups roam around extorting money and killing innocents with impunity. While the twin factors of inefficient law enforcement and inadequate economic development might have substantially contributed to the mayhem and mess in the region, the real problem lies elsewhere. The relentless hostile invasion by millions of Bangladeshis leading to competitive struggle between the invaders and the ethnic majority for scarce land and livelihood resources is the core of the problem. That has led to civil strife and lawlessness all over the region. That is the truth, though our political leaders might never admit it. Unless this menace is tackled there is little hope for peace.

Even a cursory glance at the monumental changes in the demography of north-eastern states will reveal the overwhelming population change as the most important single cause responsible for the growing ungovernability of the region. During last 30 years the entire north-eastern India has been brutely trampled upon and subjected to an unprecedented invasion by millions of alien infiltrators. It is a blight which has destabilized almost every State, every district and every town of the region and debilitated and supplanted most instruments of governance.

When millions of migrants move from one country to another, or even from one region to another, they generate extensive and earth-shaking tremors leading to social, economic and political upheavals in the land of their entry and encroachment. This is not something new. It has been the experience worldwide for ages throughout mankind's history. The recent events of the Balkans bear mute testimony to the devastating role of demography in causing widespread destabilization and disorder. In the first place, the incoming hordes of immigrants need space to live and multiply. Then comes the need for land to raise crops which is accompanied by search for jobs and ancillary occupational opportunities and resources to earn livelihood. Over a period of time all such demands, call them basic necessities, if you will, multiply with the influx of more men and women and that creates an atmosphere of hostile competition and acrimony between the immigrants and the original inhabitants of the area. The latter naturally resent the intrusion of the newcomers on their home turf, threat to their cultural ethos and the growing encroachment over their lands, factories, jobs and livelihood resources. The cultural antipathy and cut-throat competition for land and jobs makes life harsh and difficult, even nasty and brutish, for the squeezed ethnic and religious groups of the original inhabitants. The natural process of fierce competition for grabbing limited land and productive resources gives rise to tensions and frequent inter-communitarian fights, not only with the intruding immigrants, but also with sister ethnic groups and more importantly, with the law and order authorities. The mounting grievances ultimately take the shape of anger, hatred and organised militancy against the authority of the incompetent state apparatus and leads to gradual debilitation of governance. Historically that has been the natural course of socio-economic struggle and the concomitant civil strifes generated by fast-paced demographic changes in most parts of the world. That is what happened in Kosovo, Serbia, Bosnia and is now subsuming the Macedonian civilization, the last bastion of Orthodox Christianity in the Balkans. There is nothing new or unusual in it. It is a natural, but tortuous and long, process. Finally a stage comes when failure of the government to safeguard the basic requirements of security and economic wherewithals of the original inhabitants and ethnic groups comes to be perceived as the sole cause of their misery by almost every community and ethnic group driven to the margin and struggling for survival. That sets in motion a chain reaction of anger, hostility and civil strife which keeps on erupting sporadically and then occurs almost continually. It ultimately culminates in the outbreak of civil war like conditions in the affected country, or region. Let us face it, in Assam a clear warning about the impending mayhem was sounded 23 years ago by the Nellie massacre of February 1983. Somehow that was ignored by the political leadership. But the issues which resulted in Nellie killings have been allowed to simmer too long, and a stage is fast approaching when many more Nellies might be enacted. One similar blood bath is in progress in Karbi Anglong. Even now, at this late stage, the governments at the centre as well as in the north-eastern states must grow up and try to analyse and understand the events that shook Assam 23 years ago when hundreds of people were butchered in Nellie during the Assembly elections which were violently opposed by the Assamese agitators demanding deportation of illegal Bangladeshis. Unfortunately no one in the government tries to go into the elementary phenomenon of socio-economic complexities of the pulls and pressures created in a resource-starved society by the incessant flood of aggressively pushing immigrants. Often the conflicts are centred around available jobs and livelihood resources, as happened during the Assamese and Bihari confrontation in November 2003 over recruitment for 2000 placements in North-Eastern Railways. Doling out financial packages, or rushing more security forces, is nothing more than a fire-fighting operation. Such sporadic gestures will not remove the divide of cultural asymmetry, nor invest the ethnic groups with lost land and livelihood resources, nor will mere gesturing clear the primordial suspicion and growing hostility among the indigenous people towards the predators coming from a foreign land with a stamp of hostile culture.

In writing a footnote to the growing ungovernability of north-east, attention may be drawn to the fact that in November 2004 a Japanese researcher, Ms. Makiko Kimura, wanted to present her research study on Nellie massacre at a seminar being organised by the Omio Kumar Das Institute of Social Change & Development in Guwahati. Unfortunately for reasons best known to the Assam Government, the seminar was banned at short notice even though the aforesaid research paper had already been submitted to the Jawaharlal Nehru University, New Delhi.[22] After in-depth research, Ms Kimura based her findings through an analysis of the following three competing narratives :

i) The causes of the Nellie massacre as narrated by the victims of the tragedy;

ii) The causes of the conflict as explained by the attacking groups, mostly Tiwa tribals ; and

iii) The causes of the conflict leading to the massacre as explained by the leaders of the movement.

The researcher has drawn specific attention to the rise of Tiwa movement among indigenous tribes in the plains of Assam. The Tiwas are one of the ancient ethnic tribes of Assam zealously wedded to their cultural traditions and proud heritage. Pressed beyond a point they can be awfully violent. Raja Jougalbalahu was a celebrated Tiwa hero and recently a novel based on his life was published by the noted litterateur, Rita Chaudhry. The anger and resentment of Tiwa tribals against aggressive encroachment by Bangladeshi Muslims on their traditional lands and perceived threat to their cultural heritage was the prime cause of the Nellie massacre. According to Ms Kimura, the findings of the Nellie incident point to the formation of a counter-discourse in the rise of the powerful Tiwa movement. The leaders of the movement mobilise the people by using the resource of the collective memory of the Nellie massacre.[23] Briefly, Ms. Kimura, a fellow of the Japan Society for the Promotion of Science, summarised her findings as follows:

"The findings of the Nellie incident point to the formation of a counter-discourse in the rise of the Tiwa movement. It shows the way in which tribal movement in the plains, which is one of the most active movements in present day Assam, is organized and the ways in which their leaders mobilise people by using the resources of the collective memory of the Nellie massacre. In this way, the Tiwa narratives can be identified as a counter-discourse to that of the Assamese nationality."[24]

"The Tiwa narratives powerfully reveal one of the reasons why movements by the tribes in the plains are active in Assam today. The movement is backed by the sense of deprivation among majority of the peasant tribes".[25] Her in-depth research, already published in some international journals, has identified economic deprivation as the main cause of anger of the tribals against intruders and the resultant growth of violence. Decades of impoverishment, economic distress and usurpation of their lands and occupational resources by intruding hordes of predators have often led to murderous attacks and frequent killings. It may be mentioned that the Tiwa students were in the forefront of a successful bandh (strike) organised on December 14, 2004, in Guwahati and several other towns of Assam, which culminated in a virtual seige of Dispur, the seat of Assam government. They alleged that the government led by Tarun Gogoi has failed to protect the interests of indigenous communities. The protestors included the All Assam Tribal Association, the Tiwa Students Association, the Assam Tribal Entrepreneurs Association and some other outfits representing similar ethnic groups.

Thus due to prolonged neglect of indigenous people and continued failure of the government to stem the tide of Bangladeshi invasion, the tribal groups have developed a feeling that they are no longer treated as Indian nationals and therefore time has come for them to fend for themselves. Naturally now they take frequent recourse to arms for defending their hearths and homes and in the process have locked horns with the government. A preview of the shape of things to come was seen recently in May 2005 when an aggressive Bihutoli of Dibrugarh youth launched a campaign for economic boycott of Bangladeshi infiltrators and made thousands of illegal aliens flee Dibrugarh and adjoining areas. Hopefully some lessons will be learnt from that episode.

The ongoing commotion and growing strife in the region should be read as an alarm forecasting the coming avalanche of public disorder waiting in the wings to destabilize and overwhelm first the north-east and then the large tracts of eastern India, including West Bengal and Bihar, both of which are already entrapped in lawlessness. There is an uncanny resemblance between what is happening in the north-east of India today and the events which shook the Balkans in 1980s, and finally resulted in outbreak of a bloody civil war across the region.

Apart from the tragedy of the Balkans, almost similar events had taken place in Lebanon between 1975 and 1990 after massive influx of armed Palestinians led by Yasser Arafat into Lebanon in 1970 and later years. That influx coupled with high fertility of Lebanese Muslims further fueled the Lebanese civil war. It may also be recalled that during that infamous civil strife Lebanon had more than 50 militant outfits operating in different parts of the country — each group trying to protect its own turf and identity. That recall should ring a familiar bell in our mind about the likely fate of India's north-eastern region where the number of major partisan armed insurgent outfits is as large as 31, as enumerated in Appendix I.[26] To carry the analogy further, it may be added that historically foreign powers have always evinced keen interest for intervention in such destabilized countries. It had happened both in Lebanon and the Balkans, after the said two sensitive regions had been demographically destabilised. In Lebanon, the neighbouring Syria intervened militarily in 1975-76 as soon as the civil war gathered tempo. The Syrians had intervened militarily on the specious plea of restoring peace and maintenance of public order in the strife-torn country. Though the civil war ended in 1990, the Syrian troops stayed on in that country despite repetitive protests by the Lebanese government. In September 2004 the Security Council passed a resolution calling on Syria to withdraw its troops estimated to be around 15 to 17 thousand from Lebanon. The resolution calling for Lebanon's political independence and withdrawal of all foreign troops was moved by France and the USA. But even after agreeing to comply with the U.N. directive in the wake of assassination of Rafik Hariri, former Prime Minister of Lebanon, the Syrian government continued to drag their feet. Meanwhile, the notorious terror outfit, Hizbollah, has once again jumped into the fray by picking up gun. Amidst revived violence and bomb blasts the stalemate over withdrawal of Syrian troops continued at the international level. However, the Syrians finally withdrew from Lebanon only in April 2005 bowing to intense international pressure. But Lebanon is again in turmoil.

The intervention of the United States in the Balkans was more direct and devastating. Initially the Albanian militants and Kosovar insurgents were supported against the Serb militia by Islamic countries like Iran, Taliban-ruled Afghanistan and Pakistan and later on by assorted groups of Jihadis, including Al Qaeda. And when the civil war intensified and the Serb militias committed extensive atrocities in Bosnia, the NATO along with the USA intervened by resorting to relentless bombing of Serbia for more than two-and-a-half months. We must remember that apart from the keen interest of both Pakistan and Bangladesh to destabilize and annexe the north-east, lately the USA too has evinced interest in the events taking place in the region. The US government overstepped diplomatic etiquette in October 2004 when their Ambassador, David Mulford, wrote a letter making a direct offer of assistance in investigation to the government of Assam in the wake of bomb blasts and violence in Assam and Nagaland. The offer was naturally frowned upon by the Government of India. Prima facie the upping of ante by the USA in the north-east reveals their growing interest in the region. For India it could be a worrisome development. Apart from America's growing interest in Christian church organisations, the region also witnessed commissioning of Project Ploughshare, a research venture by the Institute of Peace and Conflict Studies, Canada, which inter alia dealt with the number of deaths caused by violence since 1995, the activities of insurgent groups and the action taken by the government. Under the head 'Parties to the conflict', the study discussed the role of the Government of India, especially the Indian Army which undertook military operations against the insurgents based in Bhutan in December 2003 with active support of Royal Bhutanese Army. These developments have already caused considerable disquiet among India's defence forces and security agencies.[27]

As far as the north-east is concerned, everyone is aware of the nefarious designs of the ISI and the machinations of the Bangladeshi government. They have been fishing in the troubled waters for decades by promoting multiple insurgencies facilitated by rapid demographic changes in the region. To put it bluntly, they are working on a well coordinated plan to balkanize the north-east and then gobble it.

Let us take a close look at the problem of breakdown of law and order due to widespread economic distress. During the last three decades, there has been a quantum jump in unemployment throughout north-east, more importantly in Assam. As already mentioned, in November 2003 when some Bihari youths went to Guwahati for seeking jobs in the Railways, there was widespread violence against the entire community. But that too did not awaken our slumbering government. According to rough estimates and as reiterated by the Chief Minister of Assam in August 2004, presently there are more than two million unemployed youth in Assam alone — an abnormally high figure by national standards. The State's economic survey for 2003-2004 revealed that the employment exchanges had 15,71,996 job-seekers as against 15,24,616 in late 2001.[28] During his November 2004 visit to Assam, the Prime Minister, Dr. Manmohan Singh, too had referred to the need for providing gainful employment to 16 lakh unemployed Assamese youth. As a rule, the figures recorded in employment exchanges are underestimates to the extent of 30 per cent because lakhs of unemployed youth living in rural areas do not register themselves with exchanges. It is therefore safe to assume that the State has more than 20 lakh unemployed youth. And guess what could be the quantum of the estimated number of jobs and livelihood resources usurped by Bangladeshis and their progeny in the State? On a conservative estimate the number of Bangladeshis in Assam could be anywhere between 60 lakhs and 90 lakhs; it could be even more. According to Census 2001 the total population of Assam is 2,66,55,528 and out of them less than 40 per cent are Assamese-speaking. That should give us an idea of the mind-boggling dimensions of Bangladeshi influx! For all practical purposes the Assamese have already become a helpless minority in the land of their birth. Even if we take the figure of Bangladeshis in Assam at a conservative estimate of 70 lakhs, that would mean that a minimum of 30 to 35 lakh jobs and livelihood resource opportunities have been grabbed by Bangladeshis in Assam alone. It is well known that both in India and Bangladesh, among the poorest sections of society, at least two adult members of a family work to keep the kitchen fires burning. Basing our estimates on that simple fact, a ground reality, the quantum of jobs and livelihood resource opportunities usurped by illegal Bangladeshi immigrants could be around 35 lakhs, as against the estimated figure of 16 to 20 lakh unemployed youth in Assam. Similar is the unemployment scenario in other states of the north-east. Needless to point out that the socio-economic turbulence caused by the growing numbers of unemployed youth invariably causes public order problems. Unless the situation is remedied speedily, its cascading effect will create many more upheavals primarily due to large scale migration of job-seekers from rural areas to towns and cities and even from one state to another. If only the government had paid adequate attention to the prevention of illegal immigration, the anger caused by deprivation of land and economic distress due to unemployment among the indigenous people of the north-east might not have flared up so much and so fast. That would have saved the sensitive border region of India's north-east from turning into the tinder-box which it is now. The only hope of restoring law and order in the infiltration ravaged region is to stem the tide of illegal influx and implement a bold, no-holds-barred programme to secure our territory by throwing out as many Bangladeshis as possible and settling ex-servicemen belonging to north-eastern region along the border to provide relief to the local indigenous population. But will any government show that kind of determination and courage? Looks well nigh impossible in our vote-bank contaminated polity!

6

Crescent Corridor Across Yadava Turf

"Arise and awake, O mighty one, this sleep does not become you".

Swami Vivekanand

It may be recalled that in the years immediately preceding India's partition, some top leaders of the Muslim League and their hard-line followers had consistently demanded that a corridor should be provided through India's heartland, i.e., via Uttar Pradesh, Bihar and West Bengal, to join West Pakistan with East Pakistan (present Bangladesh). The protagonists of the 'corridor lobby' had assiduously argued, both through media and at political fora, that since the two wings of the nascent Islamic nation will be separated by more than one thousand miles, it was imperative to provide a corridor to link them geographically for facilitating proper communication and regular means of transportation between the two wings. The preposterous demand was, however, summarily rejected both by the British government and the Indian National Congress. But now just fifty-eight years after independence, the broad contours of a crescent corridor are clearly visible, originating in Assam and running through West Bengal, Bihar and Uttar Pradesh and onwards towards India-Pakistan border. Its lengthening shadow over the states of U.P and Bihar is manifestly visible all over.

This alarming development has taken barely five decades to materialize - facilitated as it is by the massive infiltration of Bangladeshis coupled with the higher fertility of Indian Muslims. The long term implications of this adverse population change are likely to be grim and foreboding not only for the unity and economic progress of the country, but also for peace in the sub-continent. Any further adverse demographic tilt in the four strategic states of Assam, West Bengal, Bihar and Uttar Pradesh should be a matter of deep concern to every Indian.

The emerging crescent corridor across the Yadava heartland has encouraged the Islamic fundamentalists of Bangladesh and Pakistan to dream about the birth of another Muslim state which they have already started calling as Mughalistan. Forces inimical to India have silently worked overtime towards achieving this goal as would be seen from the map below which runs along the 'crescent corridor' and has been taken from an Islamic website hoisted by one Gulbaz Khan. The map originated in Pakistan and has Lahore 2000 as dateline. The project "crescent corridor" running through the Yadava heartland has the potential to re-write India's history. It could ultimately translate into an obituary of Indian democracy.

Map of Mughalstan

by Gulbaz Khan

Pan Islamic Mughalstan
Lahore 2000

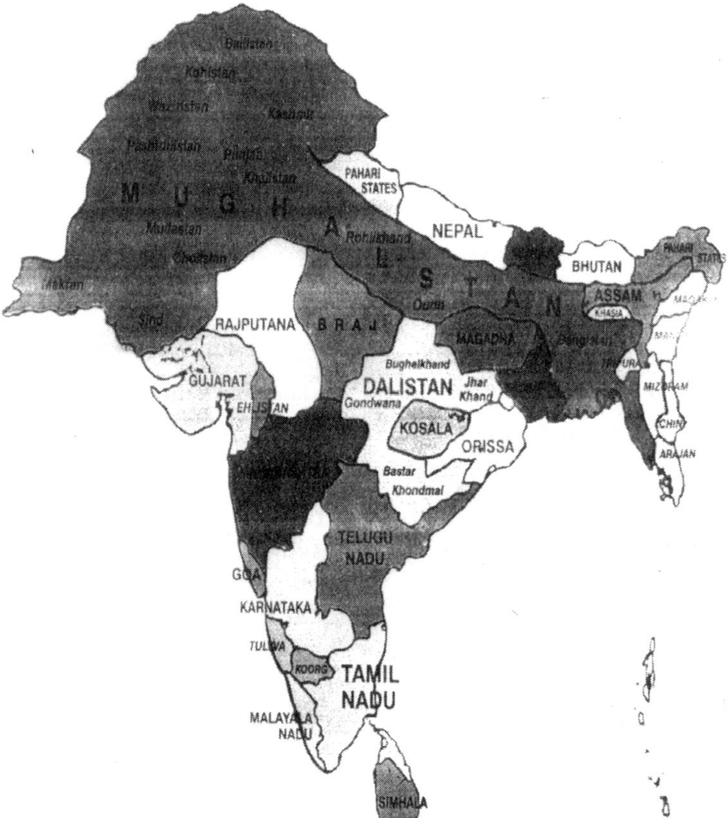

(Map not to scale)

Proposal for the Ethnic Partition of India

We have shown in the previous chapters how the Islamists have already created favourable conditions in the north-eastern region in a planned bid to fulfil their goal of using the region as 'lebensraum' for the burgeoning population of Bangladesh. The crescent corridor could also pave the way for achieving Al Qaeda's grand vision of a South Asian caliphate in furthering their campaign for conquering the world for Islam.

Apart from the demographic upheaval in Assam and the adjoining states, the Census 2001 has revealed certain far-reaching and disquieting population trends in the politically sensitive states of Bihar and Uttar Pradesh. The growing impact of illegal Bangladeshi influx is now highly visible in several districts of Bihar also. The following table shows the growing percentage of Muslims in the composite Purnea district on the border which was split during 1981-91. It will also be noted that these districts are strategically situated at the beginning of 'chicken neck', a small strip connecting the Indian mainland to north-east.

Table 6.1: Percentage of Muslims in Four Sensitive Districts of Bihar

Percentage of Muslims			Percentage Increase of Muslims	Decadal Increase	
District	1991	2001		HF	Muslims
Araria	40.42	41.14	0.71	32.2	36.2
Kishanganj	65.91	67.58	1.67	24.6	35.1
Katihar	39.87	42.53	2.66	21.9	39.8
Purnea	34.53	36.76	2.23	30.5	44.1

Source: Religious Demography of India, page 209, Census 2001.

These figures clearly reflect the changing demographic profile of these four districts, extensively affected by large scale infiltration of Bangladeshis through Assam and West Bengal.

The dangerous consequences of these demographic changes caused by the massive invasion of illegal immigrants have been repetitively highlighted in recent years. As pointed out by Arun Shourie in a series of incisive articles published in the *Indian Express* in October 2004, the first to highlight the impending threat in 1990s was T.V. Rajeshwar, the present Governor of Uttar Pradesh and a former Director of Intelligence Bureau. He had warned the political leadership about the growing Islamic threat.[1] Later in the year 1998 during his tenure as the Governor of Assam, Lt. General S.K. Sinha (the present Governor of Jammu & Kashmir), had sent a comprehensive report to the President on "Illegal Migration into Assam". He emphasised that after 1971 the illegal immigrants coming from Bangladesh have been almost exclusively Muslims. He warned in no uncertain terms that the illegal infiltration "poses a grave threat both to the identity of the Assamese people and to our national security".[2]

The frightening dimensions of the impending demographic threat have been known to the successive central and state governments. Yet for reasons best known to the country's political leadership, including the 6 years long regime of Bharatiya Janata Party led NDA (National Democratic Alliance), no effective steps were taken to safeguard national interests. Even the elementary requirement of erecting a fool-proof border fence was handled in a most lackadaisical manner. The partially erected fence on Indo-Bangladesh border is highly ineffective because of major design defects which render it useless for the difficult terrain. It can be easily cut to facilitate entry — as indeed it has been so often with impunity. Border fencing is a highly skilled engineering craft which India must learn from Israel who are doing a splendid job of constructing a security fence-cum-barrier to protect their people from Palestinian terrorists.

Taking full advantage of the monumental neglect of the Indian government, hordes of Bangladeshi infiltrators, after successfully overrunning several sensitive districts of Assam and West Bengal have now established a bridgehead for further westward march by establishing a "crescent corridor" through two important states of Bihar and Uttar Pradesh, the traditional Yadava heartland, presently dominated and cleverly commandeered by the two famously controversial Yadava chieftains by forging an alliance of Muslims and Yadavas, known as "MY" combination. During last forty years this new crescent shaped geographical corridor, registering rapidly rising Muslim population, has successfully managed to overwhelm a strategic portion of the Yadava heartland in Bihar and Uttar Pradesh, as is evident from table 6.2 below.

Table 6.2: Religious Profile of the Eastern Border Belt, 1951-2001

State		1951	1961	1971	1981	1991	2001
Uttar Pradesh	**Total**	9,953	11,140	12,863	15,922	19,966	25,100
	Muslim	1,533	1,837	2,373	3,054	4,087	5,028
	Population	(15.40%)	(16.49)	(18.45)	(19.18)	(20.47)	(20.03)
Bihar and Jharkhand	**Total**	15,690	19,026	23,097	28,499	35,473	45,674
	Muslim	2,285	3,349	4,389	5,670	7,448	10,194
	Population	(14.56%)	(17.60)	(19.00)	(19.90)	(21.00)	(22.32)
West Bengal	**Total**	4,697	6,282	8,189	10,231	13,061	16,117
	Muslim	1,873	2,765	3,538	4,599	6,157	7,947
	Population	(39.89%)	(44.01)	(43.20)	(44.95)	(47.14)	(49.31)
Assam	**Total**	4,409	6,107	8,496	10,480	13,267	15,865
	Muslim	1,429	2,023	2,709	3,342	4,929	6,400
	Population	(32.42%)	(33.13)	(31.89)	(31.89)	(37.15)	(40.34)
Border Belt (Total)	**Total**	34,750	42,554	52,645	65,132	81,767	102,756
	Muslim	7,120	9,974	13,009	16,665	22,621	29,569
	Population	(20.49%)	(23.44)	(24.71)	(25.59)	(27.67)	(28.78)

Source: Compiled from Religious Demography of India Summmary Version 2001, Table 46, page 70.

Starting in the north-east from Karimganj, Hailakandi and Cachar and moving westward via Nagaon, Marigaon, Darrang, Goalpara, Barpeta and Dhubri in Assam, the emerging crescent corridor forks out in two directions. One branch runs through West Dinajpur, Malda, Murshidabad, North 24-Parganas, and South 24-Parganas districts of West Bengal into Sahibganj and Santhal Pargana district of Bihar, while the main stream of infiltrators enters Bihar via Kishanganj, Katihar, Purnea, Araria and then makes inroads into Sahibganj, Santhal Pargana, Saharsa, Dharbhanga, Muzzaffarpur and Champaran districts. And from these sensitive districts this corridor runs through Deoria, Gorakhpur, Basti, Gonda and Bahraich in eastern Uttar Pradesh. It is clear from Table 6.2 above that during the last five decades, the percentage of Muslims has increased by more than 8 per cent in this belt. Thus an infiltration-powered shinakansen, (i.e., bullet train, as Japanese call it) of Bangladeshis has already arrived in Bihar and Uttar Pradesh to usher far reaching demographic changes in this important region. It is likely to move at a high speed in its westward journey after traversing the Yadava turf.

Interestingly in June 2004, the well known journalist, M.J. Akbar, had hailed the two Yadava supremos for capturing power in Bihar and Uttar Pradesh through "MY'" formula (Muslim-Yadav combine) as "Allah-Krishna alliance" in one of his columns in *The Deccan Times.* He lauded them for keeping both the Congress and the BJP at bay and referred to it as "the secular space" of rural Middle Kingdom. The truth, however, is that this so-called secular space is being dramatically over-run by Bangladeshi infiltrators!

As is well known, several districts of West Bengal including Kolkata in West Bengal and Rampur and Moradabad in Uttar Pradesh are already significant enclaves bustling with large Muslim numbers. These could be conveniently buckle-linked to the emerging crescent corridor in due course of time, as indeed happened in Kosovo, Bosnia and Lebanon during gory civil strifes and is now being replicated in Macedonia.

The Muslim population of certain districts of UP and Bihar has quantum jumped during the last three decades largely due to massive influx of Bangladeshis and their relatively higher fertility rate. An idea of the far reaching demographic changes likely to burst upon the demographic matrix of Bihar and Uttar Pradesh between 2011 and 2041 can be had by analysing the population of Hindus and Muslims in these two states among children in age-group 0-6 years. According to the Census 2001 Report on Religion Data (p. xlii, Statement 7), in Bihar the proportion of Muslims in 0-6 age-group is 22, while that of the Hindus is 19.9 thus giving a clear advantage of 2.1 percentage points to Muslims. In Uttar Pradesh the proportion of Muslim corhorts is 20.9, while that of Hindus is 18.6 again showing an advantage of 2.3 points to the Muslims. The children who were in the 0-6 years age group in 2001 will enter the reproductive age of 16 to 18 years between the years 2011 and 2016 A.D. and will remain reproductively active for the next 30 to 35 years. On top of it, the acceptance of family planning among Muslims is very low. Consequently during the next four decades, the relative percentage of children born will be higher among the Muslims than among the Hindus in these two states. This clear trend coupled with the minimal acceptance of small family norm in Muslim society has the potential of further downscaling the Hindu percentage substantially both in Bihar and Uttar Pradesh. That will further skew the demographic profile of the two Yadava dominated states against non-Muslims. We can gauge the dimensions of the growing demographic threat hovering over the Yadava heartland by adding to this dismal scenario the unstoppable invasion by Bangladeshis .

The far-reaching implications of the changed demography of Assam, West Bengal, Bihar and UP have already started registering with a vengeance on the kaleidoscope of India's mainstream politics. By frequent recourse in successive elections to "tactical voting", yet another name for communal voting, many communal leaders and Mullahs have already injected a heavy dose of communal poison into the electoral system of the country. It has vitiated the socio-political atmosphere in many regions and widened the divide between the Hindus and the Muslims. During the state elections in Bihar held in early 2005 and earlier during the Maharashtra elections of 2004, the electoral process underwent unprecedented communalisation. The pernicious role of communal politics in electioneering is evident from the pathetic begging by Laloo Yadav, Railway Minister in the central government, for Muslim votes by securing Justice U.C. Banerjee's interim report on the burning of coach S-6 of Sabarmati Express at Godhra in February 2002. This was a part of the grand strategy devised by Laloo Yadav for winning minority community's votes by inflaming communal passions. The same strategy was visible, perhaps more prominently, in parading an Osama clone, one Maulana Meraj Khalid Noor of Narpat Ganj, by Ram Vilas Paswan, leader of Lok Janashakti Party to garner Muslim votes. To be fair to him, Paswan did not hesitate to openly declare that Osama does have a good following among Muslim youth, though it is certainly questionable for a Union Minister to promote the 'Osama Cult' in a country under serious threat by Islamist terrorists. As if that was not enough, Paswan continued to shout from housetops that Bihar should have a Muslim Chief Minister.

In other words, due to growing demographic asymmetry the politics of UP and Bihar has now touched a new low of communal nadir where the notorious global terrorist, Osama Bin Laden, has become a role model for the Muslim electorate of the Yadava countryside. It only shows the growing clout of radical Islam in Bihar and Uttar Pradesh. Another glimpse of the future developments slated to take place in the Yadava domain came to notice on February 4, 2005, in Patna (Bihar) when Muslim mobsters organised an impromptu demonstration by laying siege to the High Court simply because a High Court judge had asked the district authorities to explain why a loudspeaker was being used for "Azan" during court hours in contravention of an earlier order on the subject. The tale of woes of the harassed and distressed High Court Judge, R.S. Garg, was to be seen to be believed during an interview by a television channel. It led to a sharp reaction by the lawyer fraternity of Patna who observed a one-day token strike on February 7, 2005, to register protest against the high handedness of the mob and failure of the district authorities. Soon thereafter the High Court Judge was transferred at his request from Patna High Court.

The aggressive misuse of the communal card in Bihar elections is not something new. It has happened quite often in the past in almost every election, though the scale on which it is being used so often is abnormally high–almost unprecedented. In the 2004 general elections to the Parliament, the Muslim community of UP and many other states had openly taken recourse to the so-called "tactical voting" which is nothing but an euphemism for communal voting. In UP the All India Milli Council had openly appealed to Muslims to support candidates of the Samajwadi Party for 14 seats, the Bahujan Samaj Party for three seats and the Lok Janashakti Party for one seat from among 32 parliamentary seats where polling was to be held on April 26, 2004.[3] The spokesman of Milli Council, Kamal Farouqui, openly declared that the decision was arrived at after conducting a survey of these constituencies. He proclaimed that their aim was to defeat a so-called pro-Hindu party. The same methodology of communal voting was used by the Muslims and sham-secular politicians in the elections to Maharashtra Assembly in December 2004. Apparently just for form's sake, the Election Commission keeps on shouting from housetops that communal card will not be allowed to be used by any party for electioneering. But then who bothers for an Election Commission rendered impotent by its own volition? The drama of communal voting was writ large all over Bihar and Jharkhand elections in spite of the Election Commission. Apart from copious references to Gujarat riots by the then ruling clique of Bihar, all kinds of posters alluding to the communal riots and Justice U.C. Banerjee's interim report on Godhra train fire were plastered in Bhagalpur district and many other towns. The only achievement of the Chief Election Commissioner was the registration of two cases under the Representation of Peoples' Act 1951 against an obscure organisation called Mili Jaanab Anjuman Ittihad-e Millat and Guddu Art Press for publishing and displaying inflammatory posters, after the political objective of the concerned politicians had been achieved.[4] Though ordinary folks might be impressed by the Election Commission's action, the wily politicians know very well that nothing much will come out of these two cases. Interestingly, even after registration of two cases under the

Representation of Peoples Act, the questionable posters were found in Samastipur and Jehanabad on February 5, 2005, leaving the Election Commission stewing in its juice. Now that the Election Commission has totally failed to prevent large scale casteisation of the election process, a question has been raised that why should not the fig leaf of barring the use of casteist and communal issues and not permitting religion and caste for seeking votes be altogether removed. The Chief Election Commissioner cannot be oblivious of the widespread propagation of the political mantra of "MY" combine which represents both the communal and casteist electioneering. Everyone knows it means seeking votes of Muslims and Yadavas by using the communal and casteist cards. If the election law is allowed to be transgressed by circumventing the legislation through devious means by cunning politicians, then there is no point in banning the use of communal card during elections. The removal of the bar on using the communal card will at least provide a level playing field to all political parties and religious groups. In any case, the blatant misuse of the equally perverse caste card has been seldom objected to by the Election Commission, for reasons best known to them. If use of religion for garnering votes is illegal and objectionable, so is the use of caste for seeking votes. In its present form the system of banning religion but surreptitiously allowing the divisive caste card being followed by the Election Commission is highly susceptible to misuse, though only by aggressive minority groups and cheer leaders of select casteist parties who invariably take undue advantage of this bar by openly defying the letter and spirit of the election law. This has happened repetitively in a number of states during the last few decades. Very recently the subsidy on Haj was increased on the eve of State elections ostensibly to win Muslim votes which was an indirect concession, or wanton inducement offered to woo Muslim voters. Yet no notice was taken by the Election Commission of this violation of electoral ethics. Incidentally now the Haj subsidy has been raised to Rs. 240 crores per annum, from 200 crores earlier, in the holy name of secularism! It may be clarified that the pattern of communal voting by Muslims is not something new, nor peculiar to India. It is a global phenomenon. In India, however, this communal strategy has reappeared on the electoral scene with renewed aggressiveness in recent years, perhaps in tandem with growth of Muslim population. Communal voting by the Muslim community was rampant all over India in the twentieth century in the pre-partition days. Actually the partition of India in 1947 was a direct consequence of recourse to communal voting and consequential violence and rioting in several parts of the country. Interestingly the same trend of radicalization of Muslim politics and recourse to communal voting had been witnessed in Bosnia and Kosovo in 1980s after Muslims became aware of sharp upswing in their population registered during the secular socialist regime of Yugoslavia. So when Yugoslavia broke up, a call for consolidation of Muslim community was given by the radical Islamist leader, Alija Izzetgovich. Earlier a large number of Bosnian Muslims used to be liberal and non-bigoted in outlook and most of them viewed themselves as part of the secular European society. They used to vote for the mainstream multicultural parties in large numbers. But in the 1990 general election the trend changed totally because of the new consciousness among Muslims about their vastly increased numbers and emergence of Alija Izzetgovich as their extremist leader. Thus in the 1990 elections the Muslims voted *en bloc* for Izzetgovich's separatist Muslim Party of Democratic Action, or S.D.A., which soon turned into a militant outfit. And that became a turning point in the history of Bosnia and Serbia. Meanwhile Albanian Muslims, known as Kosovars, aided by armed militant groups laid claim to Kosovo which had already become a predominantly Muslim majority area. A demand also surfaced for a separate Muslim-dominated state of Bosnia Herzegovina. Soon there were multiple religion-based faultline clashes between the Muslims and Serbs. Ultimately the situation degenerated into a bloody civil war in which thousands perished, though in the end the Bosnian Muslims suffered most at the hands of Serb militias. Recently in the UK general election 2005, the same strategy of tactical voting was adopted by Muslims, especially the members of Pakistani diaspora, in a bid to defeat the Labour Party and teach a lesson to Tony Blair for supporting the US President, George Bush, in Iraq war.

The demographic transformation taking place in the Yadava heartland does convey a loud message to India's political leadership, excepting those who have mortgaged their souls for crumbs of political power. This impending demographic disaster looming over the Yadava heartland can be ignored only at the cost of national peril, especially in the light of socio-political upheavals witnessed in the Balkans and Lebanon, but more importantly with the backdrop of India's partition in 1947 caused by the twin factors of adverse demography and Islamic penchant for jihad. Suffice it to say that both these factors have already become operative in the Yadava heartland and north-eastern region.

Taking advantage of the fast changing demography of the country, Dr. Omar Khalidi, a Hyderabad-born Indian Muslim, teaching architectural history at Massachusetts Institute of Technology, brought forward a highly questionable formula for virtual 'cantonisation' of India in an interview published in *The Times of India*, New Delhi, in June 2004.[5] On the pretext of evolving a decentralized "consociational power structure" in India, he advocated the creation of a number of Muslim-dominated autonomous sub-units or union territories (read enclaves) for empowering them politically. He pleads for carving out the Muslim-dominated state of Mewat (comprising Gurgaon and Faridabad districts of Haryana and Alwar and Bharatpur districts of Rajasthan), a Muslim dominated state in Bihar comprising Kishenganj, Katihar and Purnea districts and similar autonomous sub-states covering Bidar, Gulbarga and Hyderabad in Karnataka and Andhra Pradesh. He advocates decentralization on consociational pattern for empowering the Muslim community and promoting good governance. In Khalidi's list of Muslim enclaves the first one i.e. a new Mewat district in Haryana has already been conceded. The word 'consociational' has been borrowed from the history of Christian theology where it connotes an empowered church group. The consociational approach means adoption of a communitarian power group dominated by religious affinity. According to Khalidi, the consociational theory implies that "the society recognises that the nation consists of various segments with legitimate religious and cultural demands, though not economic and educational." Although the Muslim majority district of Mallapuram in Kerala, strategically carved out in 1969 by the veteran communist leader Namboodiripad as part of vote bank politics, is Khalidi's model, his consociational concept goes much farther. He argues that for each segment of society to be empowered, the electoral system must be revised to permit greater electability of minority candidates than is presently possible. It will entail demarcation of constituencies in such a way that "minority groups become majorities", or alternatively the "seats should be reserved on the pattern of the reserved constituencies" presently available only to Scheduled Castes and Scheduled Tribes.

Recently in an interview to *The Radiance,* a Jamaat-e-Islami mouthpiece of fudamentalist hue, Khalidi aggressively argued that Muslim majority districts were needed for three reasons. First, the concentrated presence in an area will assure them of security. Second, the Muslim majority districts will provide an environment conducive to the community's cultural independence. Third, enclaves in which Muslims constitute majority will provide a political base to the Muslims thereby facilitating their election to legislative bodies in larger numbers.[6] And Khalidi is quite brazenly open about the goals of Muslims. According to him at present electoral constituencies have been created in a way that the Muslim numbers don't add up to ensure election of adequate number of Muslim candidates. He further advocates that Ranga Reddy district of Andhra Pradesh, Gulbarga of Karnataka and certain adjoining talukas should be merged to create a Muslim-dominated Deccan province, while in Bihar the districts of Katihar, Kishenganj and Purnea should be constituted into an Urdu speaking province or a Union Territory. Charting out an aggressive roadmap seeking separatist enclaves for the Muslim community, Dr Khalidi points out, quite rightly, that a decade ago, it was not fashionable to talk about reservation for Muslims. But over the years things have changed. "Today the Muslims have reservations in Kerala and Karnataka and Andhra Pradesh. Don't judge everything from what is happening today". He exhorts his co-religionists to stand up for their rights by proclaiming that *"Haq liye jaate hain, pesh nahin kiye jaate"*, meaning thereby that rights have to be seized or snatched, perhaps as Khalidi would wish to do because no one will offer these on a platter.[7] In a nutshell, Khalidi has given a clarion call to Muslims along the lines comparable to what Jinnah used to say in pre-partition days. He has propounded a typically divisive Islamic formula for scrambling the Indian nation into semi-independent units ostensibly to provide greater political clout to the Muslim minority thereby setting the ball rolling for another partition of the country. After reading Khalidi's thesis who can doubt that India is likely to head for another partition the campaign for which has already been launched by Muslim idealogues like Khalidi in India and Gulbaz Khan in Pakistan? Because of sharp demographic changes that could happen, say latest by 2047, when India should be celebrating one hundred years of freedom!

Another instance of Dr. Khalidi's detestable agenda for radicalization of Indian Muslims was his unabashed attempt to introduce the virus of communalism into India's defence forces by using the high profile Justice Sachar Committee as a convenient tool. The committee was appointed by the Prime Minister to look into the socio-eocnomic and educational status of Indian Muslims and recommending measures for improving their lot. In January-February 2006, Justice Sachar was apparently egged on by Dr. Omar Khalidi and G.M. Banatwala, President of the Indian Union Muslim league, to exceed its brief and ask for data of Muslims serving in the country's defence services which naturally led to a high decibel controversy about the real intentions of the government. The move was roundly condemned both by the retired and serving defence officers and most intellectuals. On February 15, 2006, a conclave of ex-servicement led by retired Generals, Air Marshals and Admirals gathered at Amar Jawan Jyoti, India Gate, to register their protest. As anticipated, Justice Sachar's move received enormous support from many fundamentalist icons of Muslim community, including Syed Ahmed Bukhari, Imam of Delhi's Jama Masjid and Syed Shahabuddin who has been associated with the All India Muslim Personal Law Board. The Imam of Jama Masjid vociferously argued for recruitment of "Muslims in all services according to the population pattern of the community" thereby reminding the Hindus of the fast-paced growth of Muslim population. His statement was a grim reminder of the strategic Muslim refrain heard in the years preceding India's partition. The Sachar Committee even sought confirmation from the Army Headquarters of Khalidi's charges about some imaginary anti-Muslim measures taken during anti-Razakar operations to liberate princely state of Hyderabad in 1948 and more recently advising residents of some Muslim villages to move away from bombardment zone during the Kargil war in 1999. It is well known that Dr. Khalidi's book, *Khaki and Ethnic Violence,* is a rabid criticism of Indian police and security forces. Questions are already being raised about the growing clout of the Indian Union Muslim League working in tandem with Dr. Khalidi in conducting the affairs of the country. It is well known that the Muslim League is a partner in the UPA government and Dr. Khalidi is a staunch fundamentalist Muslim Leaguer at heart, as is evident from his divisive strategies discussed above.

What led to the appointment of Justice Sachar Committee is a million dollar mystery, especially when Muslim as a community are way ahead of Hindus in terms of three major globally accepted norms of socio-economic status, namely child mortality, degree of urbanization and life expectancy at birth, as analysed in Chapter 2 of this book. It is highly doubtful if at all under the Indian Constitution the proposed special benefits like reservations and unmerited preferential treatment can be bestowed on a religious minority when its members have better human development indices than the majority community!

Yet, the flag bearer of sham-secular brigade, Mani Shankar Aiyar, appears to be a great admirer of Dr. Khalidi as is evident from chapter 4 (The Constitutional and Legal Dimensions) of his tome, Confessions of A *Secular Fundamentalist.*[8] Aiyar claims to have imbibed considerable wisdom from "two Muslim Indian scholars — Omar Khalidi of Massachusetts Institute of Technology, Harvard University and Rafiq Zakaria... ".[9] Incidentally that shows the true crescentic colours of our esteemed friend, the 'secular fundamentalist'!

While the centre stage political dispensation of Bihar and Uttar Pradesh, mired in the caste-based petty politicking, continues to ignore the existence of any demographic threat, a fresh whiff of belated wisdom has come from the communist-ruled state of West Bengal. After decades of procrastinations, the Communist Party (Marxist) finally woke up to the threat of illegal influx of Bangladeshis in July 2003 by admitting that the illegal immigration has acquired alarming proportions.[10] The revised party stand announced by West Bengal State Secretary of CPI (M), late Anil Biswas, was largely influenced by the enlightened thinking of the State's new Chief Minister, Buddhadeb Bhattacharjee, who conceded in June 2005 at a seminar organized by the Border Security Force that Central Government's fears of demographic transformation of the border districts of West Bengal and the resultant threat to the State's security, economic development and social harmony were realistic. It may be recalled that Buddhadeb Bhattacharjee's earlier remarks against the sprouting of madrasas in the border districts had met with strong resistance from the party hardliners who had for decades cultivated the endless droves of infiltrators from across the border as vote-bank. So intense is the pressure of stark truth that even the then CPI (M) Politbureau member, Prakash Karat (now General Secretary), sang the same tune about the urgent need to prevent such infiltration by erecting a fence across the entire stretch of Indo-Bangladesh border, while denying that there was any major change in his party's stand on the subject.[11] Apparently the growing attacks on leftist cadres in Bangladesh after Begum Zia came to power in 2001 and the recent campaign spearheaded by the notorious Islamist terrorist, Banglabhai, to purge that country of all despicable atheists and enemies of Islam, especially the Purba Banglar Communist Party and other leftist groups, has sent a chill down the spine of communists of West Bengal. Though Marxists are known for their doublespeak, the very fact that now even the Bourbons of Alimuddin Street have recognized, albeit belatedly and reluctantly, the seriousness of the growing demographic threat from illegal influx should awaken the slumbering Hindus of Bihar and Uttar Pradesh. Hopefully that should serve as an eye-opener for the two Yadava chieftains of Bihar and Uttar Pradesh — the two backward states likely to be over-run by the Bangladeshi infiltrators within the next few decades, duly aided by the higher fertility of the Muslims of Yadava countryside.

Here it must be pointed out that the collapse of governance is clearly visible across the fast emerging Crescent Corridor running through the two states of Uttar Pradesh and Bihar which are overwhelmingly dominated by numerous crime syndicates, mostly promoted, finance and nurtured by the ISI of Pakistan. The law and order in the region has totally collapsed and cities and towns bristle with hundreds of fifth-columnist operatives working for the militant outfits based in Kashmir valley and Bangladesh. These terror-promoting cells are reported to be receiving active support of many prominent politicians like Mohammed Shahabuddin (an RJD Member of Parliament from Siwan in Bihar) and Mukhtar Ansari, an MLA from Mau in Uttar Pradesh, both of whom have been long suspected of association with the ISI. Public memory is proverbially short. But shorter still seems to be the memory of the ruling dispensation at the centre which has been persistently ignoring the irrefutable facts highlighted in a 77-pages report submitted by D.P. Ojha, a former Director General of Police, Bihar, nearly three years ago. The said report was prepared on the basis of documented police records and credible inputs from several central intelligence agencies.[12] In his comprehensive note, D.P. Ojha has focused on the anti-national activities of Mohammed Shahabuddin and his role in using Varanasi (the scene of ghastly bomb blasts at Sankat Mochan temple on March 8, 2006) as a transit point and hub for ferrying consignments of arms from Nepal. The controversial politician is widely considered to be a don and protégé of Lalu Yadav, Railway Minister in the central government. It has been alleged that a large consignment of arms were received at Shahabuddin's behest from Nepal-based ISI agents in the year 2001, and a part of the weapons were sent to the residence of a former minister in April-May 2001. He was also reported to have received a number of AK-47 assault rifles from Kashmir out of which some were kept by him and the rest sold to an MLA in Varanasi and a Ranchi-based criminal. D.P. Ojha's report specifically mentioned that Shahabuddin continued to travel to Kashmir, maintained good contacts with militants and "obtained illegal firearms as indicated by the confession of Hizbul militant, Mushtaq Ahmed Aga".[13] He also had close links with Mukhtar Ansari, the MLA from Mau in UP and was allegedly in contact with the nototious global Islamic terrorist Dawood Ibrahim. In a letter sent to the Home Secretary of Bihar Government on August 1, 2003, the former Director General of Police D.P. Ojha, had recommended an investigation by the Central Bureau of Investigations, but the government took no action.

There are reasons to believe that the truth about the emerging crescent corridor across Uttar Pradesh and Bihar is fully known to the central government and the concerned state governments. On January 26, 2006, around 9.30 P.M. a popular channel had showcased a programme, based on a report of the Economic Offences Wing of the Uttar Pradesh CID Crime Branch, exposing the growing machinations of the ISI agents and crime syndicates active in eastern UP and parts of central UP. Apparently the soft state that India has now become woefully lacks the will to act firmly against jihadi groups. No wonder, in a very perceptive article on Varanasi bomb blast, Dr. Gautam Sen has pointed out that India has now been reduced to a Quasi-Islamic State.[14]

As mentioned in the beginning of this chapter an outline of the crescent corridor running from Assam to Uttar Pradesh is clearly visible. This alarming development has mostly taken place within the last four decades, largely due to massive illegal infiltration from Bangladesh coupled with the higher fertility of Muslims. It has been aided by the rampant growth of vote-bank politics in the sensitive states of U.P., Bihar and Assam as well as in the Marxist ruled state of West Bengal.

It is not mere chance that the population of Muslims in Delhi has registered a quantum jump of more than ten-and-a-half times during last 40 years, rising from 155,453 in 1961 to 1,623,520 in 2001, while that of Muslims in Haryana has multiplied more than three times during the last 30 years, growing from 405,723 in 1971 to 1,222,916 in 2001. The nationwide impact of continuing illegal infiltration is pronouncedly reflected in the phenomenal growth of Muslim numbers in Delhi. Surely this mammoth increase of more than 14.5 lakh recorded in the national capital territory during the last forty years could not have been caused merely by the high fertility of Muslims who were a little more than 1.5 lakhs in 1961. According to a press report, the Delhi Police was said to have reiterated in a sealed affidavit filed in the Delhi High Court in September 2003 that nearly 13 lakh Bangladeshi infiltrators were staying illegally in the national capital. Several districts of Assam and quite a few of West Bengal and Bihar have been recording rapid growth of Muslim population.

Due to swift population changes, Muslims now form 28 per cent of the population in the border belt traversing Bihar and Uttar Pradesh. The broad contours of the emerging crescent corridor can be seen in the map below.

It looks as though vanguard of the global Islamist campaign for a South-Asian caliphate extending from Indonesia to West Asia, via Bangladesh, India and Pakistan, is speedily heading towards Delhi via Assam, West Bengal, Bihar and Uttar Pradesh. The persistent demand for a Muslim Chief Minister in Bihar, voiced by a prominent member of Dr. Manmohan Singh's cabinet, has to be viewed as a forerunner of the changing power equation in the Yadava heartland resulting from fast-paced population changes. Verily has it been said that the coming events cast their shadow before !

Map 6.1

Contours of the Emerging Crescent Corridor (Areas of Growing Muslim Presence)

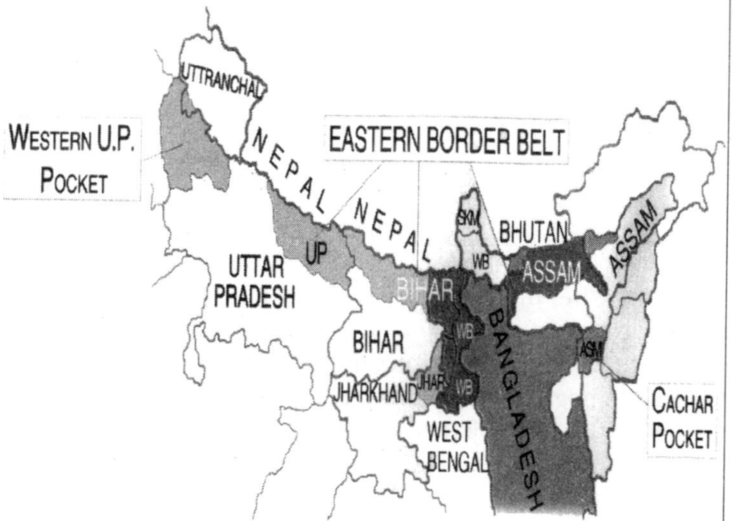

(Map not to scale)

[Source: Adapted from *An Illustrated Presentation of Religious Demography of India* (Updated upto 2001), page 22]

Notes: 1. Muslim share in the eastern part of the belt, shown in black, is now approximately 46 percent.

2. Since independence their presence in this part has increased by 11 percent.

7

The Bell Tolls

"One of the tests of leadership is the ability to recognise a problem before it becomes an emergency."

Arnold Glasgom

Unless the mainstream leadership of national parties occupying India's political matrix wakes up right now, India could face very difficult times in the decades to come. The growing demographic asymmetry, sharply accelerated by the relentless influx from Bangladesh, has the potential of changing the course of India's history. After destabilizing various regions of the country and creating widespread lawlessness, it could finally sound the death knell of the nation's unity and even our nascent democracy. Despite clumsy attempts of self-seeking politicians to conceal the truth from public it is clear from an in-depth analysis of Census 2001 data and findings of the National Family Health Survey-2, 1998, that the bell tolls for unity of Indian nation.

First, the bell tolls for India's democracy and secularism. It has been conclusively established by the population trends of Census 2001 that since independence, among all religious groups, Muslims are the only community which has been growing at a fast pace year after year and decade after decade. It has been statistically established by several studies and analyses undertaken by a number of demographers that presently on an average a Muslim woman is giving birth to at least one more child than her Hindu counterpart. At the time of partition the Muslim fertility was barely 10 per cent higher than that of the Hindus. During last five decades the difference in the fertility of the two communities has now grown to 30 per cent - and it is widening by the day. Ordinarily any minor increase in the population of a religious group may not be a matter of serious concern. But when there is a phenomenal relentless increase in the population of one single religious group seized with the radical zeal of clashing with other communities and aiming at subjugating them through jihad, it is bound to set alarm bells ringing. On their own admission the Islamists have a long term agenda of establishing one or more caliphates across the globe by defeating and overrunning all other religious groups through the time-tested strategy of jihad. And India is one of their target countries, surrounded as we are by two radical Islamist nations on our west and east. On February 23, 1998, the well known terrorist outfit, Al Qaeda, had declared a holy war on the Christians and the Jews through a proclamation signed by Osama Bin Laden, Ayman Al Zawahiri and several other fundamentalist Islamic leaders. Later on India was added to the list of target civilizations. Since then there have been innumerable attacks on the Indian civilization, including bombings of many temples and killing of Hindu pilgrims proceeding to Amarnath and Vaishnodevi though it would be instructive to include vandalisation of Bamiyan Buddhas (Afghanistan) as the most visible beginning point. Indians are proverbially known to have short memory and myopic geopolitical vision which invariably makes them soft targets of hostile nations. Unfortunately that has been our major historical failing. Perhaps not many Indians remember that in October 1998, the Al Qaeda leadership had added "the Hindu India" to the list of countries and civilizations whom the Islamists vowed to punish and destroy. The Islamists have successfully staged innumerable savage assaults, including two attacks on Raghunath temple in Jammu and one on Akshardham temple in Ahmedabad. There were attacks on Indian Parliament, the

Jammu & Kashmir Assembly and on camps of Army, the Border Security Force and the Central Reserve Police Force. In addition, conspiracies were unravelled by police disclosing the Islamist designs for assassinating the President and the former Deputy Prime Minister of India. The diabolical plot of Islamist terror outfits, unearthed in the first week of March 2005, was to attack the IMA (Indian Military Academy) at Dehra Dun, the factory of Hindustan Aeronautics Ltd. at Kanpur, and bomb several Information Technology companies in Bangalore. Fortunately by killing three Islamist terrorists, including two Pakistanis, in an encounter on March 5, 2005, the Delhi Police were able to successfully thwart their plans to undermine the morale of India's defence services by targetting the IMA and crippling the fast-growing multi billion dollar Information Technology industry by bomb blasts in Bangalore. The worst instance of terrorists' assault on Indian ethos and Hindu identity was the attempt made in July 2005 to storm and damage the makeshift Ram Janambhoomi temple in Ayodhya. Luckily the six armed jihadis, suspected to be Lashkar-e-Tayyeba militants, were intercepted well in time and shot dead by the CRPF contingent in a fierce gun battle lasting two hours. Obviously the long term objectives of Muslim terrorists continues to be to destroy the Indian nation by waging jihad, though many sham-secularists and leftists continue to preach a soft approach towards jihadi warriors. So powerful indeed is the pro-terror lobby in India that the central government readily capitulated to the demand for the abrogation of the Prevention of Terrorism Act. Ultimately that left-inspired move will facilitate the nefarious designs of terror outfits. It must be said to the credit of Al Qaeda and allied terror groups that they make no pretence about their ultimate intentions. They have clearly set forth their ultimate goal of conquering the world in the preamble of Al Qaeda Manual. It has been experienced worldwide in numerous countries that as soon as the size of the Muslim population reaches the benchmark of 30 to 40 per cent, the leaders of the community start making all kinds of demands some of which are both unreasonable and impossible to fulfil. And soon thereafter an aggressive campaign for secession is launched on the ground of non-acceptance of their religion-based demands which invariably degenerates into a no-holds-barred civil war. The familiar scenario is already unfolding in the state of Assam where the Muslims have reached the benchmark of 30 per cent and communal demands are being made quite aggressively. On Monday April 4, 2005, a huge rally was organised in Guwahati by the Jamiat-e Ulema-e-Hind, a so-called moderate Muslim organisation, in which Maulana Syed Asad Madani, President of the Jamiat, delivered a highly jingoistic speech and presented a charter of 18 demands to the Chief Minister Tarun Gogoi, who was present there. The fundamentalist Maulana (often rated as a moderate by media) served a six months notice on the Gogoi-led Congress government to meet the demands of the Muslim community failing which, he threatened openly, that the Muslims will bring down the Congress government[1]. A major demand made by the Jamiat-e Ulema was that the Illegal Migrants (Determination by Tribunals) Act must not be allowed to be scrapped. True to its vote-bank culture, the central government agreed not to scrap the obnoxious legislation, but it was struck down by the Supreme Court on July 12, 2005, and declared ultra vires. Another unreasonable demand was that citizenship cards and pattas (i.e., revenue documents) conferring permanent land ownership rights should be given to the so-called "Indian citizens" living in the char areas (sand bar islets). It should be understood that such threatening demands are not something new. This situation can be ascribed solely to the mammoth demographic change. Many more such demands will surface in due course. According to the rumour mill of Guwahati, in due course of time a demand will be made for enforcing the 'sharia law' in all Muslim majority districts of the state. Interestingly due to intimidatory tactics of the Jamiat-ul Ulema-e-Hind, the Chief Minister Tarun Gogoi caved in almost immediately. He pleaded that his government had already ensured that the Illegal Migrants (Determination by Tribunals) Act is not scrapped by making the central government agree to that proposal. He promised to consider other demands favourably and pointed out that his government had already issued land-ownership pattas to 15,000 residents of char areas (i.e., the riverine islands) and assured that more pattas will be issued soon.[2] Subsequently when on July 12, 2005, the Supreme Court declared the IMDT Act ultra vires, the Jamiat and some other fundamentalist groups threatened to plunge the State into disorder, unless another legislation was brought forward to protect the interest of Muslim community. Prima facie the state of Assam, where governance has already collapsed, is heading for a major Muslim militancy in the coming decades. The partisan demands being made by fundamentalist Muslim groups point in that direction.

Retreat of Hindus from Kashmir

These developments clearly indicate that any further decline or dilution in the population of Hindus and allied religious groups in Assam and other vulnerable states will constitute a major threat to India's unity and secular identity. Here it is pertinent to recall the devious process of ethnic cleansing in Kashmir valley which witnessed a mammoth decline in the population of the members of Hindus and allied faiths from 1981 onwards. Their proportion in population of the valley went down from 5.03 per cent in 1981 to a low of 2.77 in the year 2001. From a headcount of 5,58,000 in 1981 their presence now stands reduced to mere 1,52,000. But these figures do not tell the whole story. A detailed profile showing the gender, literacy and working status of the members of Hindus and allied faiths in the valley given below indicates that their present population in the valley consists predominantly of adult male workers:

Table 7. Profile of the Leftover Members of Hindu Faiths in Kashmir Valley in 2001.

District/ Area	Total Population	Females	0-6 Age Group	Workers	Literates
Kupwara	16,585	1,351	368	14,933	15,311
Baramula	28,091	7,539	1,690	17,480	18,715
Srinagar	62,680	10,732	2,744	47,516	48,623
Badgam	11,919	2,889	688	8,136	8,122
Pulwama	14,974	4,913	838	8,1451	8,970
Anantnag	17,364	3,820	946	12,075	12,286
Kashmir Valley	1,51,613	31,214	7,174	108,591	111,377
Percentage of Hindus and Allied Faiths in Valley		20.61	4.73	71.62	73.46
Percentage of all Religious groups		47.47	14.36	32.90	41.84

Note: The figures show the total population in absolute numbers, excepting the last two rows which list the respective percentages under various heads.

Source: An illustrated presentation based on Religious Demography of India 2005, p.33.

It is evident from Table 7 above that due to massive ethnic cleansing now among nearly 1,52,000 members of Hindus and allied faiths in the valley there are only 31,000 females and barely 7,000 children in the 0-6 age group. In other words, there are only 20.61 per cent females and 4.73 per cent 0-6 age group children respectively. While 73.5 per cent of them are literate, nearly 72 per cent are workers. The corresponding proportion for the total population of the valley (all religious groups included) works out to 42 per cent women and 33 per cent children. This data, culled from Census 2001, clearly shows that a preponderant majority of the members of Hindu faiths are single male workers, perhaps mostly non-Kashmiris. The gender profile of Hindus is severely distorted in Kupwara district recording 8 per cent females and Srinagar where females are only 17 per cent. The proportion of children in these two districts is abysmally low, even lower than the level of 6 per cent in most districts of the valley.

The gender profile, age distribution, literacy level and working status of Hindus and allied faiths shows that of the original Hindu and Sikh inhabitants only very few are now left in the valley. That indicates the diabolical sweep of the ethnic cleansing carried out by Islamic terrorists which the central and state government failed to prevent. A similar squeeze is now being experienced by the Buddhists of Ladakh region. In February 2006 there were communal clashes between Buddhists and Muslims. Obviously in Kashmir Valley the bulk of adult male workers are employed either in government departments or in the miscellaneous work slots of private sector. Astonishingly the studied silence of the hyper vocal NGOs (Non Government Organizations), numerous governmental agencies and ever pontificating mainstream media, all swearing loudly by secularism and humanitarian concerns, has added a touch of morbid poignancy to the long story of persecution in the valley. It is nothing short of a conspiracy of silence between the NGOs and the central and state governments, especially when one looks at the miserable conditions in which Kashmri Pandits have been living now for more than 15 years.

The tragic story of Kashmiri Pandits, highlighted above, has great relevance, nay even a scary lesson, for the infiltration squeezed Assamese as well as for the thinly populated Christian-dominated north-eastern states like Nagaland and Mizoram. Over the next few decades they could also meet the fate of Kashmiri Hindus primarily due to growth of pernicious vote-bank politics and the pusillanimity of the national leadership in dealing with the problem of illegal immigration.

Essentially due to their staunch commitment to "ummah", all Islamic societies are conceptually antithetical to the precepts of secularism, democracy and multiculturalism. Deriving inspiration from their scriptures and long history of innumerable jihads waged by their Prophet and holy warriors, the Islamic clergy and scholars abhor democracy and decry secularism and multicultural ethos. Frankly there never was any tradition of secularism and democracy in any Islamic country. Even in countries like Turkey and Malaysia, which often tom-tom themselves as 'secular' nations and democratic countries, there is hardly any worthwhile secularism or democracy.

Plight of Parsis

The demographic bell tolls for the enterprising Parsi community, too, which has been trapped in a perennially declining population mode for several decades. Unfortunately their rapid decline is now a highly visible trend which needs to be reversed urgently and effectively largely by the leaders of the community by reorienting their societal norms about not marrying outside the Parsi community, promoting marriages at younger age and improving their fertility level. It is time for the Parsi leadership to advise their younger generation to steer clear of the condom and abortion culture and reinvest in the system of family values. The community has always played a stellar role in the history of India. Parsis came to India in the ninth century bringing with them the glorious traditions of tolerance and enterprise nurtured by the ancient Zoroastrian civilization. They have always displayed unwavering commitment to the well-being of the people inhabiting the land of their adoption. The community also played a very significant role in India's freedom movement. Both in the pre-independence and post-independence era, they have been in the forefront of economic development of the nation. In the Report on Religionwise Data of Census 2001 pointed attention has been drawn to the sharp decline in their population which went down to 69,601 (33,949 males and 35,652 females) in 2001, from 76,382 (37,736 males and 38,646 females) in 1991. The Parsi community has a disproportionately high percentage of old people which makes the task of improving the rate of population growth of the community quite difficult. The Census 2001 report has recommended the adoption of innovative fertility improvement measures by Parsis for boosting population of their community.

Threat to Sikhs and Hindus

The bell tolls loud and clear also for the valiant Sikh community, an important constituent of the Hindu fraternity, or the 'Omkar Parivar'. The growth rate of Sikhs has recorded a steep decline during the last 3 decades, coming down drastically from 32.3 per cent in 1971 to a paltry 18.2 per cent in 2001. The last decade has witnessed another 25 per cent decline in the growth rate of Sikhs. If this falling trend continues uncorrected for sometime more, the Sikh growth rate could plummet to around 13.6 per cent in 2011 census. And God forbid, if the trend is not reversed during the next 10-15 years, by 2021 their growth rate could decline to a level as low as 10 per cent. The Sikhs are a progressive, robust and highly patriotic community and this sharp decline in their growth rate does not augur well for the future of India. Luckily they are a deeply religious and wide-awake people and hopefully they will be able to arrest any further steep fall in their growth rate. The unusually low percentage of Sikh children in the 0-6 years age group, however, foreshadows a further steep decline in their growth rate during the next 30-40 years. That should be a matter of concern to the Sikh and Hindu masses and their community leaders.

More ominously, the bell tolls for the majority community, the Hindus, whose growth rate has been continuously declining since 1951, and that too at an increasing pace, decade after decade. The 2001 census data has revealed a sharp decline to the tune of approximately 25 per cent in the Hindu growth rate. Though even now the Hindus constitute a preponderant majority of near about 80 per cent, they have already lost the majority status in as many as 7 districts of Assam, 3 districts of West Bengal, at least another 2 districts of Bihar and of course in several states of the north-east.

A mere glance at the data of Hindu children in the age group 0-6 years vis a vis Muslims in the same group makes it abundantly clear that during the next 40-50 years the percentage of Hindus will witness a more dramatic decline in several States. If the present trend continues, any time between the years 2031 and 2061, they are likely to become a minority in the important north-eastern State of Assam and possibly soon thereafter in the coastal state of Kerala in south India. According to the present demographic trends, between the years 2041 and 2061 the Hindus could lose the majority status in West Bengal as well, or at least in a large number of districts of that State.

Attention of Hindus and Sikhs needs to be drawn to the fact that as a rule, long-term demographic trendlines are seldom broken. That is one of the elementary basics of economics and statistics. Every demographer knows it. Equally important is the fact that it is a worldwide experience that no community can easily or speedily reverse the process of demographic decline once it sets in. The trend can be reversed only in about 50 years time by two successive generations of baby boomers. Thus at least for the next 40-50 years the fate of Hindus, Sikhs and other allied faiths, trapped in demographic decline, has been sealed.

A very important corollary of the changing demographic profile of India will be a steep decline in the proportion of youth among the members of Hindus, Sikhs and allied faiths compared to the Muslims. Correspondingly the percentage of old persons will register a disproportionately heavy increase among the Hindus and allied faiths. It needs no reiteration that as a rule youthful population is more productive, adventurous, aggressive and violence-prone while the old people are easy-going and inclined towards a laid-back and sedate lifestyle. Going by the experience of several European nations, notably Germany and Russia, in the not-too-distant a future, say after 2051 or 2071, there could be a steady shortfall in the availability of suitable Hindu and Sikh youth for recruitment to India's defence forces too. In view of the large difference of 21 per cent between the cohorts in the 0-6 years groups of Hindus and allied faiths and the Muslims, there is a strong possibility that after 2061 or 2071, the proportion of young men and women among the Hindus and Sikhs will sharply go down, while the percentage of old men and women in their population will dramatically increase thereby further restricting the availability of suitable Hindu and Sikh youth for defence forces — a scenario similar to the 'too-few-youth' crisis haunting the governments of Russia, Germany and several other European countries. As mentioned elsewhere in this book, even now there is a staggering shortfall of more than twelve thousand officers in our defence forces, perhaps largely due to the availability of comparatively better career opportunities in many other sectors of our growing economy. The situation will become really grim after three or four decades when the proportion of youth will decline rapidly, while opportunities in the corporate sector will continue to attract an overwhelming proportion of talented youth of Hindus and allied faiths. It could adversely impact the already inadequate availability of youngmen and women for defence forces.

Omar Khalidi's Grand Design

The latent demographic changes have the potential of starting the trend towards balkanisation of India due to the changed religious composition of States like Assam, West Bengal, Bihar and Tripura all of which are adversely affected by massive illegal Bangladeshi influx. The flood of illegal immigrants from Bangladesh is threatening to reduce the Hindus of north-eastern region to near minority status in their traditional homelands. The demand for another partition, or merger with contiguous areas of Bangladesh, is likely to emerge first from Assam and West Bengal, the two strategically important states which have witnessed the maximum infiltration of Bangladeshis. It is well known by now that the ISI controlled Islamists operating through Bangladesh have a grand design to subvert the governance of India's north-eastern region. As already mentioned, a demand for some sort of cantonisation of Muslim majority areas by creating semi-autonomous Muslim-dominated enclaves, replicating the Macedonia's divisive polity, was voiced forcefully in June 2004, in *The Times of India*, New Delhi, by Dr. Omar Khalidi, a fundamentalist, who tried to raise the pitch in an interview to *The Radiance,* a weekly brought by the Jamiat-e-Islami. Omar Khalidi's advocacy for creation of Muslim-majority union territories, or Muslim-dominated enclaves, is entirely in keeping with the two nation theory inherent in the orthopraxy of Islam which divides the world into two hostile camps, i.e., Darul Islam and Darul Harb. Also the demand for creation of Muslim majority States and districts raised by Omar Khalidi is totally in conformity with the worldwide phenomenon of Muslims wanting to form 'community-controlled enclaves' as a prelude to breaking away from the parent country on ground of religious incompatibility with other faiths in the matter of life style and cultural differences — their familiar refrain and strategic ploy. The civil society worldwide is already bewildered by the intensity of multiple jihads being waged by Muslim terrorist groups for secession from the parent countries in Cyprus, Bosnia-Herzegovina, Kosovo, Macedonia, Russian province of Chechenya, Thailand, Philippines, and nearer home in the Kashmir valley. The trial balloon for creating separatist enclaves for Muslims, floated by Omar Khalidi, is just first step in the direction of another partition of India. There should be no mistake in identifying his ultimate objective. To add more fuel to the secessionist fire sought to be lit by Omar Khalidi's thesis, on May 1 2005 in the 18th annual conference of the AIMPLB (All India Muslim Personal Law Board) held in Bhopal, a declaration was made to establish Nizam-e-Qaza, or the Islamic judicial system in every district of India, i.e., 648 districts in all, which seeks to make a mockery of the Indian judicial system. The proposed Sharia courts will deal with all family matters and property disputes pertaining to the Muslim community. The declaration made by the AIMPLB on the initiative of Syed Shahabuddin is nothing short of an open defiance of the Indian Constitution and a challenge to the majesty of Indian judiciary. It may be recalled that the Nizam-e-Qaza or Islamic judicial system, was first introduced by the third Caliph, Uthman-e-Ghani, at Madina during his 12 years tenure from 646 to 656 A.D. In India it was started in 1192 A.D. by Qutub-ud Din Aibak and thereafter continued off and on during Mughal rule. It was, however, finally abolished by the British government in 1864. Recently due to ascendancy of radical Islam worldwide and emergence of 'secularitis' as the new credo of Indian politicians, the AIMPLB has decided to challenge the Indian state and its judicial system by introducing it again in India, after a gap of 140 years. It is learnt that the so-called Shariat Courts have already been set up surreptitiously by the ulemas in Gujarat, Bihar, Uttar Pradesh, Assam and Orissa, under the guidance of AIMPLB. The Qazis (judges) of these courts have been directed not to seek publicity or attract public attention. The intention is to first make the extra-constitutional Shariat courts functionally effective and then make these fully acceptable to the Muslim community so that no government dare to dismantle these or declare them illegal. To achieve this objective the Muslim Personal Law Board has come out with a two-part booklet "Nizam-e-Qaza Ka Kayam" (establishment of Nizam-e-Qaza) which contains an outline of the proposed Islamic system of justice. The ultimate objective of fundamentalist elements is to institutionalize the office of qazi in towns and villages and motivate the Muslims to settle all matters pertaining to marriage, divorce, inheritance, etc., in Dar-ul-Qaza courts and discourage them from approaching the law courts for settling their disputes or even going in for appeals under the Indian judicial system. Their clear aim is to subvert the law of the land and undermine the authority of Indian Constitution and judicial system.[6] It is a grotesque sectarian-cum-separatist project the implementation of which needs to be curbed effectively. A typical instance of cock-eyed justice sought to be administered by Shariat courts and Dar-ul-Uloom, Deoband, was the recent case of a traumatized married women, Imrana, of village Chaitwal in Muzaffarnagar district of Uttar Pradesh, who was raped by her father-in-law, one Ali Mohammed. When a complaint was made by the outraged lady, mother of 5 children, the bizarre verdict given by the Ansari Panchayat and the Muslim clergy was that as a result of rape the victim's marriage with her husband stood annulled due to which she will have to leave her marital home. This absurd verdict was duly upheld by Dar-ul-Uloom, Deoband, the highest seat of Wahabi Islam in India and supported by some members of the All India Muslim Personal Law Board. It was claimed that according to Islamic law, Imrana had now become "haram" (illegal relationship) for her husband Noor Ilahi, even though the two wanted to stay together. There are some more similar instances of cock-eyed justice, one of Rani, wife of Iftikhar of Hadauli village in Bulandshahr district of U.P., Rukhsana of Tonka village in Mewat (Haryana) and then one Jyotsanara of Assam — all victims of the lust of their fathers-in-law. All of them — Imrana, Rani, Rukhsana and Jyotsanara were denied justice by Shariat courts and Islamic scholars.

Prima facie Shariat courts are nothing but extra-constitutional and extra-judicial fundamentalist entities. They have come to pose a serious challenge to Indian state. The unmistakable objective of Shariat courts appears to be to radicalize the Muslim community and escalate communal tensions by promoting divisive tendencies in society. Astonishingly no sham-secularist Hindu nor any leftist idealogue has shown the guts to oppose and condemn the questionable anti-national proclamations made by the AIMPLB, though the Bharatiya Janata Party and Communist Party (Marxist) did show the sagacity to support Imrana's claim to justice.

Meanwhile the Chief Minister of Andhra Pradesh has provided 5 per cent reservations for Muslims in government services and educational institutions in furtherance of vote-bank politics. Such abject surrender by political leadership to communal demands not only militates against our secular ideal, but will further exacerbate mutual hostility and promote religion-oriented divisions in society. Mercifully the communal reservations announced by Andhra Pradesh government were struck down by the High Court of Andhra Pradesh. To capitalize on the vulnerability of the central government as a quick follow up on August 25, 2005, three Muslim ministers and 26 Muslims Members of Parliament met the Prime Minister, Dr. Manmohan Singh, in a bid to pressurize him to give 5 per cent reservations to Muslims on all India basis. It is a sad spectacle, a familiar scenario recalling the pre-partition years.

Once Assam becomes a near-Muslim majority state and a call for secession is given in the north-eastern region, the sound and fury of its jihadi reverbrations will be heard in several Muslim majority districts of the country. The likely secessionist call is bound to impact West Bengal and the adjoining districts of Bihar, e.g. Kishanganj, Purnea, Araria, Katihar, etc., where Muslims have already become majority or are racing towards the near majority status, say within the next three to five decades. What will happen next, no one knows. In all probability, a civil strife like the one witnessed in the Balkans might break out. Your guess is as good as mine!

The bell tolls for the Christian community of north-eastern India, too, especially for the inhabitants of Nagaland, Mizoram and Meghalaya where Bangladeshi infiltrators have made deep inroads by occupying vast tracts of government owned uninhabited forest lands in difficult terrain. The number of Bangladeshi infiltrators in Nagaland has grown sharply during the last four years. According to *South Asian Intelligence Review*, it is widely believed that by now the percentage of Bangladeshi infiltrators in Nagaland might be near about 20 per cent of the total population which comes to four lakhs. It may be recalled that Nagaland had a total population of 2 million people in 2001, as revealed by the census. The state has vast uninhabited hilly areas some of which are reported to have been occupied by illegal immigrants. Alarmed by the growing influx of illegal immigrants, in September 2004 the Naga students had launched a campaign for throwing out Bangladeshis from their home state. Slowly but surely the realization about the impending Islamic threat emanating from the teeming population of Bangladesh to the identity of Christian population of north-east has started dawning upon the inhabitants of Nagaland, Mizoram and Meghalaya. They are realising fast that in view of the small size of their population thinly spread across certain pockets of the north-east, it will be well nigh impossible for them to fight and repel on their own the avalanche of jihadi storm-troopers let loose by Pakistan's ISI through Bangladesh. It is not for nothing that recently the Naga students decided to join hands with the North-east Students Organisation (NESO), an outfit dominated by Assamese students, to launch a joint campaign against the continuing infiltration from Bangladesh. This is a pragmatic development, a welcome change from the earlier rigid partisan postures displayed by most Christian groups of the north-east.

Leftists Muslim Spat

Let there be no mistake that the bell will also start tolling for the Marxists and leftists of West Bengal, Bihar and Kerala fairly soon. It is just a matter of time. Unfortunately the Indian brand of communists and leftists are blessed with tube-light reflex and suffer from acute myopic vision. Global experience shows that both the Marxists and the Islamist make excellent bed-fellows, but only as a temporary arrangement, i.e., only so long as the

Muslims remain subdued because of their small population. Once Islamists acquire demographic predominance, the first victims of their fundamentalist wrath have always been communists. That has been the global history of radical Islam. There are a number of examples of wholesale extermination of communists and leftist groups by Islamists, including what befell the communists of Afghanistan, Kosovo and Bosnia. One does not have to recount the prevalent atmosphere of pronounced hostility to communism in many breakaway Muslim nations of the former Soviet Union. A classic example of Islamic hatred for communists came to light recently right here in India in Kerala. After the Marxists staged a successful rally in the Muslim majority district of Mallapuram in early 2005, a "political fatwa" was issued by the Indian Union Muslim League warning the Muslims to stay away from communists failing which the faithful will face ex-communication.[7] In fact, the Muslim League activists distributed pamphlets seeking to impose a social ban on all communists within the Muslim community. The message was: "A good Muslim can never be a communist and a hardened communist can never be a good Muslim".[8] Reaching out to Muslim masses through a hate-spewing pamphet, the Karuvarakkundu Panchayat Committee of IUML (Indian Union Muslim League) called upon members of the community to avoid marrying communist activists. Titled *'Mallapuram Soil and Soul'*, the document prescribed stringent measures against communists, including the "fatwa" that a Muslim communist will have no right to his father's property, on his death the last rites will not be performed as per Islamic practice, nor would his body be allowed to be buried in the mosque premises, etc. The activists of Muslim League further exhorted the faithful that those who had married communists should terminate such alliances.[9] Thus despite self-styled Marxist leaders displaying great bonhomie with communal Muslim leadership, both in West Bengal and at all India level, the angst of Muslim clerics and community leaders against communism has been gathering momentum, not only in Bangladesh but all over India, too. Incidentally Mallapuram district was created in 1960s as a Muslim-dominated area by Comrade Namboodiripad. And now the radical Muslims of Mallapuram have issued fatwas against the same communist fraternity, their former benefactors. These developments show that the Indian communists are well past the stage of learning anything, least of all the truth. They don't understand that once Islamists attain a near majority status in north-eastern India, they will start hunting down not only the "infidel" Hindus, Buddhists and Christians, but also the communists and leftists. Apart from the first hand experience of Lebanon, Afghanistan and the Balkans, the communists ought to learn from the ready example next door in Bangladesh where Banglabhai, the recently arrested bearded fundamentalist follower of Bin Laden, and his storm-troopers have been hell bent on eliminating the cadres of Purba Banglar Communist Party and Sarbahara Party (which claims to be an outfit of have-nots). Once the Islamists take over an Indian state, or seize a predominantly Muslim region, the fate of Indian communists and leftists there is not likely to be any different from that of the so-called infidels, the Hindus.

The impending demographic change is likely to destabilize the Indian nation by further widening the historical divide between the two communities. In due course of time it could lead to major faultline conflicts and civil strife much worse than those witnessed in Lebanon during 1975-1990 and later on in the Balkans. Due to sheer size and strength of one billion plus population the religion-based faultline conflicts raging across India will have the potential to cause untold misery on an unimagineable scale. The Balkans and Lebanon still continue to smoulder because of the glowing embers of the past civil war fuelled by the sharp growth in Muslim population.

Hindu Migration from border districts

The demographically challenged Hindu community of Assam and West Bengal is facing a serious challenge. It is a deep existential crisis which needs to be handled boldly and imaginatively. Otherwise it could mean deep erosion of the Hindu identity in these two states which might cause eruption of major faultline conflicts. As and when the demand for secession is raised in India, the universally peculiar phenomenon of non-Muslims being forced to out-migrate from Muslim dominated areas will gather speed. Once it gathers momentum there is bound to be a corresponding reaction in the Hindu majority areas which could cause large scale cascading effect of migration and cross-migration by the two communities on a scale much bigger than what had been witnessed during the partition of India in 1947. At that time there were millions of uprooted people all over India running hither and thither in search of security and shelter. Unless corrective measures to forestall the coming deluge are initiated now, the secessionist campaign is likely to recur, say after 10 to 20 years, on a massive scale. Interestingly this phenomenon of non-Muslims being driven away from the Muslim-dominated areas is being witnessed even in the far-away Norway where it has been termed as the "ousting effect".[9] The expression "ousting effect" means that "when the Muslims reach a certain level in a specific area, non-Muslims begin to move out".[10] Though Norway has a small Muslim population and their percentage was only 0.90 in 1990, in recent years their numbers have grown quite fast. The abnormally high growth rate of Muslims during the last two decades has already created a fear complex among the indigenous people, both Christians and atheists. Between 1980 and 2003, within a short spell of 23 years, Muslim population grew more than 75 times in Norway, from a mere 1006 in 1980 to 75,761 in 2003. And their numbers and overall percentage are growing at a fast pace. Muslim population has already grown quite rapidly in Oslo city and Akershus area of Norway where the "ousting effect" has already started taking its toll. Even though European nations are now wide awake and gearing up to meet the threat, in July, 2004, the Princeton University Professor Bernard Lewis told the Hamburg daily *Die Welt* that Europe would become Islamic by the end of this century, at the latest.[11] According to the well known strategic analyst and contemporary historian, Niall Ferguson, Europe could be a Muslim majority continent much earlier, say in another 50 years or so. Although Norway is relatively a much safer country, tucked away in a corner of northern Europe, quite far from the first ports of call of Muslim immigrants in Italy, Spain and France, a fear has gripped the intellectuals and political analysts that Norway might become a Muslim majority country by 2046 due to sheer force of higher growth rate of Muslims.[12] Apparently all over Europe the situation is moving in the same direction as currently witnessed in Assam and West Bengal, the two Indian states over-run by infiltrating Bangladeshis, where Hindus are relocating themselves because of the "ousting effect", a very graphic though unflattering term coined by the Norwegian intelligentsia.

Selig Harrison's Forecast

It may be recalled that as early as 1960, a well known American author and strategic analyst, Selig S. Harrison (presently working for the Center for International Policy), wrote in his somewhat controversial book, *India: The Most Dangerous Decades,* that in the decades ahead India might face another split, or division into a number of states, due to the growing undercurrents of centrifugal forces.[13] He expressed the view that because of serious ethnic divide and sociological contradictions India will break into a number of territorial sub-units as a prelude to its balkanisation. Briefly, according to Harrison's assessment India faces the risk of being split into a number of totalitarian small states. Now it seems that the divisive process could start first in the north-eastern region which has multiple ethnic groups. According to Harrison, in India several linguistically and ethnically diverse people are held together in a body politic called central government over which hangs the shadow of powerful casteist and regional groups wanting to pull in different directions. Consequently, the contradictions between the deep-seated centrifugal forces and the urge for a unified national identity will have the potential to create anarchy, fascism and totalitarian trends largely due to the prevalence of casteist and regional mindset. Every region recalls its ancient past and its golden age. Similarly each caste group tries to prove itself to be more equal than the rest. As economic competition increases, the militancy of regional and caste lobbies will grow. Regional groups will assert new claims to dominance in political and administrative leadership and the steel frame of civil services will be weakened. Though Indian Constitution postulates a healthy competition for good governance between responsible national level parties, some regional or casteist parties ruling in states might not cooperate with the ruling party in New Delhi. Instead they may try to manipulate partisan grievances to get better of the central government. He felt that there could emerge a generation of narrow-minded politicians and bureaucrats who will be unable to talk to each other meaningfully at national level — a situation clearly visible in many parts of the country. While discussing the stresses of Indian politics and indiscipline of communist in chapter VII of his book Harrison pointed out that latter often manage to score success by collaborating with parochial interests and chauvinist group. Harrison correctly anticipated that communists and leftists will improve their hold on India's polity by taking recourse to political machinations and by forming alliances with subaltern parties ruling in different states. Ultimately the *coup de* grace for the likely vivisection was likely to be delivered by the communists and leftists who, according to Harrison, have no compunction in resorting to manipulative politics. He felt that the communist strategy will ultimately lead to balkanisation of the Indian state and demise of democracy. While conceding that by protecting its civilizational and cultural identity India had so far demonstrated that its power of survival was rivalled only by China, Harrison argued, fairly well and correctly, that the divisive forces operating as regional and caste lobbies, egged on by communists, have the potential of subverting the structure of governance and ultimately supplanting the democratic polity. He foresaw that ultimately sheer growth of casteism and regional imbalances might lead to disintegration of the Indian union and creation of multiple semi-totalitarian and fascist sub-nation states.

The latest manipulative instance of the communist strategy to divide and destroy the unity of Indian nation is manifest in their unethical insistence on implementing the controversial proposal for reserving 27 per cent seats for the members of OBCs (i.e., Other Backward Castes) in educational institutions with effect from June 1, 2007. The leftists and their parochial allies are fully aware that one year is too short a period for finding the requisite finances and organising the necessary infrastructure for making additonal seats available to the general category candidates in colleges, universities and medical institutions. Yet in single-minded pursuit of political power they are hellbent on dividing the fractured Indian society into "anti-reservationst" and "pro-reservationist" factions, even if it causes eruption of civil war like conditions across the country. Communists are aware that Muslims cannot be easily divided because of the iron-grip of Mullahs and fundamentalist elements on their flock. Therefore the only easy way to capturing political power lies through promoting fissiparious tendencies in the caste-ridden Hindu society.

Though Selig Harrison's prophesy about the threat of India being pushed towards balkanisation by the communists has been proved wrong till now, it cannot be denied that the communists and the sham secularists, mostly Hindus, have been trying their worst to promote caste-based divisive forces in many parts of the country and their efforts have met with resounding success. During last 45 years many forecasts made by Harrison, especially about growth of casteist and regional politics and emergence of petty politicians who are unwilling to speak to each other meaningfully have come true. By firming up their stranglehold on the central government through the strategem of outside support the communists have been able to thwart many economic reforms and undermine good governance. On top of it, many states are infested with sectarian violence and Naxalite menace which has struck deep roots in at least 125 districts of 12 states and they are working overtime on their plan to establish a Compact Revolutionary Zone starting from Indo-Nepal border in the north down to Andhra Pradesh in the south. The sharp growth in the number of ISI modules and the rising graph of Bangladeshi infiltration have substantially contributed to the political mess writ large across the country.

Divided States of India

All these developments are danger signals for India's unity and secular entity. Most of these had been anticipated by Harrison including our present march towards the dangerous decades. Largely due to the promotion of minority vote-bank and caste-based divisive politics, India now appears to be heading towards vivisection and demise of democracy. Politically speaking, India has been through very difficult times in recent years. There have been five successive general elections since 1989, yet none yielded a single-party majority in the Lok Sabha. And let us not ignore the fact that the last three Lok Sabha elections were held in a short span of nearabout six years or so something totally unprecedented in the electoral history of India. Unless a miracle happens, in the coming decades the demographic change, aided by politics of minority vote-bank and caste-oriented sham secularism, is likely to claim Indian-democracy as its prized victim. The unfortunate denouement could come soon, unless effective measures are taken right now.

By now, it is clear that the threat to India's unity and economic progress is likely to come from a different source than the one visualized by Harrison. It is likely to manifest from the jihadi groups operating from our two fundamentalist neighbours. They are already trying to take full advantage of India's adverse demography and vote-bank politics. Truly, the communists and leftists have played a predominant role, as visualised by Harrison, in promoting multiple fissiparous and divisive tendencies by undermining the cultural unity of India and supporting casteist politics in the holy name of secularism. Their hobnobbing with the ideologues of radical Islam is likely to prove the proverbial last straw on the camel's back. With sharp growth in Muslim population the fundamentalists have started clamouring for more concessions and politico-religious favours. They are already arm twisting the central and state governments to extract more concessions, as is evident from the recent decision announced in May 2005 reserving fifty per cent seats for Muslim students in the Aligarh University. More demands like proportional allocation of seats in the Parliament and state legislatures according to their population, reservations of jobs, enforcement of Sharia laws, etc., are being openly raised which will further communalise the polity. The presentation of a long charter of demands by the Jamiat-ul Ulema-e-Islami first to the Assam government for fulfilment within six months and then in the last week of May 2005 before Sonia Gandhi, the Chairperson of the ruling coalition, along with the proclamation of AIMPLB to set up Shariat courts in every district, have to be viewed in the context of the growing threat to the integrity of India. The overall politico-religious scenario in the country is totally reminiscent of the pre-partition years when communal demands were being aggressively projected and pursued with a vengeance, finally culminating in partition.

The hideous growth of Islamic militancy across the length and breadth of India is now clearly visible in mushrooming of ISI-sponsored terror cells in various States and arrests in recent years of hundreds of anti-national moles and their local collborators involved in innumerable terrorist attacks. The widespread impact of the radical ideology was felt recently in February 2006 when multiple jingoistic proclamations were made, almost with beat of a drum, during the violent protests in India against publication of Prophet Mohammed's cartoons by newspapers of Denmark and several other European countries. Although neither any Indian newspaper, nor any Hindu leader, had approved re-publication of the cartoons, the ire of the protestors was directed aginst the usual suspect, the Hindus, in several cities and towns like Hyderabad, Lucknow, Muzzafarnagar and Mau, as reflected in attacks on Hindu shops and localities. In a bizarre speactable Haji Yakoob Qureshi, a Minister of the Uttar Pradesh government, announced a reward of Rs. 51 crore to anyone who beheads the Danish cartoonists who caricatured the Prophet of Islam. Not to be left behind, Zafaryab Jilani, a prominent Muslim leader and member of the all Indian Muslim Personal Law Board, lent his support to the *supari* (or contract killing)offered by Haji Yakoob Qureshi. Under the Indian Penal Code contract killing, or even abetment of murder, is a criminal offence for which the U.P. Minister and his supporter Zafaryab Jilani ought to have been arrested and prosecuted. But that was not done in the worst (or best?) tradition of India's secularitis-benumbed political dispensation. These developments point to the shape of things to come, say within the next one or two decades, and can be ignored only at great risk to the unity and integrity of Indian nation.

Starting with Assam, West Bengal and Bihar as flash points of divisive politics, the future struggle for secession is likely to be launched by the terror groups based in Bangladesh. They will be duly aided by the spy-cells of the notorious ISI functioning in the region and spread out in many parts of the country. Its spill-over could cause major countrywide migration of population followed by major political upheavals which might culminate in seizure of political power by one or more region-based satraps some of whom may be from the hard-line Hindu-dominated states like Gujarat, Maharashtra and Rajasthan, while some other casteist or regional satraps might rise in U.P., Bihar and south Indian states. The worst strife and mayhem may be witnessed in the north-east and eastern India followed by a major spillover into Bihar and Uttar Pradesh. Frankly, at this stage it is difficult to anticipate the course of political events resulting from the likely countrywide civil commotion in which millions of people could again be uprooted creating a major law and order problem. That might emerge as a colossal challenge for India's security forces in the decades ahead. They will do well to start planning from now onwards to meet the impending grave threat to the nation's unity in the "dangerous decades" ahead.

Credit must be given to Selig Harrison for highlighting the deivisive role of Indian communists in promoting "dominant parochial interests" acsross the country to exploit local chauvinism to their advantage.[14] Their deliberate attempts to promote parochial casteist intersts and fundamentalist Muslim ideology by aligning with communal groups on the one hand, and casteist leaders on the other, is well known. Recently they were totally exposed when they unabashedly joined hands with fundamentalist Islamic outfits for mobilizing violent protests and demonstrations during the March 2006 visit of the US President, George Bush, to India. Acting in tandem with the Samajwadi Party and fundamentalist Mullahs, they undertook unprecedented mobilization of Muslims by inflaming passions over publication of prophet Muhammad's cartoons and Indian government's vote against Iran in the matter of processing nuclear fuel. The protesting rioters had full support of the Marxists and communists despite their claim to being torch-bearers of secularism. There could be no better proof of the validity of Harrison's assessment about the dubious and divisive role of communist leadership in destroying national unity.

The overall scenario of near total collapse of governance in Assam and several north-eastern states coupled with the sharp growth in lawlessness in Bihar and West Bengal should serve as a warning to our political leadership about the impending demise of democracy in India. With the benefit of hindsight it can be said that the overly delayed prophesy made by Selig Harrison in 1960 in his tome, *India: The Most Dangerous Decades*, now finally appears to be coming true — though the threat has emerged from a radically different source than the one initially perceived by Harrison. With the benefit of hindsight it appears that Harrison's assessment of the pull of the caste-based divisive forces and communists joining hands with self-seeking politicians to destroy democracy and unity of India appears to be coming true. We seem to be moving inexorably towards the 'most dangerous decades' at a steady pace and the denouement might come soon, say within the next twenty to thirty years at the most — even earlier.

But does anyone care ? Perhaps none. "The most pathetic person in the world", remarked Helen Keller once very thoughtfully, "is someone who has sight but no vision". And in the context of India's demographic predicament and divisive politics, such a person has to be a Hindu suffering from acute vision deficit. He appears to be the only one who cannot read the bold writing on the wall spelling out the looming threat of tomorrow's turmoil, violence and secessionist faultline conflicts, all combining to destroy Indian democracy and in the bargain, our ancient civilizational ethos. Time has come to remind the country's slumbering leadership of Arnold Toynbee's famous observation that "civilizations die from suicide, not murder". We are steadily marching towards the suicide cliff, unfortunately at a time when "knowledge revolution" has the potential to transform the Indian nation into an economic super power in the global arena.

8

Secular Graffiti and Hindu Dilemma

"Strategy without tactics is the slowest route to victory. Tactics without strategy is the noise before defeat."

-Sun Tzu

Famous Chinese strategist and philosopher

Barely 57 years after independence, today the Indian nation once again stands at the cross-roads of history. For centuries, nay millennia, the Hindu faith has been the fulcrum of Indian civilization. Despite one thousand years of slavery and struggle, the sacred tradition of Hindu dharma continues to be the most important connecting link between its past and present and also between the diverse people living in various parts of the country. The glory of Ramayan and Gita, as surely as the powerful preachings of Sikh Gurus and Mahavira and Buddha, resonate throughout the length and breadth of this ancient land and millions of Indians draw inspiration from the wisdom enshrined in our holy scriptures. Unlike semitic religions, Hindu dharma is not a monolithic formation; it is an all-encompassing religion. It has a unique element of elasticity and cosmic federalism. A Hindu can be a Jain, a Buddhist or a Sikh — or even an atheist. There is no central religious authority in Hindu faith which can ex-communicate or throw out anyone from Hindu fold, not even an anti-Hindu atheist. In that sense it is a unique religion and the absence of dogmas makes it almost an unparalleled spiritual faith completely free of the intolerance often encountered in many other religions. Perhaps the Hindu mode of worshipping multiple deities, like Vishnu, Siva, Lakshmi, Parvati, Ganesha, Brahma, Saraswati and innumerable other gods and goddesses, including Gautam Buddha and Jain Tirthankaras, representing multifarious strands of spiritual thoughts has made it much more tolerant of other people's religious beliefs than any other faith worldwide. If man, as they say, has cast God in his own mould, then it stands to reason that those who are prepared to live their lives ethically and by accepting harmonious existence of multiple gods and goddesses in their pantheon will have no quarrel with the existence among them of people owing allegiance to diverse beliefs. When a number of deities representing God can co-exist harmoniously, how can their followers be dogmatic and refuse to accept multiculturalism or co-existence with other faiths? The most distinctive feature of Hinduism is that it has numerous powerful components of secularism. In that sense it is much more than mere religion. It is a complete way of life, as described by that eminent philosopher and India's former President, late Dr. S. Radhakrishnan, because of its higher sensitivity and broad sweep of eternal and all encompassing humanism. The Hindu dharma has fairly intense feelings for all living beings, including the lowest of the lowly creatures, and even mundane things, both spiritual and worldly. According to Hindu scriptures the guiding principle of life is 'Dharayati iti Dharma' which means all that sustains this universe (and everyone in it) is "dharma". For a Hindu the guiding principle of life is "dharma" which entails subscribing to all those principles which are fit for adoption by householders in their day-to-day life. The Hindu concept of "dharma" is not limited to any sectarian or doctrinaire religious belief ; it consists of universally accepted moral principles, as rightly emphasised by Swami Vivekananda. It is entirely due to the grandeur of the prevalent Hindu ethos that the Indian civilization has maintained centuries old tradition of secularism and pluralism – almost unheard of in the narrow universe of semitic monotheistic creeds.

And that is how the Indian people, predominantly Hindus, Sikhs and Jains opted for a secular constitution despite going through a blood-drenched partition of their motherland in 1947. By the very nature of its cosmic beliefs, Hinduism accepts change as an important fact of life. Since times immemorial the Hindu philosophy, enshrined in the Vedas and Upanishadas, has regarded change as the only immutable law of life, a fact repetitively emphasised in several holy texts. Incidentally the strong belief in change as an important aspect of our existence alone can explain the prowess shown by the Hindus in quickly mastering the languages of even the marauding aliens, like the Mughals and the English, so fast and so well. Despite centuries of slavery and economic deprivation, this acceptance of change as an important facet of life has enabled the modern Hindu youth, spurred by the centuries old tradition of worshipping Saraswati, the Goddess of Knowledge, to burst upon the global scene as experts in Information Technology and numerous other scientific disciplines, including surgery, biotechnology and engineering. That is a tribute to the glory of Hindu dharma, the glory of India, my motherland, your motherland and motherland of one billion plus citizens inhabiting this vast country.

Unfortunately long centuries of slavery, repetitive overdoses of non-violence and abject tolerance of tyranny and irrational belief in dogmas have emasculated the Hindu society. We have touched a new low of cowardice and pusillanimity to such an extent that now Hindu masses do not react even to persistent attacks on Hindu identity and civilizational values. For instance, no punishment was meted out to Pakistan for sponsoring and sheltering the outfits responsible for attacking Indian Parliament in December 2001. Similarly the ISI trained terror groups responsible for sending out jihadi warriors to storm Sri Ram Janambhoomi temple on July 5, 2005, have managed to stay beyond chastisement by the Indian state. Earlier there were numerous attacks on Hindu temples, including two on Raghunathji temple in Jammu and one on Akshardham temple in Ahmedabad. None of the source perpetrators of these dastardly crimes has been brought to justice, nor does the Indian state show any inclination to curb the menace. No other civilization, no other nation, would have allowed the country and the jihadi outfits sponsoring such crimes to strut around without being penalised. Obviously the over-emphasis on gross tolerance, even at the cost of self-respect, carried as baggage from our historical past of long slavery, has now come to threaten the very existence of Indian civilization. Today within India itself, the Hindu society faces multiple dangers from different quarters some of which are quite daunting and mind-boggling.

Insulting Hindu Ethos

A totally inexplicable and peculiar threat to the Hindu identity comes from a motley crowd of leftist Hindus masquerading as secularists who not only try to heap scorn and insults on Hindu faith and Hindutva, but invariably use drivel and bucolic epithets against anyone trying to speak up for Hinduism. The recourse to secular graffiti, directed solely against the Hindus and no other community, has spread quite rapidly and is now threatening to assume near epidemic proportions. Anyone who reads English newspapers, or watches television programmes, can notice the widespread use of drivel against Hindu ethos, Hindu scriptures, and our ancient civilizational values. To cite just one concrete instance, on May 3, 2004, the New Delhi edition of a prominent English daily published with banner headlines a lead story captioned "No full stops in Rig Veda" alluding to rigging of polls during the general elections in a State notorious for lawlessness as "Rig Veda", thus pouring wanton ridicule over the sentiments of Hindus for whom Rig Veda is the source of spiritual solace. Apparently neither the Editor of the newspaper, nor the reporting journalist, bothered a wee bit about the insult which they were heaping on Rig Veda, a holy scripture held in high esteem by millions of Hindus, and even by scores of non-Hindu scholars and litterateurs worldwide. In March 2005 on the occasion of Mahashivaratri the same newspaper published a derogatory article about lord Shiva by alluding to his libido in a mocking manner. The editor and the concerned scribes could take this liberty, and merrily get away with it, solely because of their reassuring belief that the Hindus are quite used to tolerating any insult and every scorn without lodging any widespread or violent protest. They dare not write in a derogatory or derisive manner about the prophets and religious beliefs of any other community. Such wanton tolerance of demeaning insults by Hindus is a hang over from a thousand years long spell of slavery.

Another glaring instance of wanton pouring of scorn on the ancient Hindu ethos is the persistent devaluation and daily trivialisation of the term 'saffron' by the English media. Throughout Indian history saffron colour (known as 'kesariya' in most vernacular languages) has been the representative symbol of the Hindu and Sikh valour and their spirit of sacrifice. During medieval times when hordes of Muslim invaders plundered and pillaged cities and towns, the saffron coloured attire (or kesariya bana) invariably stood for the daring and resolve of Indian soldiers and peasantry to offer sacrifices for the protection of their motherland and dharma. The earlier generation of freedom fighters and founding fathers of our Constitution were fully conscious of this fact because of their deep association with the masses. It is not for nothing that the colour saffron occupies the pride of place in our national flag, right on top, above every other colour. Additionally, saffron, or kesar, is by far the most sweet smelling condiment, sort of a herb, extensively used in the ancient Indian cuisine. But all these ancient and civilizationally sacred aspects of saffron do not matter for the graffiti-writing leftists and sham secularists! Astonishing indeed is their monumental disdain for the historical fact that Bhagat Singh, the legendary hero of our freedom struggtle, had implored his mother to drape him in colour 'saffron' while standing in Death Row, by singing "Mera Rang De Basanti Chola". Day in and day out the sham secularists have been using the word saffron in a pejorative sense. Such indeed is their contempt for India's past that they treat not only saffron, but nearly all Hindu ethos as clap-trap fit to be thrown into the dustbin of history. Incidentally, only Islamic tradition has the distinction of holding colour saffron in contempt and utter disdain. Prophet Muhammed specifically forbade the wearing of saffron coloured garments and had reportedly chided some of his followers who dared to wear saffron coloured garments. Isn't it remarkable that the same degree of Islamic ridicule for saffron has been copied by our self-styled secular intellectuals who have reduced the word saffron to some kind of trivial trash? Just recall how during dozens of barbaric beheadings of scores of innocent civilians during the Iraq war, often the condemned prisoners were shown in terror-laden video-tapes wearing saffron-coloured clothes, as a mark of their being "dhimmies" ! The utter contempt in which leftists and self-styled secularists hold the colour saffron, the top pride of our national flag and the ancient Indian ethos of daring and sacrifice, underlines the magnitude of the threat posed by secularitis-seized political thinkers and analysts.

The greatest pity, however, is that most of those using drivel against Hindu ethos and Hindutva are Hindus, coming from Hindu parentage and carrying Hindu names. Yet they display amazing insensitivity to the Hindu sentiments. Could there be anything more disheartening than that? It needs no elaboration that the Hindu ethos and Hindutva are two sides of the same coin. And the surprise of surprises is that neither the Hindu intellectuals, nor the comatose Hindu middle class, find themselves equal to the task of countering the relentless onslaught on their faith and scriptures by Hindu-hating Hindu secularists. Granted that the Hindu intellectuals cannot and must not stoop to the low level of those who regularly take recourse to scorn and abuse for denigrating Hinduism. But not standing up even to forcefully register well-articulated protests against incessant drivel and calumny shows the Hindu society in poor light, especially those who claim to be its intellectual and political leaders.

The insertion of secularism as an essential feature of Indian Constitution in 1976 during Emergency gave a cross-eyed slant to the body politics of the country. Today secularism is by far the most misused word by various political parties and leaders of India's political theatre. In no other country you will find the mainstream politicians using the term secularism so frequently, so unabashedly and so deviously as in India. Interestingly most politicians wearing secularism on their sleeves are either leaders or supporters of patently casteist and communal political outfits and some of them are neck deep into the quagmire of blatant corruption. Yet they have no compunction in singing paean to secularism while donning skull-caps for attending religion-denominated Iftaar parties, or haranguing aimlessly in patently caste-based conferences like the Rajput Mahasabha, Yadava Sammelan, Brahmin Mahasammelan, or a Shia or Sunni congregation. They defend with great gusto the grant of religion-specific discriminatory Haj subsidy, but oppose common civil code and even support use of the funds collected from Hindu Devasthan trusts for doling out money to madarasas without batting an eyelid. And yet they and their collaborators, mostly communists and leftist obscurantists, keep strutting across the political firmament. Surprisingly these political busy-bodies consider caste-oriented political philosophy and Islam-oriented minorityism an essential components of their secular commitment. Despite their tall claims the fact remains that today India is anything but a secular country. Frankly, the Indian state does not fulfil even the two elementary postulates of secularism. First, uniform application of laws to all citizens irrespective of their caste, creed or religion; and second, the concept of equality before law. As pointed out by K. Subrahmanyam, a well known author and strategic analyst, in a very perceptive article, *Forces of Fragmentation*, "no country can call itself democratic or secular unless it has a common civil law". Democracy implies that all citizens have equal rights and are to be treated equally under the rule of law. Thus, allowing different personal laws is a negation of both secularism and democracy because it means that a person's religion determines the law by which he or she is to be governed. For that reason India cannot be termed either a secular state or a democracy.[1] Commitment to secularism entails that all social and political relationships will be governed by laws enacted democratically. It is unacceptable "that the laws will be beyond the competence of democratic governance for some sections on account of their having God's sanction".[2] He further highlighted the fact that because of the first-past-the-post system a person often manages to get elected even when he or she polls some 30 per cent of the total vote. The result is that the Parliament seldom represents the will of the majority of the electorate. This faulty system has robbed the right-thinking majority of its due rights and has ensured in perpetuity that the minority (or a coalition of caste and communal vote-banks) will dominate the majority. Those who come to power on the basis of exploitation of divisive politics have therefore no interest in promoting national unity. The result is that regional, caste-based and communal parties have gathered strength. In the struggle for political power secularism and democracy are used as slogans for seizing power.[3] Among specific instances of religion-based discrimination institutionalised by Indian politicians are the absence of a common civil code, the provisions made in Articles 30 and 370 of the Constitution which promote discrimination on the basis of religion and territorial identity. For instance, under Article 370 no law passed by the Indian Parliament is applicable to the State of Jammu & Kashmir, unless it is duly re-passed, or approved by the State legislature. Even the Governor of Jammu and Kashmir state takes the oath of office under the separatist constitution of Jammu & Kashmir, while all other State Governors take the oath under the Constitution of India. Similarly our constitution allows blatant discrimination by certain state governments between Indian nationals in the matter of purchase, sale and transfer of property on the questionable ground of domicile. The very idea of domicile-based discrimination is a flagrant violation of the conceptual ideal of secularism. Yet another example is the deliberate non-implementation for the last five decades of Article 44 which envisions the enactment of a uniform civil code for all citizens, irrespective of their religion or caste. These are some of the glaring instances of the Indian state functioning in an anti-secular and communally partisan manner. To sum up, in India almost all essential components of secularism are more honoured in breach than in observance.

Let us make a cursory comparison of our "perverse secularism" with the secular framework of the United Kingdom, a country often cited as role model for India's parliamentary democracy. In the UK uniform civil and criminal laws have been enacted for all religious groups and communities and these are equitably applied to all citizens, without making any exception. In the eyes of the law all citizens are equal irrespective of their gender, creed, religious beliefs, and modes of worship. Equal respect for all faiths and equal treatment of people belonging to diverse religious groups is the quintessential hallmark of secularism. Unfortunately that high ideal, a vital component of the secular ideology, is totally missing in the Indian theory and practice of secularism. The constitutional and legal position of secularism is more or less the same in almost all European democracies and America. Yet the British commitment to the secular ideal has not deterred the state from declaring itself a "Christian" nation. The monarch ascending the throne, whether the queen or the king, invariably assumes the title of "Defender of Faith". Interestingly in the UK all important state functions like the coronation and inauguration of the Parliament session are accompanied by a Christian prayer, often led by the Archbishop of Canterbury himself. But that does not detract from the state's commitment to secularism. In sharp contrast, the system which India has evolved is a putrid and perverse kind of secularism. It could more appropriately be called pro-Muslim minorityism because among all minorities it favours only the Muslims, while denying any favour to the Parsis and other communities. The banning of Salman Rushdie's Satanic Verses under pressure of fundamentalist groups, and overturning of Supreme Court's verdict in Shah Bano case by enacting a special law in 1986 to deny to the divorced Muslim women their rightful claim to maintenance under the law are glaring examples of rampant communal discrimination taking precedence over the basic secular principles of natural justice and equality before law. The favours to the biggest minority community are often resorted to with impunity at the highest level solely with a view to garnering their votes. While analysing the secular claims of Marxists and others of their ilk, Bhibhuti Bhusan Nandy, a retired officer of Research and Analysis Wing, has drawn attention to certain pro-Muslim traits prominently displayed by the leftist regime of West Bengal. First, the Marxists adopt a discriminating approach in practising secularism when their ministers boycott Saraswati Vandana at public functions and cut out invocation to Ganesha from Chhou dance and yet continue to sit through recitation of Quran at public functions. Second the Marxists did not have the courage to take action against fundamentalist Muslim clerics who issued a fatwa towards the end of year 2004, proclaiming social and economic boycott of twenty-odd families of Muslim bauls (traditional bards well versed in religious songs) for singing Bengali songs preaching peace and unity among followers of different faiths. The same Marxist regime had no compunction in banning Tasleema Nasreen's *Dwikhandita* under pressure from fundamentalist Mullahs. Although Nandy does not mention it, one of the Mullahs, a cleric preaching at Tipu Sultan mosque of Kolkata, openly instigated the faithful to assault and humiliate the author of *Dwikhandita* and *Lajja* by blackening her face. He even announced a cash reward to any Muslim who was willing to intimidate Tasleema Nasreen by blackening her face. Yet the self-styled secular government of West Bengal, swearing by the Marxist ideals, took no action against the Muslim cleric who was prima facie guilty of committing the serious non-bailable offence of criminal intimidation, punishable under sections 503, 504 and 506 of Indian Penal Code. The third act of blatant discrimination practised by the State government, as highlighted by Nandy, is even more astonishing. West Bengal government spends more than rupees 15 crores annually on madarasas which largely focus on teaching Quran and Hadees, including the doctrine of jihad, or holy war against infidels, to children of impressionable age. Prima facie any financing of hate-spewing communal ideology militates against the secular ideal. It also goes against the Marxist claim of promoting secular thought and inter-community peace and harmony. Interestingly the same Marxist government treats Sanskrit seminaries (known as Tols) in a highly discriminating manner by virtually refusing to support them financially. And the reason given for this indefensible discrimination, according to a former head of the Sanskrit department of Calcutta University (known for his proximity to the leftist regime), was that the teaching of Sanskrit would increase the influence of the Rashtriya Swayamsewak Sangh! For exposing the sham-secularism of Marxists, Bibhuti Bhushan Nandy deserves applause from all secular Indians. He has cited several interesting examples of Marxist duplicity. Just sample this one which takes the cake for practising the fine-tuned stratagem for deceiving the electorate. Some years ago, during an earlier Id celebration, a former State minister who is now a sitting Member of Parliament, led the namaz on the Red Road in full glare of television. Prima facie that may not be considered as something objectionable but it becomes questionable because Marxists always emphasise the need to avoid public participation in religious functions, especially those of Hindus. The most shocking instance of Marxist deception to bluff the gullible Hindu voters was seen when the same Marxist politician during the last parliamentary elections prefixed the word "comrade" to his name in the wall-writings across the areas inhabited by the majority community (read Hindus), but dropped the Marxist prefix in the wall-writings in the Muslim dominated areas where instead his name "Mohammed" was used to garner votes of his community.[5] The motto of the CPI(M) seems to be "secularism be damned, long live crescentic minorityism"! The sole aim of Marxists appears to be to garner votes for riding back to power by hoodwinking both Hindus and Muslims. Lastly, the Marxist regime has singularly failed to check Bangladeshi infiltration. According to Nandy, the subversive and criminal activities of illegal immigrants have created so much insecurity in the border areas that many original inhabitants (read Hindus) have been forced to leave the affected border areas "in droves", after selling their houses and lands at throw away prices to Muslims. All this was being done by Marxists and their so-called secular supporters to secure the crucial 23.6 per cent Muslim votes to retain political power.[6] According to Census 2001, the proportion of Muslims in West Bengal has now risen to 25.25 per cent, substantially higher than 23.6 per cent recorded in 1991. In any case, by practising sheer duplicity and open support to communal and casteist political forces the Marxists of India have emerged as frontrunners in the race for a trophy in obscurantism!

Apart from the specific provision for application of different legal systems for the citizens belonging to different faiths, one often hears frequent political pleas to introduce religion-based reservations in government jobs and educational institutions as has been done recently in June 2005 in Andhra Pradesh. The most perverse instance of Muslim appeasement was the attempt to communalise India's defence services by the Justice Sachar Committee by collecting data about the so-called shortfall in representation of Muslims – a short sighted divisive ploy resorted to in February 2006. The same strategy of communal reservations is now being openly mouthed and propagated in U.P. and Bihar to win Muslim votes. Frankly, in view of the instances cited above no more proof is needed to prove that India is patently an anti-secular country. In fact, the Indian brand of secularism emphasises only three things. First, the State and its laws must discriminate against the majority community, that is the Hindus and allied religious groups. Second, the state apparatus must be used to promote anti-Hindu thoughts and actions. And third, undue favours must be showered on only one single community and no other minority group. As a rule, secularism should have meant complete disassociation of the State and its functionaries from all religious beliefs and treating all religions in a transparently just and equitable manner. But that is just not done in India.

This new breed of left-oriented Hindus have come to pose serious challenge to Indian civilizational values. They have been on rampage now for quite sometime past. Recently Mani Shankar Aiyer, a Cabinet Minister and poster boy of sham secularism, has penned a patently anti-secular tome, *The Confessions of A Secular Fundamentalist* (Penguin Viking 2004), which highlights his anti-Hindu mindset. An objective reading of Aiyar's book gives the feeling of being led around on a guided tour of a grotesque construct of sham secularism and Islamic fundamentalism. As pointed out by R. Jagannathan, Mani Aiyar's book shows what is wrong with Indian brand of secularism. It calls for an extreme variety of secular doctrine in which the entire burden of making secularism a success in India will have to be borne by the majority community, i.e., the Hindus. He therefore concludes that Aiyar's secularism is a fraud. Jagannathan has rightly observed that apparently most Hindu critics of Hinduism are victims of their own low sense of self-esteem.[7] It goes without saying that all pseudo-secular Hindus suffer from a low sense of self-esteem because they have lost their civilizational moorings; otherwise they won't readily join the tribe of Hindu-haters. It is because of this low self-esteem that some secularitis-seized members of Hindu society want to promote crescentic fundamentalism in India. No wonder Aiyar has even a word of praise for Aurangzeb's bigoted zeal for demolishing Hindu and Jain temples. He also ignores persistent persecution of Sikhs by Muslim rulers and shows no respect for history and historians by casually dismissing the well documented atrocities by Muslim rulers on their Hindu subjects as imagined wrongs. By shunning any rational analysis of the innumerable violent attempts of Muslim rulers to subjugate and convert Hindus as events of no historical consequence, he has revealed his animus towards Hindu civilization. At the end of his book Aiyar has appended a set of 16 cleverly devised questions which he has tried to answer himself. In quite a few cases he has answered the questions by recourse to convoluted logic. For example, on the question of introducing a common civil code, as envisioned in Article 44 of the Constitution, he admits that the State of Goa has a long record of common civil code introduced by the Portuguese rulers. But in his true fundamentalist style he dismisses its propriety and usefulness by saying that "the code was imposed by a totally non-democratic foreign imperialist power that had captured Goa after defeating the ruling Muslim dynasty".[8] And then comes his Pope-like pontification : "We can never replicate the methods of these proselytizing communalists — nor would we wish to".[9] What perverse logic, what prevarication, dear fundamentalist? Pray, then explain why have we retained hundreds of good laws like the Child Marriage Act, Prevention of Sati Act, and the Indian Penal Code and Criminal Procedure Code, enacted by the equally colonialist British rulers. And one more question. Were Portuguese the only colonial and proselytizing rulers? How about the Muslims, how about the British? They too had colonized India and embarked on campaigns of large scale conversions. In fact, Muslim rulers had always used wanton violence and brute force to spread Islam throughout India, nay across the globe, on a scale much larger than the Portuguese or the English. A great part of Aiyar's book is short on logic and long on anti Hindu diatribe and his blind approval of separatist Islamic fundamentalism is writ large all over the text. There are quite a few inconsistencies propagated by Aiyar through his book which need not be commented upon here. The broad parameters of Aiyar's secular fundamentalism appear to be somewhat similar to Jinnah's deceptive secularism which invariably sought to give preference to claims of Muslim minority over the Hindu majority of the undivided sub-continent. Left to themselves perhaps, Aiyar and other members of sham-secular brigade would like to supplant the glorious Hindu civilization root and branch from Indian soil and replace it with the crescentic cactus nurtured by them for decades. Their pronounced hostility to Hinduism brings to lips an ancient prayer: "O God, save us from our friends, we shall take care of our foes."

Nevertheless credit must be given to Mani Shankar Aiyar for his frankness in openly denouncing Hindu ethos while supporting the Muslim cause to hilt, including the latter's non-acceptance of small family norm and the custom of triple talaq prevalent in Islamic societies which violently violates the principle of gender equality. Unlike other secularitis-seized Hindus he has displayed considerable candidness by rallying forth to support obscurantism of his Muslim constituency by justifying even demolition of temples and gross atrocities committed on Hindus during the long span of Muslim rule. He is openly pro-Muslim, unlike most other sham-secular politicians who often try to hide their disdain for Hindu ethos behind veiled rhetoric and inane platitudes. Frankness is undoubtedly a plus point for Aiyar, it must be conceded.

Surely there is something morbid and ugly in the present day spectacle of educated Hindus berating their ancient ethos and civilizational values. In this context, for the benefit of our younger generations, it may be worthwhile to recall the exhortations of Dr. Annie Besant, who was President of the Indian National Congress in 1917, calling upon Hindus to defend and guard their faith and motherland. In a soul-stirring call to the Hindu society she spoke thus :

"If Hindus don't maintain Hinduism, who shall save it ? If India's own children don't cling to their faith, who shall guard it ? Indians alone can save India, and India and Hinduism are one."

But in today's decadent cultural milieu, dominated by self-serving political buccaneers, who bothers for Annie Besant? The new crop of sham-secularists won't even know who she was and how enormous was her contribution to our freedom movement. The present tribe of sermonising secularists is utterly incapable of fully comprehending the intensity of Annie Besant's commitment to the Hindu ethos of India and the sacrifices made by that great patriot and lakhs of Indian foot soldiers, mostly Hindus and Sikhs, for India's freedom in the last century.

Rejoinder of Tavleen Singh

Interestingly during the recent spell of heaping wanton insults on Hindus and Hindutva, when most columnists and analysts, shrank back from picking up the gauntlet of morbid drivel, it fell to the lot of an intrepid Sikh lady, Tavleen Singh, a no-nonsense columnist, to take up cudgels on behalf of the mild-manned Hindus and wavering intellectuals of the community. In a stinging rejoinder to the relentless tirade of fundamentalist secular brigade on Hindu identity, she wrote a refreshingly punch-packed article in *The Indian Express* in June 2004.[10] Frankly without quoting verbatim from her article, it would be impossible to do justice to Tavleen Singh's facile and powerful pen. In her inimitable style she wrote:

"My inner voice is a bit of a nag and I might have told it to shut up, had Madhu Kishwar not drawn my attention to the need for someone to examine how many times the word Hindu is used pejoratively. You might find, she said ominously, that it is used mostly in pejorative terms. After this I began to read and listen more carefully to "secular" voices and found to my horror that Madhu was right, Hindu fanatic, Hindu fundamentalism, Hindu nationalist, Hindutva mostly, that is how the word Hindu gets used and nearly always pejoratively."

Tavleen continues candidly and boldly. "I am not a Hindu, but with this I have a serious problem because the debate appears no longer confined to the cloistered world of priests, or even the self-serving ones of politics; it has expanded into a challenge to Hindu civilization. So one of our new secular ministers tells us that the Sindhu Darshan festival, started by the last government to celebrate the river India gets her name from, will be made less communal." "Excuse me?"[11] She rightly points out that no Indian can be proud of our glorious heritage if he or she knows nothing about the roots of Hindu civilization. Unfortunately we Indians have denied our glorious heritage for the last fifty years. Drawing attention to the havoc caused to the world by Semitic religions, she concludes that "Hindu civilization is something of which I am very proud of. If that is evidence of my being "communal", then my inner voice tells me, so be it."[12]

Every true Indian must salute Tavleen Singh for giving a befitting reply to the reams of secular graffiti printed and circulated endlessly by self-styled secularists and rabble rousing leftists all over the country.

Demographic Threat

The most important threat to the Hindu society, however, comes from the fast changing demography of the country. Adverse demography is not merely a challenge to Hindus, it is a challenge to the entire Indian nation, including the Sikhs, the Jains, the Buddhists and the Christians. Indeed it has all the ingredients of an existential challenge for India's secular ethos. In the long run it will pose a challenge even to the existence of our pro-Muslim secular fundamentalists and comrades, as already analysed and explained in a previous chapter. The former have only to look at the happenings in the next-door Bangladesh where the recently arrested "Banglabhai", a typical Islamist phenomenon, has been busy hunting the communists and leftists, along with ethnic cleansing of the timeless targets, the Hindu infidels.

The day of reckoning for Indian society is drawing close because of the looming threat of adverse demography which could make the Hindus, Sikhs, Jains and allied religious groups lose majority status in large parts of their own homeland, or at least in certain crucial States, during the next forty to fifty years — may be even earlier. Democracy is essentially a game of numbers. Elections to govern the country will always be won or lost on the basis of population numbers. But how to convey that message to the vast majority living in villages and small towns, totally oblivious of the menace. That is the core of Hindu dilemma. Anybody seeking to administer the country through elections has to have maximum people on board and must have the long term perspective of national interest. Let us not forget that India will remain a secular country only so long as the fraternity of Hindus and allied faiths constitutes the majority population.

A mere glance at the religious composition of the cohorts in the 0-6 years age group, as given in the Census 2001, will convince even the most die-hard sceptical critics about widespread adverse demographic changes likely to envelope India in the near future. Yet there is no urgency at any level in the government, or in societal institutions, about the urgent need to devise a multi-pronged survival strategy.

It is time that Hindus reorganised and modernize themselves and threw out all dogmas, false rituals and obscurantism. The orthodox among them have not only to change their outlook but also their social mores, though the traditional Hindu ethos of "universal humanism" has to be protected. Hinduism must not become a hostage to petty and peripheral issues. The fraternity of Hindus and allied faiths, call them Omkar Parivar if you will, must make a new resolve to ensure survival of their identity and heritage at all costs. This, however, can no longer be taken for granted because of the continuous decline in their percentage share in India's population, particularly along India's borders during the last 120 years. And that adverse demographic trend has gathered a huge momentum after independence primarily because a large majority of Hindus and allied religious groups have readily adopted the small family norm. In the circumstances, the future of Hindus and allied faiths cannot be taken for granted in the face of adverse demography and growing threat of jihadi terrorism. As explained elsewhere, lately even Christians of north-eastern region have realized this threat.

In an interesting analysis of the developing threat to India, Prakash Singh, a retired Director General of Police, has referred to the viewpoint of a controversial intellectual who once said that there were only two possible solutions to the persistent problem of communal conflict in India. One solution was that all Muslims should become Hindus, while the second solution was that all Hindus should become Muslims. It was argued by the same intellectual (name withheld by Prakash Singh) that Muslims being what they are will never opt for Hindu faith and therefore the only alternative was for the Hindus to embrace Islam, if the communal question is to be resolved. Prakash Singh concedes that the proposed solution will outrage the majority community, i.e., the Hindus but candidly posits the million dollar question: are we, the Indians, not already moving in that direction?[13] The ethnic cleansing in Kashmir by driving out lakhs of Pandits, the persistent persecution of Hindus and Buddhists in Bangladesh, the massive infiltration from Bangladesh causing Hindus to become a minority in 6 districts of Assam and the sharp growth of Muslim numbers in West Bengal and Bihar clearly point to the turmoil likely to overwhelm India in the near future. Prakash Singh has referred to the resolve of an important Lashkar-e-Tyeba leader who declared that his organisation would not rest till the Islamic flag flies on Red Fort. Was he day dreaming, asks Prakash Singh?[14]

Frankly, the Indian society has yet to throw up a dynamic and daring leader willing to meet the jihadi challenge head on with equal measure of determination, albeit without blabbering and with poise and equanimity. There is certainly a drought of dynamic and daring leaders among Indian politicians, especially the Hindus.

It is time to carry the warning about the threat of fast changing demography and its far reaching implications across the country to the uneducated and ill-informed Hindu masses, mostly living in the countryside. They must be awakened to the fact that during the last century adverse demography had changed the destinies of several countries and civilizations, including India which went through the trauma of partition solely because of the numbers game in which the Hindus and allied religious groups lost. The educated middle class, opinion-maker intellectuals and semi-literate and illiterate Hindu masses must be apprised of the fate which befell the Christians of Lebanon (reduced to a helpless minority within a few decades) and the similar fate which overtook the Christian Serbs in Kosovo and Bosnia because of the sharp increases in population of Muslims. Both in Lebanon and the Balkans the population changes were accompanied by high voltage civil strife involving huge loss of life and property. Though ultimately the once-upon-a-time majority community i.e. Christians were reduced to minority status, the embers of strife continue to smoulder in Lebanon.

The impending demographic threat should be an eye-opener for all Hindus, including leftists suffering from gross vision deficit induced by the opiate of secular fundamentalism. They should realise that after Islamists take over this country, their plight will be similar to or even worse than that of the communists of erstwhile Yugoslavia, now reduced to a truncated and embattled Serbia — with the former Communist President of that country, Slobdan Milosevic, dying in prison, after being incarcerated by the International Court in Hague. It is time to tell the Hindu masses frankly that unless they counter the demographic threat and take effective steps to reform, re-engineer and reinvigorate the Hindu society, their future generations will face a bleak future. Niall Ferguson's warning that in the next 50 years Europe is likely to become a Muslim majority continent, and the suggestion made by some wisecracks to rename it as 'Eurabia' has already made the Christian Europe sit up and take notice. But there is hardly any awakening in India. Several countries are trying to re-invent and re-order themselves demographically in a bid to counter the impending threat. In a bid to step up their declining populations many European countries like Sweden, France and Italy have announced liberal cash bonuses to pressurise young couples to opt for more babies. In the U.K. serious questions have been raised about the validity of the concept of multiculturalism and the Prime Minster Tony Blair, has started advising young couples to opt for the 5 children norm, even though just now the immigrants constitute less than 6 per cent of Britain's population. In most European countries there is a complete about turn from the erstwhile emphasis on small families. The tremors of the coming demographic threat are felt even in the far away Australia, paranoid by the growing population of jihad-infested Indonesia. In Australia, too, a specific provision for cash bonuses has been introduced and young couples are being advised to have more babies, at least 3, preferably many more.

Unfortunately while the western nations have woken up, in the Hindu society, especially the masses living in rural areas, there is very little awareness about the impending demographic threat because the Hindu leadership has kept this serious threat under wraps. It is time this problem of adverse demography was brought out of closet and openly debated across the country so that the Hindu masses become aware of the difficult times ahead for their future generations. Most leading politicians at national level, especially the Muslims and secular fundamentalists, have been fully aware of the gigantic demographic transformation. Yet the Hindu leadership has withheld the sharp contours of this devastating faultline not only from the multitude of Hindu masses, but even from the middle class opinion-makers. Madhu Limaye was a well known socialist and a die-hard secularist. While referring to the explosive growth of Muslim population and decline in the Hindu percentage, he wrote way back in January 1986 a very perceptive article which was reprinted in *The Muslim India* (a journal formerly brought out by Syed Shahabuddin) saying that it looked certain that the Hindus were a dying race, as warned by Swami Shradhanand decades ago. Madhu Limaye predicted that in the coming decades there will be a sharp decline in Hindu population and may be by 2300 A.D. they might lose the majority status in India. After that there will be a precipitate Hindu decline and they will become extinct in this ancient land of theirs.[15] He bemoaned that though there was much that was bad in Hinduism (also in Buddhism, Jainism and Sikhism, according to Madhu Limaye), yet there was something priceless too. Thanks to the stupidity, social exclusiveness and cowardice of Hindus in the past millenium that 'priceless something' which is "the heritage of the entire human race will disappear and that makes me sad. ...."[16] In his controversial book, *Communal Rage in Secular India*, late Dr. Rafiq Zakaria, too has alluded to the fact that Hindus are likely to become a minority community in India by the year 2300 A.D. Yet he emphasized, perhaps by way of condescending consolation, that there was no demographic threat to the majority status of Hindus in the immediate future. The truth, however, is altogether different as is evident from our detailed analysis of population trends presented in chapter 2. Though Hindus might not become a minority in India in the near future, the dangerous denouement of Hindus losing majority status in several parts of India, including Assam, West Bengal, Bihar, etc., is likely to take place much earlier — may be even before the end of the present century. Islam being a congregational religion, the vast majority of Muslims are already aware of this developing demographic trend through the medium of mosque and madarasas. But unfortunately the Hindus and Sikhs masses are totally unaware of this danger.

It must be reiterated that Madhu Limaye and other prophets of doom forecasting decimation of Hindu identity will be ultimately proved wrong. The fact remains that the Hindus cannot and will not become a minority in India easily, not at least in the next 100 or even 300 years. The instinct for self-preservation and survival is uppermost in the consciousness of every human being and the Hindu society, approaching one billion mark, cannot be an exception to this primordial trait. It is, however, correct that dulled by repetitive overdoses of tolerance, the Hindu reflex has become so slow that unless danger stares them in the face they don't react. But once awakened they can surely take care of themselves and their civilizational values. If despite centuries of persecution first by militant Islam in the seventh century and then by Nazis in the twentieth century to annihilate them by genocide, the identity of Jews could not be obliterated, how and why will the one billion strong Hindu civilization become extinct ? Demographic changes will not sweep and dismember the entire country in one go. The impending change will surely happen, but only by stages, and after considerable civil strife and bloodshed — much more extensive and diabolical than that what was witnessed during India's partition. In first place attempts will be made by the Islamists to yank away Assam and some other north-eastern States due to demographic changes and religion-based faultline conflicts. Logically there will be resistance and some fight back leading to migration of Hindus from Assam. Then the malaise might engulf West Bengal and Bihar. Later on it might even travel to Uttar Pradesh. If the events of Lebanon and the Balkans could be taken as examples, as soon as Assam and north-eastern states reach the stage of secession there might be a cascading effect caused by large scale movement of population from one area to another — something similar to what had happened before and during India's partition in 1947. And that will shock and jolt the somnolent Hindu society into action – perhaps some belated stupid reaction which could take a terrible shape. After all, in recent years the comparable events in the Balkans did result in violence and massive mayhem. In view of the sheer size of Hindu numbers, nearly one billion plus by 2020 or 2040, it could lead to widespread civil commotion and bloody strife. Where will it end no one can forecast, not at least today. Perhaps due to civil strife India will break up into a number of states, mostly having Hindu majority, though some may be Muslim dominated. And there is a strong probability that after being fed up with the repetitive Islamic onslaughts, the second one during the last one hundred years, finally one or more militant Hindu dictatorships might come into existence to counter the fundamentalist menace and thereby rule over the divided states of India, mostly Hindu dominated. Frankly, there is already a cross-section of public opinion in the Hindu middle class nurturing the belief that only a brief spell of military rule can ward off the existential threat posed to the secular Indian identity by our two aggressively fundamentalist neighbours. Undoubtedly the day the democracy folds up in India will be a sad day. The responsibility for such a denouement culminating in decimation of democracy will, however, squarely rest with our mainstream casteist and sham-secularist political class which has no commitment, no vision and no ideal.

It may be recalled that when the Muslim population crossed the threshhold of 40 per cent in the erstwhile communist and secularitis-infected Yugoslavia, all hell broke loose. The Serb leadership was in the hands of Communists, all die-hard secularists, some even more committed than our own home-grown brand of sham-secularists. Slobadan Milosevic was the Chairman of the Socialist Party of Serbia (read Communist Party).

But when Kosovar Muslims aided by Albanian jihadis started ethnic cleansing of the minority Serb population of Kosovo, Milosevic and his select team of communists turned aggressive nationalists. That happened entirely due to a call given by 200 Serb intellectuals, retired army officers and journalists to save the Serb identity and their heritage which led to sudden revival of the instinct for self-preservation and soon self-interest got better of the communist ideology nurtured for decades among the Serbs. In a jiffy the primordial urge for survival overtook the communist leadership and obliterated all traces of Serb secularism, including the much-touted socialist ideals. Ultimately the uncontrollable violent events took such an ugly turn that Milosevic and his communist team-mates lost head and resorted to large scale atrocities on Muslims by using the Serb militia as an oppressive tool. With the benefit of hindsight soon the Serbs realized that they have paid a heavy price for their decades long foolish dalliance with secularism and communism. But in the meantime immense damage had been done to the Serb cause and Kosovo, the so-called Jerusalem of Serbia (we had better call it Haldighati of Serbs), has been permanently lost for all practical purposes. Hopefully the national leadership of India, including Marxists, will learn some lessons from the fate of the Balkans and Lebanon, even at this belated stage.

Countering the Threat

Prima facie there is no reason why those Hindus and Sikhs who are financially well off and can afford to bring up more children should limit their family size to two or three. They must understand that it is preferable to have four children and one car rather than opting for two children and three cars. Surely the development and prosperity of Indian nation is an important economic objective, but ensuring long term independence of the country and securing the future of younger generations by continuing the momentum of progress are decidedly far more important national goals. Neither independence, nor unity and security of the future generations can be mortgaged for the sake of greater prosperity of the present population of Indians. In the long run only a balanced growth of population among all religious groups will guarantee the continuation of a secular and pluralist social order. It is now admitted by economists worldwide that the real enemy of prosperity is not, repeat not, population growth. It is lack of education and skill. Population is not a liability, but an asset because it provides youthful manpower. India has a population density of 324 persons per km, while Japan has a density of 335. Yet Japan is prosperous, India is poor. Is it not a paradox that Bolivia with population density of 5 is poor and therefore overpopulated, while Singapore with a density of 5088 per km. is prosperous despite having no mineral wealth or green hinterland growing plentiful crops of grains, fruits and vegetables? And the splendid spell of prosperity forecast by economists for India during the next 20 to 30 years will be entirely due to the increase in our youthful working population. It is time we got rid of the old Malthusian notion of population being a liability. Economists worldwide now agree that population, also known as human resource, is a huge productive asset, provided it is educated and skilled. The real roadblocks to prosperity are illiteracy, ignorance and lack of occupational skills—not population numbers.

We should remember that if freedom is lost, or should the country go through another partition and spell of bloodshed, as happened 59 years ago in the sub-continent and recently in the Balkans, that will spell end of the road for India's prosperity as well as its future ambition to emerge as a global power. In any case, the entire burden of population planning need not be carried by the fraternity of Hindus and allied faiths. They have already contributed more than their proportionate share. That message must go out boldly to all Hindus, Sikhs, Jains and Buddhists, in no uncertain terms, especially in rural areas. Family planning may be practiced only by those Hindus and Sikhs who are pitiably poor and unable to earn two square meals a day.

Without trying to sound alarmist it has to be recognized that the Hindus, to use a corporate jargon, are slowly but surely being subjected to creeping mergers and acquisitions. The large scale infiltration from Bangladesh can be described as adverse merger. As mentioned elsewhere, according to a

Bangladeshi demographer, Sarifa Begum, approximately 14 million Bangladeshis had sneaked into India during the one single census decade of 1981-91. The silent invasion continues unabated and the total number of illegal foreigners and their progeny is now estimated to be over 30 millions, or more than 3 crore. And they have penetrated deep into various parts of India, including Mumbai and Delhi. In West Bengal, Assam and other States of North East such infiltration is now posing a serious and imminent challenge to the existence of local populace. Lately many Hindu families in border districts of Assam and West Bengal, overwhelmed and overrun by illegal infiltrators, are reported to have relocated to safer habitats. Many more will move out soon.

Similarly the growing campaigns for conversion, mostly of the poor and illiterate Hindu tribals, could be classified as creeping acquisitions which have to be countered and contained at grassroots level by reforming and reinventing the Hindu society.

In Jammu and Kashmir a demographic change has already been forced on non-Muslims. The religious and cultural practice of annual yatra to Amarnath which has been in vogue since times immemorial, has become a regular target of Jihadis. Even the pilgrims going to Vaishno Devi are not spared. And unless urgent remedial measures are adopted, both Hindus and Sikhs in the violent valley could end up as museum pieces.

This is a time for strategic introspection by the political and spiritual leaders of the Hindus and allied faiths. One important step towards restructuring the Hindu society could be to summon a major conclave of representatives of all sections of the Hindu community from the four corners of India, including all reform-minded religious leaders and preachers. The Hindu society must make bold to abolish all caste distinctions in one go and once for all. A Mahayagna should be organised on the pattern of the one held several hundred years ago in the Aravalli hills, perhaps at Mount Abu, when a similar crisis situation arose for the embattled Hindu civilization because of rapid decimation of Kshatriya warriors while battling the hordes of invaders. At that critical time by common consensus it was considered essential to co-opt scores of non-Kshatriya clans and tribal communities into the Kshatriya fold by baptising them as "warriors" through the medium of a formal yagna or "havan". And by that single fiat they came to be known as "Agnikula" Rajputs. The result was electrifying and the crisis was overcome by adding a new crop of youthful warriors to fight the onslaught on dharma and freedom.

It may be recalled that Muslim atrocities reached its peak during the reign of Mughal ruler Aurangzeb who resorted to senseless killings of innocent masses and razed hundreds of temples. While the renowned Hindu warrior Shivaji rallied brave Marathas to join the battle against Aurangzeb's savagery in western India and established a Hindupad Padshahi, another saviour of the oppressed masses rose in north India. Born in Patna in 1666, he was the famous tenth Guru of Sikhs, the Warrior Saint, Guru Gobind Singh, who challenged the might of Mughal empire by taking up arms. Before doing so, however, he wrote a letter to the Mughal emperor, Aurangzeb, in which he warned that when "all other means have proven ineffective, it is right then to take up the sword."[17] Those were difficult times for the hopelessly disunited Hindu society, deeply divided by caste-based discrimination and trapped in meaningless rituals. On the auspicious day of Baisakhi in 1699, the great Guru created "Khalsa" by baptising five mild and meek Hindus handpicked from different castes and regions of India whom he imbued with rare zeal to fight for dharma and justice. The five disciples handpicked by Guru Gobind Singh came from different castes, including the highest and the lowest, and belonged to different regions of Bharat Varsha. Among them were Daya Ram Kohli, a Kshatriya from Lahore in the north, Dharam Dass, a Jat from Delhi, Mohkam Chand, a low-caste washerman from Dwarka (Gujarat) in the west , Himmat Rai, a cook from Jagannath Puri (Orissa) in the east, and Sahib Chand, a barber from Bidar in the south. The significance of the transformation brought by Guru Gobind Singh was that in one go he removed all inequalities and abrogated all religious prerogatives of higher castes. By moulding them into "Khalsa" he made all Hindus sit together, eat together and take up arms together to fight for their dharma and motherland. He was indeed a very worthy son of his worthy father, Guru Tegh Bahadur, who had sacrificed his life to protect the Hindu faith and honour of Kashmiri Pandits when the latter were ordered to embrace Islam on pain of death. Guru Gobind Singh was both a warrior and a learned scholar who led by personal example. Well endowed with knowledge of ancient scriptures he was a soldier par excellence and an accomplished poet. In one of the famous stanzas of his celebrated hymns, he prayed thus to Lord Shiva (God):

"De Shiva bar mohe aiyhe
Shubh karman te main kabhun na darun
Na darun ari se jab jaiye larun
Nishche kar apni jeet karun."

Translated into English it means: "O Shiva, grant me this boon that may I never turn away from doing good deeds, that may I always join the battle against the enemy fearlessly, and by your grace may I always emerge as victor by sheer resolve to win."

To raise a committed army to fight Aurangzeb's terror and tyranny he gave a wake up call to the Hindu society calling upon every mother to donate at least one son in the service of motherland, to be baptised as Sikh. And his strategic call did bring forth a tremendous response. Soon it became a universal custom among Hindus of Punjab to baptise the first son as a Sikh and dedicate him to the service of motherland and dharma. That was how the Mughals were defeated by the Sikhs and thrown out from the Punjab. To defend "dharma" and the oppressed masses, Guru Gobind Singh had to undergo immense persecution. Apart from the martyrdom of his father, his four sons Ajit Singh, Jujhar Singh, Zorawar Singh and Fateh Singh had to bear the brunt of Mughal emperor's wrath. Two of his sons were tortured and bricked alive in Sirhind fort under orders of Aurangzeb. Years later, Banda Bairagi alias Banda Bahadur, his warrior disciple from Maharashtra, avenged the dastardly killings of Guru's innocent children, by attacking and slaughtering the Mughal garrison at Sirhind and pillaging the Mughal encampment in the fort.

The difficult times presently facing India demand that all segments of the Hindu society, including the scheduled castes, the scheduled tribes and backward classes should be brought into the mainstream by abolishing all distinctions of caste and creed. Today in the echelons of political power there is hardly any Hindu identity because the already fractured Hindu society has been totally fragmented after Mandal Commission delivered a virtual coup de grace. There are hardly any Hindus left because most would now rather identify themselves as backwards, scheduled castes, Brahmins, Kshatriyas, Yadavas, Jats, Balmikis or Marathas, Tamilians and Punjabis. In such a scenario there is absolutely no chance of the voice of Hindu masses being heard in the corridors of power. The reverbrations of the shameful atrocities committed by some misguided Jats on hapless Balmikis of Gohana (Haryana) in the last week of August 2005 should serve as a warning to the leaders of Hindu society to reform themselves and get rid of all discriminatory and decadent religious practices. It is time to boldly carry out radical reforms and reinvent the Hindu faith by holding an all-encompassing representative conclave of different sections of Hindu society. The need of the hour is to confer the status of twice-born, that is "dwijya", on all categories of Hindus by throwing out all caste labels by means of a Mahayagna. Only such a bold and dynamic step, reminiscent of the one taken in the hoary past in the Aravalis in Rajasthan, and later on successfully repeated in the seventeenth century by Guru Gobind Singh at Anandpur Sahib in Punjab, is the pressing need of the hour. All community leaders and intellectuals of Hindu faiths should be involved in this national endeavour to unite, restructure and galvanize the Hindu society. A national level conclave of Hindus needs to be organised to take stock of the situation arising out of the double whammy of adverse demography caused by skewed acceptance of family planning by different religious groups and incessant influx of Bangladeshis which has tilted the balance against the Indian civilization. Later on, similar conclaves and yagnas could be held in every State to create mass awareness. Decades ago the murmurs of a folklore could be heard in the dusty villages located around Kala Amb in Haryana (close to the notorious battleground of Panipat) about how the Marathas had lost to the army of Ahmed Shah Abdali in the third battle of Panipat. According to the folklore, just the night before the day of the battle, when Abdali went around among his camping soldiers he saw a number of kitchen fires burning in the Maratha encampment across the river. Out of sheer curiosity he asked one of his commanders that why were there so many kitchen fires burning in the enemy camp. He was told that the Hindus were divided into a number of castes due to which they did not cook and eat together. His instantaneous response was: "Insha Allaha, then I will surely win tomorrow". The rest is history. And those who do not learn from history, as they say, are condemned to repeat it. That folklore at least should awaken the slumbering Hindu society.

It will do further good to the Hindu society if for the time being all controversial and peripheral issues are placed on the backburner.The focus should be on unifying the Hindu society by winning back into the Hindu fold all those who deserted it by opening the doors for return to their ancient faith, i.e., "ghar wapasi". For the time being there is no harm in adopting a rationalist approach, as was advocated by Swami Vivekananda and Veer Savarkar. Wisdom and sagacity should be the key watchwords in these times of existential crisis. The proposal to delete all objectionable references to lower castes from Hindu scriptures is a laudable initiative taken by the Chairman of the National Commission for Scheduled Castes, Dr. Suraj Bhan. It must be followed to its logical conclusion in order to stamp out untouchability and unify the Hindu community. The Chairman of the Commission for Scheduled Castes claims to have secured the support of the Sankaracharya of Sringeri Peetham in this endeavour and hopes to get similar response of from other Sankaracharyas and Dharmacharyas by "generating awakening" on the subject. It is a bold step in the right direction which must be supported by all sections of Hindu society.[18]

There is no point in ignoring the fact that in the ongoing global conflict between Islamist terror groups and civil society the Hindu masses and the Christian nations have been unwittingly cast in the role of long term partners. This global compulsive alliance is likely to last for many decades to come. A conscious effort should be made to eradicate the wrong impression being created all around that the Hindus are an anti-Christian community which surely they are not.

Need for Public Discourse

It is essential to bring out the questions relating to demographic changes out of closet for threadbare analysis and discussion. The impending demographic threat requires a country-wide candid discourse on religious and secular platforms, at national and state levels, in which Hindu masses as well as intellectuals of all hues, including the sham-secularists and leftists, should be encouraged to participate. Without such a "samvad" or open public debate it will be difficult to awaken the self-styled secularists and their camp followers to the true dimensions of the demographic threat facing India. Otherwise they will continue to mislead the gullible Hindu masses by deliberately belting out their trade mark dope-laced lullabies from multiple bandstands.

The proposed Hindu conclave must also consider various other options for evolving an effective national strategy, including the need for a more dynamic, energetic and vibrant leadership which will not shrink back from grappling with the multipronged assaults on Indian civilization. One of the most important steps to revitalise the Hindu society would be to assign a more dynamic and purposeful role to women whose participation in nation-building has to be substantially increased. It is not a difficult task because traditionally India has been the continent of Shakti and Hindus have worshipped Mother Goddess for thousands of years. Therefore all gender discrimination should be ruthlessly put down and weeded out. Obscurantist and discriminatory practices should have absolutely no space in Hindu homes. Let us not forget that for centuries Lakshmi, Durga and Saraswati have been our role models. Therefore vesting more power in Hindu women and ridding the Indian society of gender bias is an important goal which brooks no more delay. A frontal campaign must be launched to eradicate all evil practices. It is disgusting to read newspaper reports about occasional attempts to glorify the abhorrent cult of 'sati'. It is time to send out a clear message through opinion-makers, including Sadhvis, Dharamagurus and other religious preachers to illiterate Hindu masses that the 'sati pratha' is highly violative of the basic tenets of our scriptures. For enlightening the ignorant masses it must be highlighted that after the demise of Raja Dasarath, father of

Maryada Purushottam Ram, neither Kaushalya, nor any other queen took recourse to sati. They continued to live as householders and waited for the return of Sri Ram to see him ascend the royal throne. If mother of the Maryada Purushottam was not required to opt for 'sati' where is the justification for glorifying the medieval custom of sati now ? As pointed out in an illuminating article by O.P. Gupta, a Sanskrit scholar and serving diplomat, according to a shloka in Rig Veda (X.18.8) a Hindu widow was advised to return to the world of living beings and return alive to her home and return alive to her children. She could even take a new husband. Similarly the right of a Hindu wife to her matrimonial home is enshrined in Rigvedic Richas X.18.8 and X.85.42 which have to be recited at the time of marriage vows. The rights to matrimonial home of a Hindu wife are also reconfirmed in another marriage richa of Rig Veda (X.85.42).[19] This true path laid down in Vedas must be made known to millions of ignorant and illiterate Hindu masses, mostly spread out in rural countryside.

There is a widely prevalent foolish belief among urban middle class Hindus that since they have been living in this ancient land for the last 5000 years no one can harm them or overwhelm their identity. They don't realize that barely 1100 years ago Hindus and Buddhists were there in Afghanistan and beyond. More importantly during the last 59 years Hindus and Sikhs have been ethnically cleansed from Pakistan and Bangladesh and the last 15 years have seen the Hindus retreating from Kashmir Valley and fleeing from border districts of Assam and West Bengal.

Lastly, time has come to boldly remind the Hindu masses by relaying the wake up call to every village, every hearth and every home that those who don't learn from history will ultimately end up as bad history. That important lesson all Hindus and Sikhs must learn from our eerie, troubled past.

It is time to wake up to the call of history, our history and civilization whose very continuance is in peril. To listen to it is to live; to remain deaf or diffident, is to die. Each votary of our great anicent land has to make a choice - and act.

9

The Looming Threat Ahead

"There was a siege going on; it had been going on for a long time, but the beseiged themselves were the last to take notice of it".

Paula Fox

India seems to be moving inexorably towards turbulent times. No sane person could have imagined that the second publication of Prophet Muhammad's cartoons in some European journals in February 2006 and the subsequent visit of the US President, George Bush, to India in the first week of March, 2006 will cause widespread eruption of violent demonstration by the Muslim community across the country. As usual, the Muslim street embarked on the path of mindless violence in many cities and towns. But the concerned state governments made no attempt to meet the anticipated contingency of aggressive Muslim mobsters directing their ire against members of the majority community. The onslaught on Hindus was entirely in keeping with the long standing tradition of fundamentalist groups, unable to reach the real or imaginary culprit, taking recourse to venting their ire on the majority community. Similar violence had manifested way back August-September 1969 in attacks on Hindus in Ahmedabad (Gujarat) in the wake of a clash between the Jews and Palestinian Muslims over Al Aqsa mosque. Similarly in October 2002 five innocent persons lost their lives in a communal riot in Solapur (Maharashtra) when Jerry Falwell, an Irish clergy, wrote disparagingly against Islam in a French journal. In response to a call given by some Muslim organizations violent demonstrations were held over some slanderous remarks made in a French journal by Jerry Falwell, during which Hindus were targeted for no rhyme and reason.

The demonstrators agitating against Danish cartoons and their mentors knew very well that no Hindu had anything to do with the drawing or publication of the objectionable cartoons which first appeared in the Danish newspaper, *Jyllands-Posten*, in September 2005. Yet it was the Hindus alone, and members of no other community, who bore the brunt of the unprecedented mobilization of Muslim mobs by the community's leadership acting in cahoots with ever-opportunistic leftists. The spate of attacks on Hindus in several cities and towns like Hyderabad, Lucknow, Meerut and Muzaffarnagar conclusively proved that in recent years there has been a massive radicalization of the Muslim community. The scale of mobilization and deliberate targeting of Hindus further indicated that in many cities prior preparations had been made to unleash violence on unsuspecting citizens. In Lucknow the riotous mobs carrying unlicensed arms opened fire killing one hapless shopkeeper on the spot and then fought pitched battles in streets, not with police but with Hindus, because the former appeared to be absent as if by design!

At least four innocent persons were killed in the communal flare up in Lucknow alone. The demonstrators in many cities and towns hurled foul invectives at the visiting U S President, while unashamedly lionising the notorious terrorist Osama bin Laden whom they proclaimed as their role model. To the chagrin of sham-secular Hindu elite, in many towns thousands of demonstrators carried aloft kingsize photographs of bin Laden thus openly displaying their commitment to the cult of terror. Here and there one could also see streaming banners proclaiming the desire of demonstrators to resort to suicide bombing. The weird and horrifying spectacle of thousands of demonstrators carrying banners proclaiming their desire to act as suicide bombers and high-pitched slogans eulogizing Osama bin Laden gave a direct lie to the charade frequently mouthed by the sham-secularist lobby that there are no terrorists among Indian Muslims. Though publishers of cartoons were European Christians, the attacks of mobsters were directed solely against Hindus. No Christian was harmed.

The extensive participation by lakhs of Muslims in these demonstrations was nothing short of an open invitation to further terrorist attacks. Frankly speaking, the inexplicable recourse to widespread violence by aggressive Muslim rallyists was remniscent of the community's hostility against Hindus in the pre-partition years.

Jihad against Hindus

As if responding to the praises showered on bin Laden and his tribe of suicide bombers by thousands of Muslim demonstrators, within the next four days the Islamic terrorists struck with a vengeance on Tuesday, March 7, 2005, at the famous Sankatmochan temple in Varanasi. The three bomb blasts in the most sacred temple town of Hindus, easily comparable to what Mecca is to Muslims, resulted in death of 20 worshippers and injuries to nearly another 100 Hindus. The dastardly crime bore an uncanny resemblance to the bomb blasts which had rocked Delhi and caused heavy loss of life and property on the eve of the most important Hindu festival, Deepavali, in the last week of October 2005. It was yet another attack on the Hindu identity of the silent majority. It is jihad proper, raw and gory in its primitive form.

Time has come to speak out openly that a regular jihad is being waged by militant Islamic groups against Hindus in a bid to annihilate the centuries old civilizational ethos of India. The unending series of attacks on Hindus and their temples have all the trappings of a regular jihad ordained against infidels in the Islamic scriptures often cited by terrorists. Even though the soft Indian state and secularitis-benumbed media invariably try to conceal the truth, the fact remains that the ongoing repetitive targeting of the places of worship of Hindus and their pilgrims are part of a bigger design, perhaps a global design of the Muslim terror groups, to overrun India. It may be recalled that in October 2001, barely five weeks after the 9/11 attack on WTC, an announcement was made on Al Jazeera television by a representative of Al Qaeda proclaiming that in addition to the Crusaders and the Jews, the Hindu India shall be their target because of the alleged occupation of Kashmir and the so-called atrocities committed on Muslims. And within two months of that announcement the jihadi militants attacked the Indian Parliament on December 13, 2001. Yet no effective steps are being taken to meet the growing challenge of Islamic terrorism.

It is well known that during the last few years Hindu temples, religious festivals and pilgrims have been targeted with impunity by jihadi groups. Last year on July 5, 2005, a group of Lashkar-e-Tayeba goons tried to storm Ramjanambhoomi temple. Luckily they were killed by the alert CRPF contingent protecting the sacred shrine. In August 2003, Mumbai was rocked by twin bomb blasts near the Mumba Devi temple in which more than 50 people lost their lives. On September 24, 2002, an attack was mounted on Akshardham temple in Ahmedabad resulting in death of more than 30 worshippers. Earlier on August 6, 2002, nine innocent pilgrims proceeding to Amarnath temple in Kashmir valley were killed in a terrorist attack on Nunwan camp (near Pahalgam). Sri Raghunath temple at Jammu was targeted twice by jihadi groups once on March 30, 2002, and a second time on November 24, 2002. Over the years the terror groups, now deeply entrenched within India, have sent innumerable messages through regular bomb blasts and senseless killings that they will not allow the Hindus to live peacefully in their ancestral homeland. Their avowed objective is to convert India into Dar-ul-Islam and for achieving that goal they draw inspiration from the classic Quranic injunctions to attack and destroy all temples and idols of the infidels. Irrespective of the changing colours of the ruling political dispensation at the centre, the response of Indian government to the growing menace of jihad has been absolutely timid and weak-kneed - at times even cravenly submissive, as was evident in hasty repeal of the Prevention of Terrorism Act in 2004. The real tragedy, however, is that despite centuries old violent encounters with radical Islam, neither the Indian government, nor the Hindu society has learnt any lessons.

In sharp contrast to the timid response of the Indian state to the threat of Islamist terror, the USA, the UK and many other European governments have displayed better understanding of the threat posed to civil society by radical Islam. They have demonstrated their resolve by taking on the jihadi groups in a no-nonsense manner. The non-response of Indian government has naturally whetted the appetite of Islamic terrorists to attack Hindu civilisational ethos more ferociously and with greater determination. Indian government's monumental failure to decode the jihadi matrix and analyse their militant mindset is both intriguing and deplorable.

In openly trying to kill the so-called Hindu infidels and obliterate their religious identity the jihadi groups draw sustenance from the Preamble of Al Qaeda which proclaims that "Islamic governments have never been and will never be established by peaceful solutions and cooperative councils. They are established, as they have always been, by pen and gun, by word and bullet, by tongue and teeth". That is the real, raw and destructive face of militant Islam, now aggressively trying to overwhelm and subdue India.

Threat of Civil War

Despite shenanigans of naysayer secularist defenders of radical Islam, the fact remains that a feeling has grown in the Hindu community that India is moving in the direction of a civil war. Till recently the low-key discourse about the likelihood of a civil war erupting across the country was confined to hush-hush conversations in the drawing rooms of Luteyn's New Delhi and across sun-kissed lawns of South Delhi farmhouses. For a change, the possibility of the simmering discontent among Hindus caused by relentless attempts of Jihadis to destroy their religious identity culminating in a civil war was brought out, rather boldly, by the editor of *The Economic Times*, New Delhi, by initiating a debate on this politically shunned subject.[1] Despite divergent views expressed by the three experts selected by the editor, including Ved Marwah, a former Commissioner of Police, Delhi, who also held gubernatorial posts, Prof. Neerja Jayal of Jawaharlal Nehru University and Dr. Ajai Sahni of the Institute of Conflict Management about terrorism spiraling into a civil war, no one dare completely rule out the possibility of a civil strife engulfing the country.

Ordinarily a serious subject like the growing threat of civil war should have first received attention of prominent strategic analysts and mainstream politics-oriented newspapers and journals, especially because in recent months it has been frequently alluded to at informal gatherings not only in the national metropolis, but even in many other cities and mofussil towns. Unfortunately the prevalent culture of minority-appeasement afflicting our English-speaking middle class and leading lights of English media have not allowed the sensitive but highly relevant issue to be brought out of the closet of political correctness. That is how it fell to the lot of an unconventional, but bold editor of India's premier economics-oriented daily to break the deafening silence of perverse secularism. He has done well in throwing open this topical subject for public discourse.

The much feared civil war, spiralling out of widespread communal strife, is likely to be powered by the twin factors of fast growing jihadi attacks and galloping increase in the percentage of Muslim population. The religion-based faultline conflicts caused by the demographic decline of Hindus and allied faiths is bound to widen the growing communal divide. Anyone having his ears close to the ground can hear the rumblings of the coming strife in many parts of the country. Recently a friend had an occasion to visit certain rural areas of western Uttar Pradesh and what he saw and heard there was both revealing and alarming. Apart from the growing fear generated by whispers, hush-hush talk and rumours about collection of weapons and ongoing preparations for self-defence, the atmosphere of apprehension and hostility is visibly writ large across many rural areas of Muzaffarnagar, including Shamli and its neighbourhood, and in the countryside of Meerut and Ghaziabad districts. The unanimous call given by the Kerala Assembly seeking release on parole of the ace terrorist Abdul Nasser Madani of ISS (Islamic Sewak Sangh) and the recent outbreak of communal violence in Mau and then in Aligarh (Uttar Pradesh) in the first week of April 2006, during Ramnavami celebrations, did not come as a surprise to those who have been watching with dismay the galloping growth of radical Islam in India. Another good friend living in Kolkata informs me that similar conditions of fear and trepidation prevail not only in border areas of West Bengal, but in Kolkata city itself which has witnessed frequent sales of Al Qaeda sponsored Jihadi cassettes and CDs. Unless the central government comes down heavily on Islamic terrorists and their local collaborators boldly and effectively, the law and order situation is likely to get out of hand, sooner or later - perhaps much sooner than one can imagine.

Unfortunately there appears to be a political conspiracy of silence about protecting the identity of the majority community. How else could one explain the Goebblesian falsehood propagated day in and day out by proclaiming that there are no followers of Al Qaeda in India and that Islamic terrorists have no support base among Indian Muslims? Pray, then who were those thousands of demonstrators who eulogized bin Laden and offered to become suicide bombers during the March 2006 demonstrations against the visit of American President, George Bush? Let us not forget that according to intelligence sources there have been more than 700 terrorist attacks, some big some small, in various parts of the country during the last 5 years in which more than eight hundred Indian Muslims were involved. Many of them had been trained in Pakistan and Bangladesh. For instance, one of the key Jaish-e-Mohammed terrorists involved in July 2005 attack on Ramjanambhoomi temple was Maqbool Hussain, a resident of Dhubri in Assam. He had spent 5 long years (1992-97) studying in Deoband and had travelled to Bangladesh and Pakistan on strength of forged travel documents to receive training and instructions from jihadi masters. Quite a few among the perpetrators of the dastardly attack on Sankatmochan Temple in Varanasi are Indians and some of them had reportedly studied at Deoband (UP). Many more Indians have been found to be involved in terror attacks from time to time.

According to intelligence sources, the harmed militant outfit, SIMI (Students Islamic Movement of India) alone has thirty to forty thousand members, all bin Laden supporters, mostly working underground.

Defying the widely practised culture of political correctness, M.K. Narayanan, India's National Security Adviser, acknowledged in an interview to a television channel in the second week of March 2006 that jihadi groups have been recruiting Indian nationals for their operations.[2] Referring to Pakistan's strategy of involving Indian Muslims in acts of terror, he stated that there "is a very distinct attempt to alter the mix, if I may say so".[3] "We do find, here and there, individuals who are Indians who are getting involved in these offences", was his candid admission.[4]

The incompetence and dismal record of Indian government in firmly curbing terrorism has received flak in the latest United States Country Reports on Terrorism released in the last week of April 2006. It points out that in previous years terrorists staged hundreds of attacks on people and property and further records that "India's counter terrorism efforts are hampered by its outdated and overburdened law enforcement and legal systems". Frankly, it is beyond the political will of our weak-kneed government to smash hundreds of terrorists cell embedded within the country and punish their pay masters in our immediate neighbourhood.

Unfortunately despite centuries old experience of violent encounters with jihadi Islam neither the Indian government, nor the Hindu society, has learnt any strategic lesson. In sharp contrast to the Indian indifference, the USA and most European nations have shown better grasp of the problem. Immediately after the bomb attack on Sankatmochan temple in Varanasi, the well known spiritual leader, Sri Sri Ravi Shankar, was compelled to publicly state that the Hindus feel threatened in India. Horrified by the killings of praying worshippers in the Kashi temple, even the secular columnist, Renuka Narayan, made an appearance on a television channel and wailed that what Mecca was to Muslims, Kashi (Varanasi) was to Hindus.

The tragedy is that the Hindus want to protect their religious identity without standing up for it. That won't work. It is time Hindus realised that to meet the challenge of powerfully organised Islamic terror, backed by the worldwide ummah, they have to revitalize themselves by infusing massive doses of action-oriented energy, after getting rid of casteism, passivity and indolence. Unless that is done, it will be difficult to save India's civilisational identity. All true Indians must realize that today Jihad is the only fully globalised enterprise across the world. And Jihad Inc. have millions of shareholders and franchises in more than 60 countries. Therefore, time has come for Hindus to seize the initiative and reinvigorate and re-equip themselves for meeting the challenge in the difficult and dangerous decades ahead. It is foolish to expect that the *effete* political leadership alone at national level, irrespective of outward labels, will be able to protect India's civilizational identity.

India has already moved into dangerous decades, and turbulent times lie ahead. To the growing demographic challenge and jihadi terrorism, has been added the spectre of politically resurrected divisive caste conflicts recently witnessed across the country during the anti-reservation agitation.

Endnotes

Chapter - 1

1. Michael Meyer, Birth Dearth, *Newsweek*, October 11, 2004, pp. 40-42.
2. Ibid, p. 42.
3. An article titled 'Into The Woods', Stefan Theil, *Newsweek*, July 4, 2005, pp.31-32.
4. Ibid, p.32.
5. Ibid, p.34..
6. Michael Meyer, Birth Dearth, *Newsweek*, October 11, 2004, p.43.
7. Ibid, p.45
8. Ibid, p.43.
9. Source: BBC news, http://newsvote.bbc.co.uk.
10. Samuel P. Huntington, *The Clash of Civilization and The Remaking of World Order*, p.117
11. Source: BBC news, http://newsvote.bbc.com.uk_.
12. Ibid.
13. Source: http://www.mail.com/? sr=signup.
14. Ibid
15. Ibid.

16. Source: Population Reference Bureau, http://www.prb.org/template.cfm?.
17. Pentagon Files— Population Control as a Military Issue: Source: http://www.africa 2000.com/INDX/pentagon.htm. .
18. Ibid
19. Ibid.

Chapter – 2

1. Source: *Census of India, Report on Religion Data*, Statements 7 and 8b, pp. xlii and xiv respectively.
2. Source: Ibid. Statement 8a, p. (xiiv) of the Report.
3. Zoya Hasan and Ritu Menon, A Woman is a Woman is a Woman, *Indian Express*, September 22, 2004, p.9.
4. P.N. Mari Bhat and A.J.Francis Zavier, Role of Religion in Fertility Decline: The Case of Indian Muslims, *Economic & Political Weekly*, Mumbai, January 29, 2005, p.398.
5. Ibid.
6. Ibid.
7. News Item 'Delimitation: Mallapuram gets 4 more constituencies', *The Pioneer*, New Delhi, March 25, 2005, p.9.
8. N.H.F.S.-I report, pp. 97-98.
9. Ibid, p.138.
10. Ibid, p.149.
11. Ibid. *N.F.H.S-I Report, p.xxii.*

    (Ibid, p.xxv).

    (Ibid, p.65).

    (Ibid, p.69).

    (Ibid, p.84)

    (Ibid, p.109)

    (Ibid, p.117).

12. P.N. Mari Bhat, A.J. Francis Zavier, Role of Religion in Fertility Decline: The Case of Indian Muslims, *Economic and Political Weekly*, Mumbai, January 29, 2005, pp. 385-402.
13. Ibid, p. 385.
14. P.N. Mari Bhat, Trivialising Religion, *Economic and Political Weekly*, Mumbai, March 26, 2005, p.1376.
15. Ibid, p.1378.
16. Ibid, p.1379.
17. P.N. Mari Bhat and A.J. Francis Zavier, Role of Religion in Fertility Decline: The Case of Indian Muslims, *Economic and Political Weekly*, Mumbai, January 29, 2005, p.399
18. Macedonia on the edge, A vote on municipal boundaries threatens to open old conflicts. *The Economist,* October 16,2004, p.46.
19. *The Week*, London, July 31, 2004, p. 5.
20. Macedonia on the edge, A vote on municipal boundaries threatens to reopen the old conflicts, *The Economist,* October 16, 2004, p.46
21. Forum Mot Islamisering, The Demographic Bomb — When will Norway become a Muslim Country? [Source: http://fomi.ytring.dk/English/DemoBomb-E.htm.]
22. Alexander Nicoli, U.S. think tank's rosy picture, *Business Standard*, New Delhi, February 11, 2005
23. *Religious Demography of India*, p.37.

Chapter – 3

1. Rafiq Zakaria, Malic Mongers, and Abusaleh Shariff, Muslims Outnumber Hindus? Never, *The Pioneer,* New Delhi, October 2, 2004, p.7.
2. *Census of India 2001, The First Report on Religion Data,* Statement 1-a, p. xxviii.
3. Syed Shahabuddin, Muslim Indians in Census 2001: Rise in National Proportion and Fall in Growth Rate, *Mainstream,* October, 23, 2004.

4. Ahtesham Qureshi, *Hindustan Times,* New Delhi, July 9, 1995.

5. Varinder Singh, Dwindling Sikh population worries minorities panel, *The Tribune,* New Delhi, November 1, 2004, p.5.

6. Samuel Huntington, *The Clash of Civilizations And the Remaking of World Order*, p.117; Source: Spangler, Decline of the West I, pp.93-95.

7. A news item 'Do it for Country', *Hindustan Times,* New Delhi, May 13, 2004, p.1.

Chapter – 4

1. Bibhuti Bhusan Nandy, Space Invaders, *The Sunday Hindustan Times,* New Delhi, February 14, 2003.

2. Prakash Singh, Bangladeshi Immigration: Are we heading for another Partition?, *Dialogue*, New Delhi (a journal of Astha Bharati), October-December 2001, Vol.3, No.2, p.37.

3. Bibhuti Bhusan Nandy, Space Invaders, *The Sunday Hindustan Times,* New Delhi, February 14, 2003.

4. Ibid.

5. Onkareshwar Pandey, ISI and New Wave of Islamic Militancy in the N.E., *Dialogue,* New Delhi (a Journal of Astha Bharati), Volume-3, No.3, January-March 2002, p.98.

6. Source: *Religious Demography of India*, 2001 Revision, Appendix Table A-3, p. 187 (Religious Profile and Decadal Growth).

7. Jayanta Kumar Ray, Migration from (East Bengal/East Pakistan) Bangladesh to India, *Dialogue*, New Delhi, Vol.3, No.3, January-March 2002, p.34.

8. A news item 'Bengal CM speaks BJP lingo, assails influx from Bangladesh', *The Times of India,* New Delhi, June 24, 2005, p.1.

9. Ibid.

10. 'Census mirrors Buddha's concern: Numbers Prove Illegal Entry by Bangladeshis' *The Times of India*, New Delhi, June 25, 2005, p.11.

11. Source: Salam Azad, *Status of Minority Communities in Bangladesh,* a Paper read at the Internation Conference organised by CAAMB (Campaign Against Atrocities on Minorities in Bangladesh) at Kolkata on January 22-23, 2005.

12. V.K. Shashikumar, When the Right does wrong, *Tehelka,* December 18, 2004, p.12.

13. Ibid.

14. Ibid.

15. Ibid.

16. Subir Bhaumik, *Flowergarden or Fluid Corridor: A Conceptual Framework for Refugee Influx, Migration and Internal Displacement in Northern India, The Elsewhere People,* published by Lancer Books, 2003.

17. Ibid.

18. A news item, 'True lies: MOS Jiswal eats his words on Bangla issue' *The Times of India,* New Delhi, July 28, 2004. p.13.

19. A news item Bangladeshi influx: 'Aliens taught Assamese before pushed into State', *The Assam Tribune,* Guwahati, March 4, 2005, pp.1-3.

20. Ibid.

21. Bhadra Sinha, Can't deport Bangladeshi immigrants, *The Times of India,* New Delhi, September 25, 2003.

22. A news item "S.C. notice on Bangla influx", *The Statesman,* New Delhi, December 11, 2004, p.8.

23. Pioneer News Service, 'SC notice to Centre on illegal Bangladeshi migration', *The Pioneer,* New Delhi, December 11, 2004, p.4.

24. Abraham Thomas, HC ties Centre's hand on deporting B'deshis, *The Pioneer,* New Delhi, March 17, 2005, p.1.

25. A news item, 'HC raps Centre on Bangladesh migrants issue', *The Economics Times,* New Delhi, March 19, 2005, p.2.

26. Subhash Kapila, Bangladesh: New base of terror?, *The Kashmir Telegraph,* May 2004; Source: http:// kashmirtelegraph.com/ 0504/eight.htm.

27. A news item 'Ulfa has 7 hotels in Bangla: BSF; *The Pioneer,* New Delhi, June 4, 2005, p.1.
28. An editorial captioned 'Bangla blueprint and NE', *The Assam Tribune,* Guwahati, March 21, 2005, p.1.
29. A new item 'Non-Muslims in Bangladesh under threat, says report, *The Pioneer,* New Delhi, August 23, 2005.
30. A news item, 'Entry to UK is going to get tougher', *The Times of India,* New Delhi, June 22, 2005, p.1.
31. Ron Duarah, Suspected Bangladeshi exodus continues, *The Assam Tribune,* Guwahati, May 15, 2005, pp.1-3.
32. Sanjoy Hazarika, North by North-east, *The Statesman,* New Delhi, May 21.

Chapter 5

1. Rana Ajit, 'N-E erupts, 45 blown off', *The Pioneer,* New Delhi, October 3, 2004, p.1.
2. *The Pioneer,* New Delhi, October 4, 2004, p.1.
3. A news item captioned 'Ulfa issues extortion notices', *The Asian Age,* New Delhi, December 20, 2004.
4. Ibid.
5. Rahul Karmakar, Manipur Univ officials punished', then freed, *Sunday Hindustan Times,* New Delhi, December 19, 2004, p.13.
6. Ibid.
7. A PTI news item, Ulfa Harkat Links, *The Statesman,* New Delhi, December 21, 2004, p.1. (source: PTI)
8. *South Asian Intelligence Review (SAIR),* Volume 3, No. 15, October 25, 2004.
9. Ibid.
10. Ibid.
11. Ibid.
12. Ibid.

13. Ibid.
14. Ibid.
15. Ibid.
16. BJP: Faultlines Stay, Migration Is Still Hot, *The Economic Times,* New Delhi, August 14, 2004, p.3.
17. Ibid.
18. News Item titled 'Daimary confirms Ulfa's active ISI link, *The Economic Times,* New Delhi, December 24, 2003, p.2.
19. Ibid.
20. Ibid.
21. A news item 'Minority population in Bangla going down' *The Assam Tribune,* Guwahati, June 23, 2005, pp.1-3.
22. Assam Bans Nellie Case Paper Presentation, *The Asian Age,* New Delhi, November 14, 2004.
23. Ibid.
24. Ibid.
25. Ibid.
26. Appendix I p. ....
27. Seema Mustafa, US access to N-E worries defence officer, *The Asian Age,* New Delhi, December 21, 2004, p.3.
28. *The Times of India,* June 16, 2004.

Chapter 6

1. Arun Shourie, Right on Course, *The Indian Express,* New Delhi, October 9, 2004, p.9.
2. Arun Shourie, Further warnings, further calumny, *The Indian Express,* New Delhi, October 10, 2004.
3. A news item captioned Milli Council splits U.P. Muslim votes five ways, *The Asian Age,* New Delhi, April 21, p.1.
4. A news item 'Godhra posters: EC files FIRs against 2 bodies, *The Economics Times,* New Delhi, February 2, 2005, p.2.

5. M.A. Siraj, Minority View, *The Times of India,* New Delhi, June 15, 2004, p.16.
6. Dina Nath Mishra, let us be open about it, Frankly Yours, *The Pioneer,* New Delhi, Feb.27, 2005, p.13 (Foray).
7. Ibid.
8. Mani Shankar Aiyar, *Confessions of a Secular Fundamentalist,* (Penguin Viking 2004) pp. 112-117.
9. Ibid.
10. A news item 'Bangla migrant issue alarming, says CPM finally', *The Economics Times,* New Delhi, July 15, 2003, p.2.
11. Ibid.
12. Binay Singh/TNN, Varanasi a storehous of illegal arms: *The Times of India,* New Delhi, March 12, 2006, p.14.
13. Ibid.
14. Gautam Sen, Death in Varansi, *The Pioneer,* New Delhi, March 10, 2006, p.9.

Chapter 7

1. 'Sheer blackmail' the second editorial in *The Pioneer,* New Delhi, April 7, 2005, p.6.
2. Ibid.
3. Ibid.
4. *The Assam Tribune,* March 3, 2005, pp.1-3.
5. A news item 'Secret plan to make shariat courts legit', Kanchan Gupta, *Sunday Pioneer,* July 3, 2005, pp.1 and 4.
6. Ibid.
7. S. Sanandkumar, a news item 'IUML asks Muslims in Kerala to keep off Left', *The Economic Times,* New Delhi, March 7, 2005, p.3.
8. Ibid.

9. Ibid.
10. Source: The Demographic Bomb — When will Norway become a Muslim Country?, http://fomi.ytring.dk//English/Dem Bomb-E.htm.
11. Ibid.
12. Ibid.
13. Selig Harrison, *India: The Most Dangerous Decades*, Oxford University Press, 1960.
14. Ibid, ch.II, pps. 246-247.

Chapter 8

1. K. Subrahmanyam, Forces of Fragmentation: Behind the Fig Leaf of Secularism, *The Times of India,* New Delhi, April 18, 2002.
2. Ibid.
3. Ibid.
4. Bibhuti Bhusan Nandy, Secular Claims, A Marxist Blend of Duplicity and Deception, *The Statesman,* New Delhi, January 21, 2005.
5. Ibid.
6. Ibid.
7. R. Jagannathan, Microview, Why Mani Aiyar is wrong, *The Business Standard,* December 4, 2004, p.11.
8. Mani Shankar Aiyar, *Confessions of a Secular Fundamentalist,* Penguin, Appendix, p.256.
9. Ibid.
10. Tavleen Singh, 'This inner voice too needs hearing', *The Indian Express,* June 13, 2004, p.7.
11. Ibid.
12. Ibid.
13. Prakash Singh, In search of lebensraum, *The Pioneer,* New Delhi, February 1, 2005, p.7.

14. Ibid.

15. Baljit Rai, *Is India going Islamic,* p.108, B.S. Publishers Chandigarh.

16. Ibid.

17. J.S. Bains, *Political Ideas of Guru Gobind Singh,* p.23.

18. A news item, 'Delete Dalit Slur from scriptures, *The Times of India,* New Delhi, July.21, 2005, p.13.

19. O.P. Gupta, It has all been said before, *The Indian Express,* New Delhi, May 21, 2005.

Chapter 9

1. Debate: Could Terrorism spiral into a civil war?, *The Economic Times,* New Delhi, March 14, 2006, p. 15.

2. Pakistan aiding jihadi terror, says NSA, The Economic Times, New Delhi, March 20, 2006, p. 2.

3. Ibid.

4. Ibid.

Appendix 1

Proportion of Population age 0-6 to Total Population by Religion Communities-2001 (India, States and Union Territories)

India/States U/Territories	All religious communities	Hindus	Muslims	Christians	Sikhs	Buddhists	Jains	Others
India	15.9	15.6	18.7	13.5	12.8	14.4	10.6	18.0
Jammu & Kashmir	14.6	13.3	15.4	11.6	10.6	11.7	10.9	15.5
Himachal Pradesh	13.0	13.3	16.2	12.8	12.1	10.6	10.5	13.2
Punjab	13.0	13.2	16.3	16.1	2.8	13.4	10.2	13.5
Chandigarh	12.8	13.4	17.1	12.1	9.1	7.7	10.0	9.7
Uttaranchal	16.0	15.4	21.2	11.7	14.8	9.1	9.8	14.7
Haryana	15.8	15.4	24.5	12.4	13.0	16.2	11.3	11.7
Delhi	14.6	14.3	18.5	11.4	10.8	13.5	11.3	10.1
Rajasthan	18.8	18.8	21.0	14.6	15.1	18.2	10.7	15.9

India/States U/Territories	All religious communities	Hindus	Muslims	Christians	Sikhs	Buddhists	Jains	Others
Uttar Pradesh	19.0	18.6	20.9	14.6	14.1	19.9	11.9	17.0
Bihar	20.2	19.9	22.0	14.8	14.2	19.4	11.0	20.3
Sikkim	14.5	14.6	13.2	14.6	2.0	14.4	11.5	15.0
Arunachal Pradesh	18.8	17.1	18.8	20.5	7.6	19.8	15.7	19.1
Nagaland	14.6	12.7	19.2	14.6	8.3	11.9	11.7	12.8
Manipur	14.2	13.2	19.8	14.0	8.5	18.4	10.1	14.8
Mizoram	16.2	9.2	10.1	16.1	9.8	20.5	16.8	15.8
Tripura	13.6	13.0	18.6	15.7	4.5	17.9	11.9	12.1
Meghalaya	20.2	14.2	21.2	21.1	12.3	14.4	13.5	21.5
Assam	16.9	14.5	21.8	17.6	9.9	14.3	10.5	15.5
West Bengal	14.2	12.7	18.7	13.4	10.1	10.6	9.6	15.4
Jharkhand	18.4	17.9	21.2	16.2	11.1	16.8	11.1	19.0
Orissa	14.6	14.4	16.5	17.8	10.8	13.3	10.8	17.8
Chhatisgarh	17.1	17.2	15.5	15.3	12.3	13.4	11.7	19.0
Madhya Pradesh	17.9	18.0	17.9	13.3	12.9	14.5	11.3	18.1
Gujarat	14.9	14.9	15.8	12.8	12.7	17.3	9.2	12.7

India/States U/Territories	All religious communities	Hindus	Muslims	Christians	Sikhs	Buddhists	Jains	Others
Daman & Diu	13.0	13.2	12.3	9.8	11.0	13.5	10.8	8.7
Dadra & Nagar Haveli	18.2	18.3	16.1	19.3	11.4	18.6	13.8	13.3
Maharashtra	14.1	14.0	16.2	10.3	11.6	14.1	10.1	13.1
Andhra Pradesh	13.3	13.2	14.9	12.3	12.4	16.2	11.3	13.8
Karnataka	13.6	13.3	16.1	11.1	11.9	15.3	12.0	13.8
Goa	10.8	10.9	15.2	9.6	10.0	12.0	11.5	11.9
Lakshadweep	15.0	3.6	15.5	3.1	-	-	-	-
Kerala	11.9	10.8	15.0	11.2	10.0	12.7	9.7	15.9
Tamil Nadu	11.6	11.5	12.9	11.2	10.4	12.0	10.8	11.1
Pondicherry	12.0	12.0	13.1	11.0	8.3	5.5	11.6	12.6
Andaman & Nicobar Islands	12.6	12.7	11.3	12.7	12.4	5.9	13.0	15.1

[Source: Census of India 2001, Religion Data Report, Statement 7, p.xlii]

Notes: 1. Population figures for India and Manipur exclude those of Mao Maram, Paomata and Purul sub-divisions of Senapati district of Manipur.

2. The column All religious communities includes 'Religion not stated'

Appendix 2

Proportion and growth rate of population of religious communities in India 1961-2001.

	Proportion									
Religious Communities	**Unadjusted**					**Adjusted***				
	1961	1971	1981	1991	2001	1961	1971	1981	1991	2001
1	2	3	4	5	6	7	8	9	10	11
All religious groups	100	100	100	100	100	100	100	100	100	100
Hindus	83.4	82.7	82.6	82.0	80.5	84.4	83.5	83.1	82.4	81.4
Muslims	10.7	11.2	11.4	12.1	13.4	9.9	10.4	10.9	11.7	12.4
Christians	2.4	2.6	2.4	2.3	2.3	2.4	2.6	2.5	2.3	2.3
Sikhs	1.8	1.9	2.0	1.9	1.9	1.8	1.9	2.0	2.0	1.9
Buddhists	0.7	0.7	0.7	0.8	0.8	0.7	0.7	0.7	0.8	0.8
Jains	0.5	0.5	0.5	0.4	0.4	0.5	0.5	0.5	0.4	0.4
Others	0.3	0.4	0.4	0.4	0.6	0.3	0.4	0.4	0.4	0.7
Religion not stated	Negligible ------------------------- Negligible -------------------- Negligible ----------------									

Contd.

	Unadjusted				**Adjusted*** (i.e. Fudged Data)			
	1961-71	1971-81	1981-91	1991-2001	1961-71	1971-81	1981-91	1991-2001
All religious communities	24.8	21.4	26.0	22.7	24.8	24.8	23.8	21.5
Hindu	23.7	21.3	25.1	20.3	23.4	24.2	22.8	20.0
Muslims	30.8	22.9	34.5	36.0	31.2	30.8	32.9	29.3
Christians	32.6	13.7	21.5	22.6	36.0	19.2	17.0	22.1
Sikhs	32.3	26.0	24.3	18.2	32.0	26.2	25.5	16.9
Buddhists	17.1	23.8	35.3	24.5	17.0	25.4	36.0	23.3
Jains	28.5	23.1	4.6	26.0	28.5	23.7	4.0	26.0
Others	45.7	26.6	18.2	103.1	97.7	26.6	13.2	111.3
Religion not	-68.1	66.9	590.1	75.1	-65.7	67.1	573.5	76.3

*Excludes Jammu & Kashmir and Assam for all decades from 1961 to 2001.

Note: 1. The census figures for India and Manipur exclude those of Mao Maram, Paomata and Parul sub-divisions of Senapati district of Manipur.

2. No census conducted in Assam in 1981 and in Jammu & Kashmir in 1991.

[**Source:** Census of India 2001, Religion Data Report, Statement 1-a, p. xxviii.]

Appendix 3

Major Militant Groups Operating in North-Eastern Region

1.	National Socialist Council of Nagalim (Isaac Swu-Muivah) NSCN (IM)	Nagas
2.	National Socialist Council of Nagalim (Khaplang) - NSCN (K)	- Do -
3.	United Liberation Front of Assam (ULFA)	Assamese
4.	National Democratic Front of Bodoland (NDFB)	Bodos
5.	Bodo Liberation Tigers (BLT)	- do -
6.	Bodo Security Force	- do -
7.	National Liberation Front of Tripura (NLFT) suspected of ISI connection	Tripurris
8.	All Tripura Tiger Force (ATTF)	- do -
9.	People Liberation Army (PLA)	Meities
10.	United National Front (UNLF)	- do -
11.	People's Revolutionary Party of Kangleipak (PREPAK)	- do -
12.	Kanglei Yaol Kanba Lup (KYKL)	- do -
13.	Revolutionary Peoples Front (RPF)	- do -

14.	Metei Erol Eyek Loinshillon Apunba Lup (MEELAL) (a militant forum for safeguarding Manipuri script against Bengali script)	- do -
15.	Kangleipak Communist Party (KCP)	- do -
16.	Islamic Liberation Army of Assam (a suspected ISI sponsored outfit)	Assamese Muslims
17.	Muslim Liberation Tigers of Assam (MULTA)	- do -
18.	Muslim Security Force	- do -
19.	Adam Sena (a suspected ISI sponsored radical group)	- do -
20.	Al Jihad-e Islami (a new suspected ISI supported militant group)	Assamese Muslims
21.	Kamtapur Liberation Front (a North Bengal based Gorkha outfit)	Gorkhas
22.	Hmar Peoples Convention (a Mizoram-based ethnic Hmar outfit)	Hmar
23.	Achik National Volunteers' Council	Garo
24.	Kuki National Army (KNA)	Kukis
25.	Kuki Revolutionary Army	- do -
26.	Kachin Independence Army (KIA) (operating on Indo-Burma border	Kachin Group
27.	Chin National Front (CNF) (a militant group on Indo-Burma border)	Chin
28.	United Peoples Democratic Solidarity	Assamese
29.	Adivasi Cobra Force (ACF)	- do -
30.	Dima Halim Daogah (DHD)	- do -
31.	Karbi Anglong National Liberation Front (KNLF)	- do -

(a new militant outfit based in Karbi Anglong district which has been allegedly extorting 4 percent as tax in the name of freedom for Karbis).

Appendix 4

Census 2001 - Population of Districts of Northeast & Eastern States

No	District	% HF	%Others	No	District	% HF	%Oth
	Assam						
1.	Kokrajhar	65.9	M 20.4	16.	Sibsagar	89.1	M 8.2
2.	Dhubri	24.9	M 74.3	17.	Jorhat	93.4	M 4.8
3.	Goalpara	38.4	M 53.7	18.	Golaghat	86.6	M 7.9
4.	Bongaigaon	59.4	M 38.5	19.	Karbi Anglong	83.3	C 14.5
5.	Barpeta	40.3	M 59.4	20.	Nrth Cachar Hills	70.8	C 26.7
6.	Kamrup	73.5	M 24.8	21.	Cachar	61.7	M 36.1
7.	Nalbari	76.3	M 22.1	22.	Karimganj	46.8	M 52.3
8.	Darrang	58.0	M 35.5	23.	Halaikandi	41.4	M 57.6
9.	Marigaon	52.3	M 47.6				
10.	Nagaon	48.1	M 51.0				
11.	Sonitpur	77.2	M 15.0				
12.	Lakhimpur	79.7	M 16.1				
13.	Dhemaji	97.0	M 1.8				
14.	Tinsukia	91.1	M 3.5				
15.	Diburgarh	91.7	M 4.5				

Notes: 1. HF stands for Hindus & allied Faiths
2. M stands for Muslims
3. C stands for Christian
4. Oth stands for Other Communities

No	District	% HF	%Oth	No	District	% HF	%Oth
	Arunachal				**Bihar**		
1	Tawang	98.6	C 0.8	1.	Madhubani	82.1	M 17.9
2	West Kameng	95.2	C 3.3	2.	Supaul	82.5	M 17.4
3	East Kameng	73.9	C 25.5	3.	Araria	58.8	M 41.1
4	Papum Pare	65.7	C 30.0	4.	Kishanganj	32.2	M 67.6
5	Lower Subhansiri	74.7	C 24.5	5.	Purnia	63.1	M 36.8
6	Upper Subhansiri	93.2	C 5.9	6.	Katihar	57.3	M 42.5
7	West Siang	79.2	C 19.4	7.	Madhepura	88.6	M 11.4
8	East Siang	81.5	C 15.3	8.	Saharsa	85.5	M 14.5
9	Upper Siang	85.6	C 12.9	9.	Darbhanga	77.3	M 22.7
10	Dibang Valley	85.0	C 10.6	10.	Bhagalpur	82.5	M 17.5
11	Lohit	92.1	C 5.8				
12	Changlang	81.6	C 21.9				
13	Tirap	49.2	C 50.0				

No	District	% HF	%Oth	No	District	% HF	%Oth
	Jharkhand				**Meghalaya**		
1.	Giridh	79.3	M 20.1	1.	West Garo Hills	36.3	C 54.6
2.	Deogarh	80.6	M 19.0	2	East Garo Hills	9.5	C 89.0
3.	Godda	77.8	M 20.1	3	South Garo Hills	7.6	C 89.7
4.	Sahibganj	62.4	M 31.3	4	West Khasi Hills	9.5	C 89.5
5.	Pakaur	61.8	M 32.4	5	Ri Bhoi	19.6	C 79.7
6.	Dumka	85.2	M 11.6	6	East Khasi Hills	37.5	C 61.0
7.	Dhanbad	84.4	M 15.2	7	Jaintia Hills	34.0	C 65.3
8.	Bokaro	88.3	M 11.0		**Manipur**		
9.	Ranchi	78.4	M 12.5	1	Senapati	14.8	C 85.0
10	Dibang Valley	85.0	C 10.6	2	Tamenglong	3.8	C 94.9
11	Lohit	92.1	C 5.8	3	Churachandpur	5.3	C 93.5
12	Changlang	81.6	C 21.9	4	Bishnupur	90.2	M 6.8
13	Tirap	49.2	C 50.0	5	Thoubal	74.4	M 23.9
				6	Imphal West	91.6	M 4.3
				7	Imphal East	78.1	M 15.9
				8	Ukhrul	4.2	C 95.2
				9	Chandel	5.8	C 92.2

No	District	% HF	%Oth	No	District	% HF	%Oth
	Mizoram				**Nagaland**		
1	Mamit	17.7	C 80.5	1	Mon	3.9	C 95.4
2	Kolasib	7.4	C 89.6	2	Tuensang	1.7	C 97.9
3	Aizawl	5.1	C 93.3	3	Mokochung	4.6	C 94.5
4	Champhai	2.7	C 96.9	4	Zunheboto	2.2	C 97.5
5	Serchhip	2.2	C 97.5	5	Wokha	3.1	C 96.2
6	Lunglei	19.9	C 79.6	6	Dimapur	30.8	C 61.2
7.	Lawngtlai	55.0	C 44.7	7	Kohima	9.2	C 89.9
8.	Saiha	2.0	C 97.6	8	Phek	3.1	C 96.5
	Tripura						
1	West Tripura	89.8	M 8.3				
2	South Tripura	91.8	M 5.1				
3	Dhalai	93.0	C 4.8				
4	North Tripura	80.2	M 13.9				

No	District	% HF	%Others	No	District	% HF	%Others
	West Bengal						
1	Darjiling	88.5	C 6.2	11	North 24 Parganas	75.6	M 24.2
2	Jalpaiguri	84.8	M 10.9	12	Hugli	84.8	M 15.1
3	Koch Bihar	75.7	M 24.2	13	Bankura	92.4	M 7.5
4	Uttar Dinajpur	52.1	4 7.4	14	Puruliya	92.6	M 7.1
5	Dakshin Dinajpur	74.5	M 24.0	15	Medinipur	88.5	M 11.3
6	Maldah	50.0	M 49.7	16	Haora	75.4	M 24.4
7	Murshidabad	36.1	M 63.7	17	Kolkata	78.9	M 20.3
8	Birbhum	64.7	M 35.1	18	South 24 Parganas	66.0	M 33.2
9	Barddhaman	80.0	M 19.8				
10	Nadia	73.9	M 25.4				

Note: '%Oth' is the percentage of the other major community in the District; M- Muslim, C- Christian

Appendix 5

Census 2001 - Population of Districts of U.P. and Bihar

No	District	% HF	%M	No	District	% HF	%M
	Bihar						
1	Pasch Champarn	78.6	21.3	19	Samastipur	89.5	10.5
2	Purba Champarn	80.8	19.2	20	Begusarai	86.6	13.4
3	Sheohar	84.5	15.5	21	Khagaria	89.7	10.3
4	Sitamarhi	78.8	21.2	22	Bhagalpur	82.5	17.5
5	Madhubani	82.1	17.9	23	Banka	88.0	11.8
6	Supaul	82.5	17.4	24	Munger	92.1	7.9
7	Araria	58.8	41.1	25	Lakhisarai	95.6	4.4
8	Kishanganj	32.2	67.6	26	Sheikhpura	92.7	7.2
9	Purnia	63.1	36.8	27	Nalanda	92.5	7.5
10	Katihar	57.3	42.5	28	Patna	92.1	7.8
11	Madhepura	88.6	11.4	29	Bhojpur	92.7	7.3
12	Saharsa	85.5	14.5	30	Buxar	93.8	6.2
13	Darbhanga	77.3	22.7	31	Kaimur (Bhabua)	90.4	9.6
14	Muzzafarpur	84.7	15.3	32	Rohtas	89.9	10.1
15	Gopalganj	82.9	17.1	33	Jehanabad	91.8	8.2
16	Siwan	81.8	18.2	34	Aurangabad	90.3	9.7
17	Saran	89.6	10.4	35	Gaya	88.4	11.6
18	Vaishali	90.5	9.5	36	Nawada	88.7	11.3
				37	Jamui	87.5	12.2

No	District	% HF	%M	No	District	% HF	%M
	Uttar Pradesh						
1	Sahranpur	60.7	39.1	19	Budaun	78.6	21.3
2	Muzzafarnagar	61.8	38.1	20	Bareilly	65.9	33.9
3	Bijnor	58.2	41.7	21	Pilibhit	76.1	23.8
4	Moradabad	54.2	45.5	22	Shahjahanpur	82.0	17.9
5	Rampur	50.5	49.1	23	Kheri	80.8	19.1
6	Jyotiba Phule Ngr	60.3	39.4	24	Sitapur	80.7	19.2
7	Meerut	67.2	32.6	25	Hardoi	86.8	13.1
8	Baghpat	75.2	24.7	26	Unnao	89.0	11.0
9	Ghaziabad	75.9	23.8	27	Lucknow	79.1	20.5
10	Gaut Buddha Ngr	86.6	13.0	28	Rae Bareli	88.1	11.8
11	Bulandshahar	78.8	21.1	29	Farrukhabad	85.0	14.8
12	Aligarh	82.1	17.8	30	Kannauj	84.2	15.8
13	Hathras	89.8	10.1	31	Etawah	92.8	7.2
14	Mathura	91.8	8.1	32	Auraiya	92.9	7.1
15	Agra	90.9	8.9	33	Kanpur Dehat	90.6	9.3
16	Firozabad	87.2	12.7	34	Kanpur Nagar	84.0	15.7
17	Etah	88.4	11.5	35	Jalaun	89.9	10.1
18	Mainpuri	94.6	5.3	36	Jhansi	92.2	7.4

No	District	% HF	%M	No	District	% HF	%OM
	Uttar Pradesh						
1	Sahranpur	60.7	39.1	19	Budaun	78.6	21.3
2	Muzzafarnagar	61.8	38.1	20	Bareilly	65.9	33.9
3	Bijnor	58.2	41.7	21	Pilibhit	76.1	23.8
4	Moradabad	54.2	45.5	22	Shahjahanpur	82.0	17.9
5	Rampur	50.5	49.1	23	Kheri	80.8	19.1
6	Jyotiba Phule Ngr	60.3	39.4	24	Sitapur	80.7	19.2
7	Meerut	67.2	32.6	25	Hardoi	86.8	13.1
8	Baghpat	75.2	24.7	26	Unnao	89.0	11.0
9	Ghaziabad	75.9	23.8	27	Lucknow	79.1	20.5
10	Gaut Buddha Ngr	86.6	13.0	28	Rae Bareli	88.1	11.8
11	Bulandshahar	78.8	21.1	29	Farrukhabad	85.0	14.8
12	Aligarh	82.1	17.8	30	Kannauj	84.2	15.8
13	Hathras	89.8	10.1	31	Etawah	92.8	7.2
14	Mathura	91.8	8.1	32	Auraiya	92.9	7.1
15	Agra	90.9	8.9	33	Kanpur Dehat	90.6	9.3
16	Firozabad	87.2	12.7	34	Kanpur Nagar	84.0	15.7
17	Etah	88.4	11.5	35	Jalaun	89.9	10.1
18	Mainpuri	94.6	5.3	36	Jhansi	92.2	7.4

No	District	% HF	%M	No	District	% HF	%M
	Jharkhand				**Neighouring States**		
1	Garhwa	84.4	14.4			**Delhi**	
2	Palamu	86.2	11.6	1	Delhi	87.3	11.7
3	Chatra	87.7	11.7			**Haryana**	
4	Hazaribag	84.2	14.8	1	Gurgaon	62.6	37.2
5	Kodama	84.8	15.0	2	Faridabad	88.4	11.3
6	Giridh	79.3	20.1			**Rajasthan**	
7	Deogarh	80.6	19.0	1	Bharatpur	87.4	12.6
8	Godda	77.8	20.1	2	Dhaulpur	93.9	6.1
9	Sahibganj	62.4	31.3	3	Karauli	94.5	5.5
10	Pakaur	61.8	32.4			**Uttaranchal**	
11	Dumka	85.2	11.6	1	Dehradun	88.3	10.9
12	Dhanbad	84.4	15.2	2	Nainital	88.2	11.3
13	Bokaro	88.3	11.0	3	Udham Singh Ngr	79.1	20.6
14	Ranchi	78.4	12.5	4	Hardwar	66.7	33.1
15	Lohardaga	75.9	20.1				
16	Gumla	64.0	C31.6				
17	Pasch Singhabhm	93.2	3.5				
18	Purbi Singhabhm	89.3	9.3				

Note: HF = Hindu Faiths M= Muslims In Gumla Christians are 31.6%

Index

Notes

Notes

Notes

Notes